Process-Driven Applications with BPMN

Volker Stiehl

Process-Driven Applications with BPMN

Springer

Volker Stiehl
SAP SE, Walldorf, Germany

Translators
Rachel Raw
SAP SE, Walldorf, Germany

Paul Smith
SAP SE, Walldorf, Germany

Translated from the German language edition:
Prozessgesteuerte Anwendungen entwickeln und ausführen mit BPMN by Volker Stiehl
Copyright © 2013 dpunkt.verlag GmbH
All Rights Reserved.

ISBN 978-3-319-35506-1   ISBN 978-3-319-07218-0 (eBook)
DOI 10.1007/978-3-319-07218-0
Springer Cham Heidelberg New York Dordrecht London

Springer is part of Springer Science+Business Media (www.springer.com)

Foreword

I met Volker Stiehl two or three years ago at an SAP Tech Ed conference where he was talking about SAP Process Orchestration's use of BPMN in the integration layer. I was surprised to see this, as up to that point process automation vendors had used the Business Process Model and Notation standard only for the "business-visible" process logic. Whatever really happens between an activity *Create Order* in the BPMN diagram and the ERP system that actually creates the order was of interest only to developers and technical architects, so using some language other than BPMN to define the integration details was simply expected. Nevertheless, using a common diagramming language to define and monitor the entire solution, from the business-oriented flow of human tasks down to the minutest details of interactions on the message bus, seemed an intriguing idea.

Volker was surprised to see me at his talk, as well. Why would someone whose main interest was teaching nontechnical users how to communicate process logic effectively in BPMN care about the integration layer? What unites his interest and my interest in BPMN—and, I hope, yours as well—is the potential of a common process language that is shared by business and IT. Already, BPM solutions exhibit a much greater degree of close business-IT collaboration throughout the implementation cycle than other applications, and BPMN is largely to thank for that. Used properly, BPMN can be more than simply a means of gathering business requirements. It can provide the backbone of the actual solution implementation!

In principle, the same diagram prepared by the business analyst to describe the business's desired To-Be process can be used to automate the execution of that process on a modern process engine. That has been the basic "promise" of BPMN since its beginnings over a decade ago. In practice, however, that rarely happens. This book not only explains why that is the case, but provides a detailed prescription for fixing it. The prescription takes the form of a new *process-driven architecture*, based on principles and rules aligned with the spirit of service-oriented architecture but often diametrically opposed to the way SOA-based BPM has been practiced. The architecture is layered in a radically new way that preserves simplicity and stability in the business-oriented *process-driven application layer* while maximizing flexibility and agility in the underlying *service contract implementation layer*.

BPM solutions fundamentally are about accommodating *change*—changing business requirements that in turn require changing process logic, as well as changes in the system landscape brought about by mergers, system consolidations, and new technology, such as cloud. Faced with increasing demand from the business to deliver change faster, IT has long pinned its hopes on SOA's promise of service reuse. By packaging system functionality in reusable units with standard interfaces, IT could become more agile.

But this has not worked out as hoped. SOA in practice is inherently bottom-up, driven by the details of the underlying systems. The SOA architect tries to define service interfaces that will maximize reuse of system functionality, even though the future applications that will supposedly reuse them are yet unknown. In reality, these services can rarely be simply snapped together to create BPM solutions, because they rarely match up with the business requirements. Moreover, these services assume a stable system landscape, not the ever-changing technology infrastructure that is more often the reality. Thus the BPMN diagram developed with the business inevitably must be modified by the developer, as the details of reusable services "leak back" to modify the original flow logic. The business thought they were specifying the solution, but they may not even recognize the BPMN as ultimately implemented.

Fixing this problem requires instead a top-down approach, in which the business—not the SOA architect—determines the required interfaces. Reuse is not a consideration. In fact, the underlying system landscape is not a consideration, either. Ideally, the process-driven application logic should not need to change to accommodate changes in the system landscape. So how is this even possible?

The answer, as laid out brilliantly in detail in the book, is via a service contract implementation layer interposed between the process-driven application and the system landscape. Its job is to map the business-defined service interfaces to the underlying business systems that ultimately provide those services. The process-driven application layer never interacts directly with systems; it always goes through the service contract implementation layer. The interfaces called by the process-driven application represent a *service contract* intended to insulate the application from details of those systems. If the solution is architected properly, the process-driven application is unaffected by changes in the underlying system landscape. What changes is the logic of the service contract implementation layer.

This layering sounds like adding complexity, but what makes it all work is *model-driven execution* based on a common language. BPMN is used for both the process-driven application layer and the service contract implementation layer. Actually the latter is broken out into a stateful integration process and a stateless messaging process, both using BPMN but constrained to specific integration patterns.

I need to emphasize that this is a book about BPM architecture, not about a specific SAP stack and toolset. It provides clear principles for what should and should not be in the process-driven application layer, and similar guidance for constructing the integration layer. It approaches process automation in an entirely new way, based on principles of loose coupling but specified top-down, starting from requirements as seen by the business as opposed to the bottom-up reusable-component thinking at the center of SOA. In effect it is SOA turned on its head.

I recognize it is not easy to change habits and patterns of thinking, but BPM architects and developers need to give this book serious thought. In my own BPMN Method and Style training (http://www.bpmessentials.com), I continually face a similar challenge: asking business analysts and process improvement teams to describe their process logic top-down, starting with the end-to-end process first— How does it start? What are its possible end states?—and then decompose that into a handful of high-level activities and their possible end states, and so on.

This is completely opposite to the "What comes next?" approach of most process improvement methodologies. It is difficult to take people used to thinking bottom-up and concretely and get them to start thinking top-down and abstractly. So why bother to try? In my case, the goal is to create models that communicate the process logic clearly and consistently through the printed diagram, and you just can't do that by recording "what comes next." You need a different methodology and additional conventions, or "style." There is a learning curve, but in the end it's justified by the benefit. Once people learn to do it, their models become understandable to others who don't already know the process logic or even the terminology it uses. Here clarity of visual communication is the goal, and learning this new methodology is the price of achieving it.

In the case of *Process-Driven Applications with BPMN,* I see a similar possibility. BPMN can actually fulfill its original promise of process automation solutions driven directly by the business. Developers and technical architects continue to play a critical role, but their goals must include insulating the process-driven application from the details of integration. This requires new principles of BPM architecture that often run counter to long-standing practice, and a corresponding implementation methodology. But the end result, I believe, is worth the trouble. Volker Stiehl has laid out both architectural principles and an implementation approach that not only will increase business-IT collaboration but insulate the process-driven application from inevitable unknown changes in the system landscape.

When BPMN was first developed, the book *BPM: The Third Wave* by Howard Smith and Peter Fingar hailed it as a revolution because it would for the first time enable ordinary business people to create executable processes themselves. While that promise seems laughable today, its underlying premise—that business is frustrated by the functionality, brittleness, and delays in IT-delivered BPM solutions—still rings true. This book offers new hope, the chance to take process solutions as envisioned and modeled by the business, and make them directly executable. Layered architecture is the key. If that appeals to your organization, you need to read this book.

Pasadena, CA   Bruce Silver
May 2014

Preface

This book is about building and sustaining a competitive advantage for your company, thus contributing to its value and, not least, to your own personal success. We can think of business processes as the central nervous system of a company, but they are often sorely neglected in company strategy. Of course, a company must offer excellent products and/or services to have any chance of long-term success, but there is also enormous potential for differentiation and innovation in a company's business processes, and concentrating efforts in this area can make the difference that sets your company apart from the competition. Process innovations also have the unique advantage that they are not as visible to your competitors as products and services are, and they are much more difficult to copy. Just think how innovative Apple's iPhone was when it was first released, but how quickly competitors brought out their own imitations. Focusing on process-oriented innovation helps you protect and sustain growth and success.

How can we tap into this precious resource? How can we optimize business processes and exploit their full potential? These are the questions I want to answer in this book, and with the BPMN (Business Process Model and Notation) standard we now have new possibilities for planning, implementing, and monitoring processes. I particularly want to address the transition from business process planning to implementation. You have probably experienced cases yourself where business BPMN models have been altered beyond all recognition in their implementation as executable BPMN models, but this *can* be avoided. The BPMN standard enables you to create a *single process model* for both business and IT departments. I want you to seize this opportunity and use BPMN to extract the maximum benefit from the processes in your company. The approach I present here shows you how to use BPMN effectively, without having to sacrifice a common business process model, and ultimately makes the BPMN objective of executable business processes a reality.

We must also look at the transition from business process planning to implementation from another angle: The decisions we make at this early stage have far-reaching implications on resources (and of course costs), so we have to think very carefully about how to ensure that strategic processes can be implemented successfully. I favor a process-driven approach combining a process-driven methodology, a process-driven architecture, and a process-driven application. Ultimately, we have to rise to the challenge of developing applications in heterogeneous IT landscapes, as most end-to-end processes involve a number of different systems and partner connections. This is what originally inspired my interest in this topic.

My own journey into the world of application development for complex distributed system landscapes began more than 10 years ago. I was working at Siemens Business Services (SBS) in a department that developed Java-based applications. At that time, our team was developing new software that would implement new business processes for managing software licenses. The software would keep the licenses required by a company in a central license pool. When new computers were purchased, the IT department would install the software relevant to the role of the employee that the computer was intended for, taking it from the license pool. Conversely, whenever a computer was retired or an employee left the company, the license would return to the pool, where it would then be available for further installations. The processes that we were developing also had to interact with a number of existing systems. For example, new licenses were ordered using an SAP system, employee information was stored in an LDAP (Lightweight Directory Access Protocol) system, and workflow notifications were sent using an e-mail server. To top it all off, the application had its own JDBC-based persistence for saving information about who the computer belonged to and what software was installed on it. To sum up, it was a classic, distributed, Web-based application for implementing new processes spanning numerous different systems.

Our team developed a solution based on the prevalent JavaEE methodology, using the whole palette at our disposal: session beans, entity beans, message-driven beans, servlets, Java Server Pages, Apache Struts as a Web framework, and Web services. Our architect also insisted on a modern software architecture. I can remember him coming over to my desk one day and proudly telling me how many Gang-of-Four patterns (Gamma et al. 1995) he had managed to put to good use in the software (of course, more patterns does not necessarily mean higher quality software!). The software ran on a BEA Weblogic server and eventually found its way onto an SAP Web Application Server (Stiehl 2004). Customer feedback to our new solution was certainly positive, but before long it became clear that potential customers were storing their data in systems other than those we had envisaged when creating the software. How could we tackle this problem and keep our software attractive to as many customers as possible? Should we create a new variant for each customer, perhaps? Considering the sheer number of possible combinations of back-end systems, this proposal was not very encouraging. It was obvious that our solution was very vulnerable to changes in system landscapes. To put it another way, we had relied too heavily on a fixed and stable IT landscape. How did this happen? Why did we not abstract the solution from the back-end systems from the very start? But how do you actually implement this abstraction? And to what extent? How do you distribute the tasks across the abstraction levels? And above all: shouldn't a service-oriented architecture solve exactly this problem? All these issues culminated in one central question: How can I create robust applications for distributed IT landscapes that are becoming ever more fragmented as the number of on-demand and cloud solutions increases?

I wanted to get to grips with this problem: I analyzed projects, read technical articles, and attended conference lectures discussing these challenges. The more I learnt, the clearer it became that the architectures that were being presented all had similar shortcomings. Talking to project managers, I often hear other reasons for these inadequacies: They face intense pressure in their projects, and tight deadlines and budgets mean that they cannot invest the resources required to be able to produce a sufficiently robust software architecture. This, in spite of the fact that they are well aware of the consequences: short-term savings in development swallowed up in the long term by significantly higher costs for maintenance, support, and further development. Long-term goals are being sacrificed for the sake of short-term targets. Therefore, it is no surprise that software is being widely criticized for not being agile enough to adapt to the business strategies set out by management; we are overwhelmed by the task of untangling the complex web of increased dependencies between end applications and the system landscape.

In this book, I present an approach for implementing an architecture for end applications that strives to find a sensible balance between development and maintenance costs, sustainability, scalability, and error tolerance; an approach that meets flexibility requirements, while at the same time not being too complex itself; an approach that keeps the end application as abstract as possible from the system landscape in which it operates. In my search for this solution, I happened to come across the process modeling standard BPMN. This had started life as a graphical notation for modeling business processes, but had since developed into an outstanding instrument for implementing application architectures just like those I was faced with. My understanding of application architecture is a solution for end applications based on heterogeneous IT landscapes, which differentiates business and integration-centric processes. The most recent version of the BPMN standard (version 2.0) also had semantic enhancements that made it possible to execute process models created in this way, so I decided to start using BPMN to create and run complete application architectures. I do not use BPMN to model just the business processes of the end application, as the "B" in BPMN might suggest; I also use it to model and execute the integration processes between the systems. Although seemingly contradictory, these two uses of BPMN do fit together, as I will explain in this book.

With the application architecture I propose, I hope to present architects and software developers with a detailed blueprint, whose principles they can then use to plan and implement distributed applications in their companies. If application development adopts this approach, the solutions developed will help to gradually release companies from the stranglehold of dependencies and system connections mentioned earlier. In this regard, I see process-driven applications as contributing towards enterprise architecture management (EAM); however, it must also be said that this book is not about EAM; it covers areas outside the EAM spectrum.

The book is aimed at software architects, IT managers, managers with a technical interest, software developers, project managers, and also students of information and business technology. I assume that readers have a basic knowledge of BPMN. I introduce the notation briefly, but I do not go into detail about each BPMN element. Likewise, I also assume my readers have a basic understanding of service-oriented architectures, as my approach also relies on reusable services in back-end systems.

Walldorf, Germany   Volker Stiehl

Acknowledgments

This book is the product of the combined effort of many people over a long period of time. I would like to express my heartfelt thanks to all the people who have accompanied me on this journey: my Ph.D. supervisor Professor Erich Ortner, my tutors Professor Hartmut Wedekind and Professor Mathias Weske; my managers Gunther Rothermel, Dr. Achim Kraiss, and Sindhu Gangadharan, and my colleagues Dr. Udo Paltzer, Dr. Alexander Bundschuh, and Waldemar Befort. I am also greatly indebted to the following people (in alphabetical order): Sascha Alber, Professor Thomas Allweyer, Dr. Dirk Ammermann, Sascha Bertsch, Dr. Gero Decker, Marcus Elzenheimer, Dr. Matthias Fischer, Professor Elisabeth Heinemann, Nicolai Josuttis, Holger Koschek, Dr. Marco Link, Dr. Daniel Lübke, Dr. Christoph Neumann, Professor Gunther Piller, Peter Schwab, and Nicole Zeise.

Special thanks to Rachel Raw and Paul Smith for their outstanding translation and to the team at Springer, especially Ralf Gerstner. Above all, none of this would have been possible without my family, who supported me throughout, even when deprived of my time and attention: Christa, Clara, and Vera—you are all just wonderful—thank you!

If there is anyone I have neglected to thank, which I undoubtedly have, I apologize, and hope that you can forgive me!

I would point out that, although I am currently employed by SAP SE and refer to the software package SAP Process Orchestration for the implementation of the proposed architecture in Chap. 4, this book is not an official SAP publication. I would emphasize that all statements and recommendations made in this book represent my own personal opinion alone. I have intentionally kept my recommendations generic so that they can be implemented on any comparable platform.

Lastly, to my readers: I hope you enjoy the book and, of course, I hope that you can take my suggestions and apply them in your own work, to create truly flexible applications for your company and customers!

Contents

Introduction

1.1   Enterprise Application Software in the Age of Globalization

Without a doubt, today's companies are facing increased competition as a result of globalization. In their daily fight for survival with their competitors, their reaction to change must be swift, yet sustained. The following quote from Charles Darwin is particularly valid in this context:

> It is not the strongest of the species that survives,
> nor the most intelligent that survives.
> It is the one that is the most adaptable to change.

It is a company's ability to find effective solutions in response to changes that will ultimately guarantee its survival. Information technology (IT) is an important contributory factor here. Efficiently providing new software solutions is not the main problem, thanks to enormous advances in software engineering:

- Model-driven software development,
- The standardization of communication and interface technologies,
- The modularization of business functions in the form of reusable services,
- Productivity improvements for software developers due to highly integrated development environments,
- The deployment of agile development methods.

As far as the total cost of ownership (TCO) is concerned, it is the maintenance, enhancement, and adaptation of software to changing conditions that are proving to be much greater hurdles. The adaptability of software systems is becoming ever more important, but efforts to reflect this in software architectures are being thwarted by time and cost pressures. This is particularly true for software that needs to integrate existing business functions with new applications spanning multiple systems and applications in line with the service-oriented architecture (SOA) approach. Service-oriented architecture originally promised to leverage

V. Stiehl, *Process-Driven Applications with BPMN*, DOI 10.1007/978-3-319-07218-0_1,
© Springer International Publishing Switzerland 2014

the potential of increased agility, lower costs, reusability, and a rapid implementation of business strategy into software, but results in projects have been disappointing. Anne Thomas Manes has even predicted the death of SOA in her now almost legendary blog (Manes 2009). There are surely many reasons why results have fallen short of expectations, and this is no doubt at least partly due to the fact that SOA does not have, indeed has never had, a precise definition. Another reason, perhaps not immediately obvious, is that developers, when creating applications in the service-oriented world, draw on the expertise they have gained while programming tightly coupled solutions. Unfortunately, architectures that function perfectly well for tightly coupled stand-alone applications are completely unsuitable for loosely coupled, distributed applications. It doesn't matter if you are dealing with data types (working with only one data type system in contrast to working with several data type systems), communication between systems, or transaction behavior: a distributed environment requires different solutions. This means that developers need to change their way of thinking; as with any paradigm shift, a new approach is necessary. Be it a change from machine language programming to structured programming, from structured programming to object-oriented programming, or the current trend towards developing service-oriented architectures; at each stage of this evolution the degree of abstraction increases, and developers must adopt and adapt to the new paradigms if they are to fully exploit their potential. Clinging to old habits in this new world is more of a hindrance than a help. Process-driven applications or composite applications (composites for short)—I use these terms synonymously in this book—are no exception; there is no longer sole control over the resources involved (for example, database systems or ERP systems). Rather, we work in heterogeneous system landscapes where we are tasked with combining existing services and new business logic; application developers need to be much more aware of the problems that this presents.

The list of requirements goes on: Flexibility is another aspect that must not be underestimated. We can illustrate this by looking at two specific requirements:

1. Need for changes within the process-driven application itself, particularly changes to business processes
2. Ongoing changes within the system landscape on which the process-driven application operates

Changes to Business Processes Business processes, understood in the classic sense as "a series of specified operations (activities, tasks) executed by humans or machines to achieve one or more objectives" (see for example Hammer and Champy 1993), play a special role in process-driven applications. To differentiate themselves from their competitors, companies must constantly fine-tune those business processes that give them a competitive edge. Inevitably, successful processes are copied by competitors, so the competitive lead is short-lived. Let us look at an example from the airline industry: self-service check-in terminals. The airline that first introduced this idea could offer their customers the advantage of shorter waiting times (leading to higher customer satisfaction), and the airline itself benefited from personnel savings leading to lower costs. Today, almost all airlines use this service, so the competitive advantage has disappeared. Companies also have to change their processes as quickly as possible to adapt to changing market conditions. Whatever the trigger for the change, the consequences are always the same: A new innovation cycle compels companies to optimize their business-critical processes yet further, to ensure their continued success. The quicker these changes can be implemented, the higher the chances of a successful outcome. To ensure that software has this flexibility and agility, readiness for change must underpin the architecture of process-driven applications.

Changes in the System Landscape   Process-driven applications must likewise be prepared for a constantly changing system environment. It is one of the central characteristics of composite applications that they function in a heterogeneous system environment. Reusability, as we have already met in SOA, plays an important role here as well. However, we should not try to reinvent the wheel. If established, functioning business logic is already in place, then it should be used accordingly. This does present a particular challenge though, since system landscapes are not stable. When designing process-driven applications, you must take into account from the very start that changes to landscapes are inevitable. There are at least three reasons to expect that system landscapes will continue to change in the future, perhaps at an even faster rate:

1. System consolidations
2. Company mergers
3. Software as a service (SaaS), on-demand, cloud

Let us examine these three points in more detail. IT departments in companies are subject to enormous cost pressure. Executive management demands constant cost optimization from IT managers. *System consolidations* are a proven tool for reducing costs; the more systems and functions that can be pooled, the greater the cost-saving potential. For this reason alone, system landscapes will continue to change and develop. For process-driven applications, this means that calls that were previously made to several systems now have to be processed by a reduced number of systems.

On one side of the coin, retiring systems and moving diverse processes to standard software does indeed simplify the IT landscape. The flip side of this coin is *company mergers*. In order to reach growth targets, companies supplement their organic growth with corporate takeovers. Fusing companies together in this way swells the number of systems and applications in the landscape. In such cases, the composite application must be adapted to the increased number of services in the new environment.

Let us also not forget the newest trends: *software as a service* (SaaS), on-demand, and cloud providers. These offer IT managers further optimization potential by providing cost-effective business services. You can now farm out non-critical functions, thus contributing towards an optimized IT cost structure.

However, this scenario does demand a higher degree of flexibility from the architecture of process-driven applications. All of these scenarios, be it system consolidations, the addition of new systems, or the outsourcing of functions, belong to the daily challenges that process-driven applications must face, and must be considered as an integral part of their design right from the start. In other words, in spite of the havoc they wreak on system landscapes, profitable innovation processes are not something that companies are willing to forgo. Nor should they have to. With the right architecture, they can rest assured that changes to their system landscape, which are both inevitable and necessary if a company is to innovate, will have almost no negative impact on process-driven applications. Their capacity for innovation is not impaired.

Process-Driven Applications for SMEs and ISVs So far, this introduction may have given the impression that process-driven applications are only a matter for large companies, but this is certainly not the case. Even though constantly changing system landscapes are less of an issue for small businesses and midsize companies (SMEs) (although SaaS will surely leave its mark), the same principles still apply: Only successful processes that differentiate them from their competitors will guarantee survival. The demands placed on them in this respect are just the same as for large enterprises, and the readiness for change in application architecture discussed above is just as vital.

It is not just within companies that the new generation of process-driven applications has an important role. Independent software vendors (ISVs) can also use composite applications to gain entry to lucrative new markets. The business model for ISVs usually focuses on developing solutions as extensions to the products of well-known vendors such as SAP, Oracle, or Microsoft that can only connect to these standard solutions (think back to the example mentioned in the preface of an application for managing software licenses). The problem with this business model is obvious: Even if a customer shows interest in the vendor's business solution, a business deal is not possible quite simply because the customer does not meet the technical requirements. That is, the customer does not use the standard application required and has no plans to do so in the near future. Many potential customers are ruled out at the outset, because the solution stipulates a particular vendor. If software could be created that could be adapted to a customer's system landscape, this would open up a whole new avenue of possibilities for ISVs. Process-driven applications meet exactly this requirement. Once created, their architecture allows them to be adapted to the customer's landscape, without affecting the actual business solution. This is only possible if we can make the business application and the system landscape as independent of one another as possible. This book discusses in detail how this goal can be achieved.

Design and Implementation Approach for Process-Driven Applications The attributes, problems, and scenarios mentioned above form the starting point for this book. The emergence of the SOA idea and the accompanying hype around it led to a flood of books and articles elaborating on the various aspects of this topic.

Unfortunately, they did not manage to actually solve the challenges at hand; in my opinion this is largely due to, among other things, the bottom-up approach for interface determination and the strong focus on services and their reusability. In this book, we will propose a top-down methodology instead and shift the focus to the business processes that are implemented.

Another element I felt was missing was a detailed and comprehensive description of the architecture of business-oriented (process-driven) applications and their actual implementation, exploiting the full potential of the service-oriented idea and keeping the SOA promise. To provide such a description, the individual aspects that are relevant to process-driven applications, such as loose coupling, transaction handling using compensation, error tolerance, the role of service repositories, the requirements that services need to meet to support process-driven applications, and so on, need to be combined into a harmonious ensemble. To this aim, this book sets out a practical architecture proposal that takes these aspects into account and asserts the separation of business and technical processes. This book is also a plea for sustainable architectures that are robust yet flexible, that can adapt swiftly and effectively, in a way that exactly reflects management's business strategy. With a well thought-out architecture, the time lag between the announcement of a new (business) strategy and its implementation can be reduced to a minimum.

I will also consider new possibilities for the implementation already mentioned. I will explain how the latest version of Business Process Model and Notation (BPMN) (version 2.0) can be used for exactly this purpose, since there have been interesting new developments as regards the implementation of collaborative but also integration-centric processes. I will examine these new developments with reference to actual examples, and assess their potential and their limitations.

To summarize, the design and implementation approach presented in this book is based on the following three pillars:

1. The use of a *top-down methodology* (I also use the term *process-driven methodology*) to determine the main components/artifacts of the solution. The business processes are undoubtedly the drivers of the solution; hence the term *process-driven* in the title of the book. Throughout the book I also refer to solutions created in this way as *process-driven applications*, to emphasize this point.
2. A *sustainable architecture* (the same as a *process-driven architecture*) for process-driven applications that separates the actual business processes at the level of the end application and the technical processes of the so-called service contract implementation layer. The assignment of tasks to the two layers is clearly defined, as is their interaction with each other. The separation by a service contract protects the business processes from the constant changes at the system level.
3. The *use of Business Process Model and Notation (BPMN) throughout* for modeling as well as for implementing all process components at the business application level and at the level of the service contract implementation layer. As you will also see, a differentiation can be made in the service contract implementation layer between stateful and stateless processes.

1.2   Book Structure

To help achieve our goals of flexibility, scalability, and fault tolerance, this book will explain the concept of the process-driven application in more detail (Chap. 2). We will look at the typical properties of these applications and how they differ from other application types such as tightly coupled stand-alone programs, project-specific solutions, and pure integration applications. I will use examples to illustrate the ideas that composite applications are based on.

Once you have an understanding of process-driven applications, Chap. 3 moves on to the basic architecture of composite applications and the method for determining the main components of a composite (processes, user interfaces, data in the form of business objects, the required and provided services, and the service contract itself). Chapter 4 looks at an actual implementation of a process-driven application. BPMN, the standardized graphical notation for modeling business processes, plays an important role here, as already mentioned, and will be discussed in detail. As well as covering the theory, I will also use an example to demonstrate that the desired effect can actually be achieved. I will use a purchasing process as an example to demonstrate the implementation in software using SAP Process Orchestration, briefly describe the main implementation steps, and evaluate the experiences.

Process-driven applications encompass your critical business processes, they handle distributed architectures and a host of potential error situations. Still, to ensure that they can match the robustness and reliability provided by conventional tightly coupled applications, they need more than just a solid architecture. There are numerous additional technical concepts that you can use to help stabilize the overall solution, such as optimized locking in the involved systems, idempotence support in services, transaction processing using compensation, a troubleshooting concept close to the participating back-end systems, and so on. Chapter 5 investigates how these additional measures interact and how you can model them using BPMN.

Chapter 5 also introduces typical BPMN process fragments (patterns), which you can use to connect process-driven applications to systems in IT landscapes. In this context I will also present an enhancement proposal for BPMN that will make it possible to model integration processes in particular even more precisely. Chapter 5 continues with a discussion of the different approaches for increasing the flexibility of the process-driven application itself, and also the integration with the back-end systems. Business rules and analytical applications have an important role here.

Chapter 5 concludes with an analysis of the current discussions about structured and unstructured processes (keyword: adaptive case management), as well as their possible effect on process-driven applications.

Chapter 6 sums up the findings of the book and concludes by examining how customers can enhance composites like a product, without making any modifications. I will briefly cover the new developments that are emerging in this area.

The appendix contains an overview of the BPMN elements and an excursus on different approaches to managing services.

At this point, I would once again emphasize that this book does **not** address all facets of the development of service-oriented software. Neither is it a comprehensive introduction to BPMN. There is already excellent literature available on this topic, such as *BPMN 2.0* by Thomas Allweyer (Allweyer 2010b) and *Real-Life BPMN: Using BPMN 2.0 to Analyze, Improve, and Automate Processes in Your Company* by Jakob Freund and Bernd Rücker (2012). In his book *BPMN Method & Style* (Silver 2011), Bruce Silver describes very well how to implement BPMN correctly on the business side and how, in this way, you can distribute even complex processes into manageable components that can communicate with each other.

The focal point of this book is how to create an architecture for business applications that span multiple business processes, based on a process-driven methodology and producing solutions that exploit the full potential of SOA, and how to implement it using BPMN. You can, of course, deviate from the architecture proposed, and develop your applications using only selected parts of the recommended approaches. The book informs architects who choose to do so of the possible disadvantages if they deviate from the solution described here, thus enabling them to make an informed decision about how best to proceed.

I have intentionally left out subjects that have little relevance for the architecture of a process-driven application, such as the following:

- Organizational aspects of an SOA
- Service lifecycle
- Version management
- SOA and security
- Enterprise Service Bus
- SOA governance
- SOA project management
- Searching for services

These are covered quite adequately as individual topics in the SOA literature. In this regard, I would refer you to the (in my opinion, best) book about SOA, entitled *SOA in Practice*, by Nicolai Josuttis (Josuttis 2007). I can also strongly recommend *Enterprise SOA—Service-Oriented Architecture Best Practices* (Krafzig et al. 2004) by Dirk Krafzig, Karl Banke, and Dirk Slama.

1.3   SOA and Process-Driven Applications

Process-driven applications certainly share many properties, values, and goals with SOA, and you will encounter many commonalities throughout this book. However, the two approaches differ fundamentally with regard to the following: the *focus* of the approach, and *how* the applications and, in particular, the service contract are created. I am often asked what the actual differences are between the two approaches, so I would like to address this important aspect at the very start of the book. However, I must insert a disclaimer before I begin my comparison: Since SOA does not have an exact definition, but is rather an architecture paradigm (Josuttis 2007), all I can do is compare process-driven applications with *my interpretation of SOA* (and this applies to all comparisons with SOA in this book). And this is the crux of the matter: SOA is a moving target and each person has a different interpretation of one point or another. Even SOA experts find it difficult to pin down the term SOA and its characteristics. This is evident from the SOA manifesto (Erl et al 2009), which was formulated by industry thought leaders who came together "to hash out a formal declaration of the vision and values behind SOA and service orientation" (Erl 2013). Thomas Erl describes the process of negotiating the wording for the SOA manifesto. One participant, Nicolai Josuttis, published a German brochure called *Das SOA-Manifest. Kontext, Inhalt, Erläuterung* (Josuttis 2010), in which he writes about the particular difficulties they faced when searching for suitable formulations for the SOA manifesto. On page 7 of his brochure he explains:

> "Discussions were quickly reduced to the question of whether we could live with a specific formulation. We found that it was still possible for us to have different opinions about one point or another, because we could interpret the formulations that we decided on in different ways."

It is exactly this room for interpretation that is my main criticism of SOA, and this is probably where it differs most from the process-driven applications discussed in this book. Whereas SOA leaves a great deal open to interpretation (which, unfortunately, leads to unnecessary and time-consuming debate about the basic principles of the approach), I want this book to be as practical and unambiguous as possible. I want a specific application category (process-driven application) with a specific application architecture (process-driven architecture) to solve a specific problem (process-driven application development based on a distributed IT landscape), with a specific method (process-driven methodology).

However, since the SOA manifesto is the closest thing we have to a characterization of SOA, I do make reference to it in the following comparison. The SOA manifesto itself has three sections: a preamble, a value system, and the SOA principles upon which the aims of SOA as well as the value system are based. The preamble introduces the terms *service orientation* and *SOA*, and sets out the aims of SOA. The preamble is followed by a list of value statements, in which the authors compare and prioritize particular values. The final section sets out 14 guiding principles that underlie the statements in the preamble and the value system.

1.3.1   Commonalities

First, I'd like to look at the commonalities. We can keep this section relatively short, since I would go along with nearly all of the statements in the SOA manifesto. For example, I agree completely with the following sentence in the preamble:

We have been applying service orientation to help organizations consistently deliver sustainable business value, with increased agility and cost effectiveness, in line with changing business needs.

This sums up the aims beautifully, and concurs fully with those of process-driven applications. Let me also take a few examples from the value system. I agree with these as well, and also rate them as particularly important (this does not imply in any way that the values that I do not mention are wrong or insignificant):

Business value over technical strategy

Strategic goals over project-specific benefits

Flexibility over optimization

Evolutionary refinement over pursuit of initial perfection

There is also a degree of agreement in the principles. The following principles are also very important for process-driven applications:

Products and standards alone will neither give you SOA nor apply the service orientation paradigm for you.

SOA can be realized through a variety of technologies and standards.

Separate the different aspects of a system that change at different rates.

Reduce implicit dependencies and publish all external dependencies to increase robustness and reduce the impact of change.

We can apply these principles unchanged to process-driven applications. Simply replace SOA with PDA (process-driven application). You can already see that we can draw many parallels between SOA and PDA. There are of course differences as well, as discussed below.

1.3.2 Differences

I touched on the two main differences at the beginning of this subchapter: setting the focus and how, on this basis, the resulting applications and the required service contract result. Let us take SOA first. A focus on services is clearly expressed at several points in the SOA manifesto. The preamble states:

> Service-oriented architecture (SOA) is a type of architecture that results from applying service orientation.

Josuttis expands on this in his commentary (loosely translated):

"Apart from stating the obvious, that is, that the focus is on services or service-related concepts, it is very difficult to come up with an exact definition (of service orientation)."

This concentration on services is a recurrent theme throughout the manifesto. Other examples:

> Shared services over specific-purpose implementations.
>
> Identify services through collaboration with business and technology stakeholders.
>
> Maximize service usage by considering the current and future scope of utilization.
>
> At every level of abstraction, organize each service around a cohesive and manageable unit of functionality.

This focus on services is intended to create a foundation upon which processes spanning multiple systems can *then* be built. Josuttis expresses this as follows (Josuttis 2010, p. 5, loosely translated):

"It is about creating a useful and appropriate *foundation* for business processes that are distributed across multiple systems or entire system landscapes."

These statements bring me to the second aspect, where I see a significant difference. The above quotations imply a bottom-up procedure: Only once services are established can you work on innovative processes. Accordingly, the SOA literature lends great importance to matters such as identifying services, selecting the right services and interfaces, service management, service governance, and the reusability of services defined in this way.

Process-driven applications, on the other hand, put the focus firmly on the new business processes to be implemented. This inevitably results in a different procedure: top-down, starting from the business processes (I call this *process-driven methodology*). This top-down approach also defines the service contract, which ultimately determines the external representation of the process-driven application in the form of interfaces, and encompasses the business functions that are provided and those that are required. These interfaces contain only the fields that are absolutely necessary, from the application perspective. The data types of the interface fields are based on a canonical data model. An important point to consider here is that, to start with, the interfaces of the service contract are not even expected to be reusable. They are tailored individually to the process-driven application. This embodies the objective of process-driven applications to be able to reuse the business functions themselves, but not their interfaces. In other words, the interfaces of the back-end system themselves do not play a role in the process-driven application. It is the business functions that are important. How they are actually called, is secondary. Our application requirements first meet the interfaces of the back-end systems in the form of the service contract at the service contract implementation level that implements the service contract. It is in this layer that mapping takes place.

This important aim, to reuse *business functions* and not *interfaces*, is summarized in the following note:

Note
Process-driven applications build on the reuse of existing business functions, but not on the direct reuse of the associated interfaces (for example, WSDL).

Therefore, process-driven applications are not at all concerned with the issues that are so essential in SOA (see the list above). Of course, they are based on the reuse of existing business functions, but they do not need to reuse the service interfaces at the level of the end application. Therefore, the service contract neutralizes all existing interfaces with the application. This method leads to different content and a different task distribution within the resulting architecture. At first glance, the application architecture may look very similar (the separation into layers and the distribution of the functions that are to be performed across these layers is crucial in both SOA and process-driven applications), but it differs considerably in its details. Consequently, I will talk of a *process-driven architecture*, to differentiate it from SOA. To sum up, process-driven applications represent a different method, which results in a different architecture with a different distribution of tasks within it, a different approach to services and, therefore, a different management. The book contains detailed discussions of all of these topics:

- Procedure: Sect. 3.1
- Architecture and distribution of functions: Sects. 3.3, 3.3.3 and 3.3.5
- Services: Sects. 3.2.6 and 3.3.1
- Management of services in repositories: Sect. 3.4

Finally, I would like to draw your attention to yet another positive effect between SOA and process-driven applications. If you have already established SOA in your company, a process-driven application will definitely benefit from the services that have been developed as a result of the SOA initiative. After all, they simplify the implementation of the service contract implementation layer significantly; the effort invested in their development is certainly not wasted.

1.3.3   Process-Driven Application, Process-Driven Architecture

The term *process-driven architecture* is not new. It has appeared in many articles
and scientific publications (Margulius 2005; Strnadl 2006; Togliatti 2008, to name
but a few) in which the authors recognize the significance of business processes in
application development. However, these authors treat the business process part
simply as a *complementary enhancement* to the service-oriented architecture; an
SOA is a prerequisite, upon which you can implement the business processes.
This is discussed by Krafzig et al. (2004) in Appendix A.2 entitled "BPM and the
Process-Enabled SOA". The term *process-driven architecture* is used, but essentially this is an SOA that is used as a basis for implementing processes (we can
express this as a formula: process-driven architecture = BPM + SOA). Whether this
alone justifies a new label is another matter. In my opinion, it does not adequately
reflect the influence of the business processes as the drivers of the design of the
architecture (and therefore the application), as described in my book. For me, the
terms *process-driven application*, *process-driven architecture*, and *process-driven
methodology* form a unit and one cannot exist without the others. I want to use this
book to explore the differences from the approaches mentioned above, and elaborate on the details of the methodology, the architecture, and the applications that
result. Let us begin.

Definition of Process-Driven Applications

This chapter will give you a better understanding of process-driven applications before we move on to look at architecture in the next chapter. The concept of process-driven applications is itself nothing new. SAP, in particular, has been using this application type for many years, under the name "composite application" (see the box below). At this point I would like digress briefly to summarize the milestones in its development.

Two Names for One Concept: Process-Driven Application and Composite Application

You may well be wondering what the difference is between process-driven applications and composite applications. As I mentioned in the previous chapter, I use these terms synonymously. For me, both names describe one and the same application type, which comprises several new business processes that access existing business functionality residing in back-end systems. They compose a new application from a pool of existing solutions, hence *composite application*. If this is the case, why do I not simply use the name composite application? Why do I prefer the term process-driven application? The term process-driven application emphasizes a characteristic that is not visible in either composite applications or SOA-based solutions, namely the importance of business processes as the drivers of solution development and in the definition of external-facing interfaces (the service contract). As we will see, all decisions about the design of the service contract can be made on the basis of the target processes. This is a recurrent theme throughout the book. In the SOA literature, it is referred to as a "top-down approach". However, the SOA-based discussions about the creation of service interfaces have a bottom-up emphasis. (Maybe you yourself have pondered how best to create an interface so that it has maximum reuse potential. If so, you have already fallen into the "bottom-up" trap.) As will become

(continued)

V. Stiehl, *Process-Driven Applications with BPMN*, DOI 10.1007/978-3-319-07218-0_2, 13
© Springer International Publishing Switzerland 2014

clear, process-driven applications follow a different approach: They are intentionally detached from the interfaces of the existing landscape, and their external representation is defined purely from the perspective of the end application to be created (which data does the solution require and which data does it provide?). I place great importance on this aspect and want to emphasize this by using the name "process-driven application". Keep this in mind as you make your way through the rest of the book.

2.1 A Brief History: From xApps to Process-Driven Applications

In 2002, at their Sapphire customer conference, SAP announced a new generation of applications called "cross applications" (xApps), based on the principles of the composite application (SAP 2002a). This announcement also included the four important properties of these applications. These properties are still valid today and warrant a mention here (SAP 2002a):

1. xApps are cross functional, connecting multiple applications from any vendor, even across company boundaries.
2. Second, these applications are composite, supporting end-to-end processes by adding functionality through components.
3. Third, xApps are collaborative, unleashing the power of teams to drive change and innovation in a shared business context, and providing qualified information to enable collaborative decision making.
4. Finally, xApps leverage the mySAP™ Technology platform for the integration of people, information, and business processes, allowing the applications to support heterogeneous IT landscapes using industry standards. In these ways, xApps go beyond collaborative applications, extending the capabilities of a functional area (e.g. collaborative planning in supply chain management).

In the same year, the first technical details of the architecture were published at the developer conference SAP TechEd (SAP 2002b). In 2003, the book *Packaged Composite Applications* by Dan Woods (Woods 2003) was published. This was produced in close cooperation with SAP and describes the composite concept in detail. It included the basic principles of composite applications, their definition, and their characteristics. However, none of these early publications included a detailed technical blueprint that would guide SAP development departments and SAP partners through the actual implementation of these ideas.

It wasn't until 2005, when the project iCOD (Industry Composite Development) was launched, that practical suggestions for how to build composite applications using SAP technologies, tools, and frameworks were put forward. The results were initially compiled in various SAP internal papers, and then made generally available in a revised form (Schuller 2007a, b, c). In the years that followed, the concepts were also presented at various SAP TechEd conferences. These ideas are the foundation of this book as well. In particular, the distribution of composite functionality to process layers, user interface layers, and business logic layers is identical, as you will see. However, when it comes to connecting the back-end systems that are to be integrated, which is the central topic of process-driven application development, there are significant differences. Schuller makes the following recommendation (Schuller 2007a, p. 9):

> As composite applications are defined as applications built on top of other applications which reuse existing functionality via service calls, the question is how the consumption of those services actually works. The recommended solution is the (synchronous—author's note) web service technology.

This recommendation no longer stands today. With hindsight, it can only be justified by the fact that, under the influence of the SOA movement, the integration of external systems was generally portrayed as using primarily synchronous mechanisms, to illustrate the simplicity of the integration. This underestimates the importance of the integration, especially in an SOA, which is predestined for use in heterogeneous environments. In their book about enterprise integration patterns, Gregor Hohpe and Bobby Woolf provide an excellent discourse on why synchronous communication was preferred in the SOA environment (Hohpe and Woolf 2004). They ascribe this to an integration approach that attempted to reduce communication with external systems to the same semantics as for local method calls (Hohpe and Woolf 2004, p. 10). The authors put forward two obvious reasons for this:

1. Application developers are well versed in handling local calls. Why venture into unknown territory?
2. Using the same syntax for local and for remote method calls allows you to wait until the point of deployment before deciding which methods to call locally and which remotely.

In their paper *A Note on Distributed Computing* in 1994, Waldo et al. assert that remote calls are not comparable with local calls and must be handled differently. Gregor Hohpe and Bobby Woolf draw the following conclusion from this (Hohpe and Woolf 2004, p. 11):

> In summary, trying to portray remote communication as a variant of a local method invocation *is asking for trouble*. Such architectures typically result in brittle, hard to maintain and poorly scalable solutions. *Many Web services pioneers recently (re-) discovered this fact the hard way.*

The first SAP papers did entertain the idea of using a message broker, but did not expound further on its functions or tasks. Instead, they proposed a back-end abstraction layer (BAL), which is part of the composite application itself, to abstract the SAP back-end systems (see Fig. 2.1). I analyze this point in detail as well in this book, but I come to quite a different conclusion.

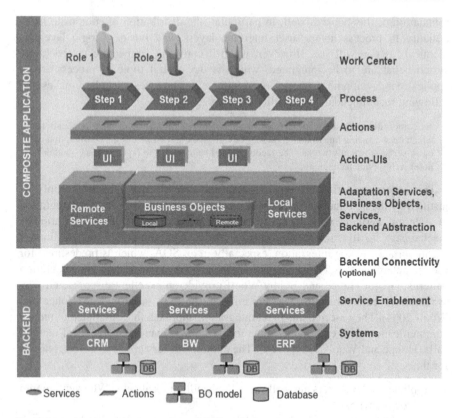

Fig. 2.1 Architecture of a composite application (Original from Schuller 2007a, p. 8)

The main idea behind BAL, which is implemented using Enterprise Java Beans (EJB) technology, was to abstract the various interfaces that are provided by SAP for accessing business logic in SAP systems. At the time, the enterprise services that had recently been established by SAP were often not available during the development of a composite application. Even though the enterprise services interface was used directly in the composite, the business functionality often had to be realized by calling remote function call modules (remote function calls (RFC) are SAP's implementation of remote procedure calls (RPC) using remote function modules (RFM) implemented in ABAP). BAL provided the abstraction required to be able to switch from the RFC module to a finished enterprise service at a later point in time. As illustrated in Fig. 2.1, the architecture includes a separate development step in the back-end systems to provide the business logic in the form of enterprise services (labeled as *Service Enablement* in the figure). This book, on the other hand, prescribes a non-invasive approach that does not require any changes in legacy systems. Furthermore, the architecture developed by SAP relies heavily on SAP technology and SAP business applications, and is therefore only of limited use for other scenarios. We can already identify some significant differences between the architecture in Fig. 2.1 and the architecture presented in this book. The xApps described by SAP attach importance to the following properties:

1. Strong orientation towards Web services
2. Back-end services are called directly from the composite application
3. Only synchronous calls from the composite; no explicit solution for asynchronous scenarios
4. Strong focus on SAP technologies and business applications
5. Direct use of very complex enterprise service interfaces in the composite application
6. Modifications required in back-end systems to provide services

The following chapters will address all of these points and suggest alternative solutions incorporating the aims mentioned at the outset.

2.2   Process-Driven Applications in Comparison with Alternative Application Categories

How do process-driven applications differ from other application types? I will compare composites with pure integration scenarios, mashups, and classical business applications. I also want to take a look at the general challenges faced by enterprise application software in a heterogeneous environment.

Integration Applications As described in the introduction, a company's composite applications should encompass the business processes that give it a competitive advantage. In this respect they differ from pure *integration applications*, which focus primarily on the technical integration between applications or business partners, for example, to ensure optimized communication between the company and its suppliers and partners. Solutions of this type were developed during the Enterprise Application Integration (EAI) era, producing a new generation of infrastructures that enabled a smooth execution of largely message-based data exchange. Optimization of the technical processes rather than the business processes was the focus.

Mashups We should also make a distinction between composites and the new generation of *mashup* solutions. Mashups are predominantly user interface programs that provide end users with screens fed with content from a wide variety of data sources. Often, these are simply a collection of existing interfaces with a shared semantic connection; these are linked to a new UI, with each reused screen appearing in its own window on the interface.

As a rule, each screen section or window is assigned exactly one data source. Of course, a single section could tap several sources, but this type of architecture is more of an exception than a rule. A screen compiled in this way results in an interface that provides end users with the data they need for their roles within a company. This is often referred to as a task-oriented user interface. Task-oriented interfaces are also created in process-driven applications. The fundamental difference is that a composite application assigns *interface definitions* rather than actual systems to the screen sections. The interfaces that have to be implemented and the systems that have to be involved to provide the required functionality are not defined at the outset; this ensues from the system landscape in which the process-driven application is to be used. Chapter 3 discusses this in detail.

Classical Enterprise Application Software A composite is different from *classical enterprise applications* such as SAP standard software, which are used mainly for business processes in companies that either operate within one industry or that span several industries but whose processes run in a uniform way. These are universal processes and, to a certain extent, can be adapted relatively easily to suit a target company and its requirements. These solutions generally work with exactly one database. The developer has full control over the required transaction behavior. This is undoubtedly the right approach for standardized processes, but it does have its limits. When it is a customer's own procedures that give it its competitive advantage, this throws up a whole new set of challenges.

2.2.1 Requirements for Enterprise Application Software in Distributed Environments

The above comparisons have pointed out all the things that a process-driven application is not. On the other hand, we have noted some parallels with SOA-based applications. In particular, the idea of creating applications that reuse existing business functionality is identical. This presents a special set of challenges, which I would like to address here. I refer to the book *Enterprise SOA—Service Oriented Architecture Best Practices* by Krafzig et al. (2004), which, right at the start of Sect. 1.2 *Enterprise Software Is a Different Animal*, discusses the challenges of creating software in an enterprise environment. I summarize the main aspects of this book below. This type of software must take into account a company's internal organization, its processes, and its business model, which presents architects of enterprise applications with a multitude of challenges. Enterprise application software must incorporate intercompany and intracompany relationships, and, as a result, it must reconcile a host of contradictory and vague requirements to come to an optimal solution. This is exacerbated by the fact that requirements change as markets, organizational structures, and company targets change; you are often chasing a moving target. All these factors of a company and its business have to be accounted for in enterprise application software, making it extremely complex.

Add to this the fact that business processes can span several departments or systems, including partners and suppliers as well, and we can see the true extent of the demands placed on software systems. Not only do we have to integrate a heterogeneous system landscape (application systems and integration solutions); the teams responsible and corporate policies differ widely as well. And let's not forget non-functional requirements such as response time behavior, scalability, reliability, availability, and security.

A well-thought-out software architecture helps with another problem: the tendency of enterprise application software to become more complex and resistant to change over time (see also Josuttis 2007; Krafzig et al. 2004, p. 4/5). Software architects have to identify and address increasing complexity in their IT projects in order to maintain the agility and efficiency needed to implement new requirements. Service-oriented architectures (the concept on which our process-driven applications are based), together with a consistent approach to componentization, help to keep IT ready and able to act.

2.3 Definition and Properties of Process-Driven Applications

On the basis of what we have covered so far, I can now (at last ☺) present a definition for a process-driven application. I would also like to list the properties typical of process-driven applications. The following definition summarizes the main aspects and opens the gates for further discussion:

> **Definition of a Process-Driven Application**
> Process-driven applications are business-oriented applications that support differentiating end-to-end business processes spanning functional, system, and organizational boundaries by reusing data and functionality from platforms and applications.

We can derive the following properties from this definition:

- First of all, process-driven applications are stand-alone applications that provide new business functionality. They are geared towards highly innovative business processes that give a company an advantage over its competitors. It is these distinguishing processes that differentiate composites from standard applications à la SAP: the aim is not to implement standard functions in a new way. Instead, the focus is on profit-making processes that supplement the standard processes with new functions. The drivers and starting point of the composite definition are the business departments that strive for process optimization. The user interfaces that are assigned to the interactive steps of a business process follow more of a lightweight, Web-based approach, which means that no extensive installation effort is required on the user side to use a process-driven application, in contrast to monolithic rich client applications (RCA). The use of RCAs is by no means excluded, however. Process-driven applications do support alternative interfaces and channels (for example, mobile end devices) and are not defined exclusively on Web interfaces.

At a lecture at an SAP event, Alexander Grobe (Coca Cola Erfrischungs-getränke) presented a very useful checklist that you can use to quickly check whether a scenario is suited to implementation as a process-driven application. I would like to present this list to you here. It lists typical scenarios for process-driven applications:

- Company-specific processes or gaps in processes that are not covered by any existing (standard) applications
- End-to-end scenarios that extend beyond system, application, and company boundaries
- Scenarios that involve a high communication, coordination, and collaboration effort, which to date has been by e-mail, Office documents such as Word or Excel files, or on paper
- Solutions with a high demand for reusable and low-maintenance business rules
- Scenarios where it is necessary to simplify or recombine separate processes, process steps, transactions, user interfaces, and IT technologies
- Processes with both interactive and automated activities
- Scenarios with lightweight B2B integrations, that is, without excessive routing and data mapping or extensive data transformations
- Self-service scenarios such as leave or travel requests (within a company) or public services such as passport applications or damage reports in the public sector (outside the company)
- Processes where frequent changes have already been observed or are expected in the future
- Scenarios with real time requirements

• Process-driven applications are by their nature largely user-centric and collaborative, that is, we want users to participate in the processes. For companies, the main objective remains to automate its processes extensively with as little human involvement as possible. It is no different for composite applications. However, particularly with company-specific processes, it is often the case that experts from business departments are involved in the processes. Unfortunately, this tends to be somewhat uncoordinated, and is often simply a matter of exchanging e-mails or Office documents. These processes are the perfect candidates for optimization.

• Since composite applications address the processes that distinguish a company from its competitors, there is of course a copycat effect (remember the example of airline self service check-in terminals in the introduction), which means we can expect a high rate of change for these processes: To maintain a long-term competitive advantage, companies must constantly adapt their processes to ever-changing conditions. This dynamic state of affairs must be taken into account during the design of process-driven applications.

• Process-driven applications extend beyond system, application, and company boundaries, which makes them very different to other solutions. It is in the nature of composites to cross boundaries, as they need to cover the complete value chain, for example, order and payment processes (order-to-cash) or procurement processes (procure-to-pay). This necessitates the involvement of various different systems inside and outside the company, and process-driven applications must be designed to deal with this.

- Process-driven applications are based on the reusability of existing functionality. Without this, they could not exist. One of the core ideas of process-driven applications is to build on existing business logic and use it in new, different processes. The SOA concept and the componentization of business functions address exactly this point. Together they represent the prerequisites for building composites. These components, equipped with a complete business function, are provided as services that process-driven applications can access when realizing innovative solutions. However, do not expect that you, or even the business department itself, can simply snap the existing functions together to build a new process. For business-critical software, which is what process-driven applications are, this is unrealistic. We need more sturdy concepts and methods, as will be discussed in more detail in the course of the book.
- As shown in the diagram of a process-driven application in Fig. 2.2, the application follows a layer model comprising a process layer, a user interface layer, and a service or business object layer. The process layer handles the innovative business processes already discussed. In order to implement these, the business processes access the relevant user interfaces or services and business objects.

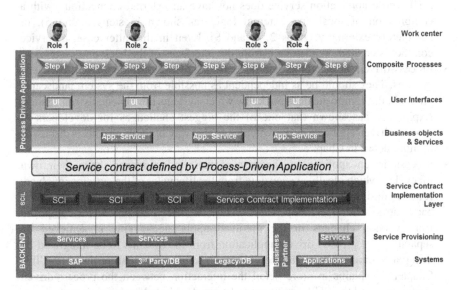

Fig. 2.2 Diagram of a process-driven application

- The end-user perspective is represented by task-oriented user interfaces. They are tailored specifically to the needs of the users in their respective process roles.

To realize their tasks, the interfaces and also the process layer avail themselves of the services of the business object and service layer. The notifications that are generated for the process participants during execution of the process appear in a worklist, which is usually on a company portal (labeled as Work Center in Fig. 2.2).

- The business object and service layer provides all the services that the process and interface layer needs to perform the necessary functions. This includes providing completely new, composite-specific business logic, data persistence for new business objects, and the reuse of existing external services.
- Even if process-driven applications use services that are provided externally, they first of all define their business requirements independently of the IT landscape in the form of a *service contract*; this looks only at the business aspect and contains only the fields that are absolutely necessary for the application. This service contract is the external representation of the process-driven application and contains not only outgoing calls (from the composite to the service contract implementation layer) but also incoming callback interfaces.
- The individual steps of the process in Fig. 2.2 are connected either to user interfaces (steps 1, 3, 6, and 7) or to service calls (steps 2, 4, 5, and 8). The service calls cover the business functionality. They are automated and do not require any user interaction.

  Figure 2.2 also illustrates how the business logic is provided: This is done either completely within the process-driven application (as indicated in step 7 by a UI whose application service does not have an external connection), with a combination of local and external logic (as shown in steps 3 and 5), or completely externally (steps 2, 4, and 8). Even in the latter case, a service contract is created, to abstract it from the interfaces of the back-end systems.

- Process-driven applications are loosely coupled with the called back-end systems. They should be as independent as possible from the system landscape. After all, the composite does not know which systems it will actually run against. Experience has shown that one of the biggest challenges for developers of process-driven applications is switching to this way of thinking; this is discussed in more detail in Chap. 3.
- Process-driven applications, because of their independence, have their own lifecycles, which ideally are separate from the lifecycles of the systems involved. It is also desirable that the versions of a composite and the versions of the called back-end systems are independent of one another. This protects a composite from version changes in the involved applications. This is achieved by separating the process-driven application from the systems to be integrated by using a separate layer, the service contract implementation layer (SCIL). Chapter 3 explains in more detail the interaction between the process-driven application and the SCIL, and how tasks are distributed between them.
- Process-driven applications work only with the data that they need to meet their business requirements. The architect plans the data model that the composite works on around the business process or processes that are to be implemented. Using these, the architect identifies the business objects and attributes that are

required. The aim is to keep the number of attributes of a business object within a composite to a minimum.

- Process-driven applications work with a canonical data type system, which enables a loose coupling with their environment at the data type level. They intentionally abstain from reusing data types and interfaces that may already exist in the back-end systems used, for example, since this would compromise their independence, which we want to avoid as far as possible. This point is discussed in more detail in Chap. 3.
- Process-driven applications are not invasive. Using a composite should not, therefore, require any kind of adaptation or modification in the connected systems in order to use the functionality of a process-driven application. From this we can also conclude that services in the systems to be integrated should be used exactly as they are.

I have selected some examples to show the functional scope that the processes of process-driven applications typically cover, but first of all the next subchapter looks at the fundamental role of BPMN, the standardized notation for graphical modeling of processes, in connection with process-driven applications.

2.4   The Role of BPMN (Business Process Model and Notation) for Process-Driven Applications: Basics

I would now like to examine the important role that BPMN plays in process-driven applications. This is not only because BPMN is used to implement all the process models in this book, but in particular because its executability has become an important part of the newest version 2.0 of the BPMN specification. BPMN has become an implementation language that can be applied not only to business processes but also to technical integration processes. Until now, companies have primarily used event-driven process chains (EPC) to model business processes and Business Process Execution Language (BPEL) for the technical processes. However, this means that when you implement the processes later, you are faced with the unpleasant and difficult task of setting up transformations between these two worlds. For this reason, I stick with BPMN throughout the book, thus avoiding any difficulties that could result from transformations between different types of notation.

You should not underestimate the influence of BPMN generally on process modeling and its implementability. It standardizes the notation used by business experts on the one hand and IT specialists on the other, thus resolving communication difficulties. BPMN provides a common language and so serves as a bridge between the two worlds. In my opinion, this deserves far more attention than executability and the other issues that are so often discussed. Of course, BPMN has its own flaws as well, but it can already be used, today, as an effective means of communication between the business and the IT world. This has immediate implications for education and training, where BPMN is currently only given a cursory mention or is neglected altogether. BPMN should be a mandatory part of the curriculum for anyone studying business studies or business information technology, and IT students taking business studies modules. If a business information and computer science graduate has to mediate between the EPC models used by business experts and the BPEL programs favored by IT experts, this role becomes much easier, at least at the process model level, if BPMN is used uniformly. This allows more time to concentrate on the essential issues, namely the business functions.

Introduction to BPMN I will now present a brief overview of the notation to enable you to understand the BPMN models used in this book. If you would like a more detailed introduction to the BPMN standard, I would refer you once again to the publications of Thomas Allweyer (2010b) and Freund and Rücker (2012). I will go into more detail about the particular importance of BPMN for process-driven applications later on in the book.

BPMN (OMG 2011) was a product of the Business Process Management Initiative (BPMI), whose aim was to design a graphical notation to represent process descriptions; a notation that would be used and understood on both the business and the technical side. Since BPMI has now been merged into the Object Management Group (OMG), the further development of BPMN is OMG's responsibility. The following quote from the BPMN 2.0 specification (OMG 2011) sets out the primary objective of BPMN:

> The primary goal of BPMN is to provide a notation that is *readily understandable by all business users*, from the business analysts that create the initial drafts of the processes, to the technical developers responsible for implementing the technology that will perform those processes, and finally, to the business people who will manage and monitor those processes. Thus, *BPMN creates a standardized bridge for the gap between the business process design and process implementation.*

Essentially, BPMN is used to design a range of different diagrams. Version 2.0 contains the following different diagram types:

- Sequence diagram
- Collaboration diagram
- Choreography diagram
- Conversation diagram

The most important diagram type for describing processes is the sequence diagram, where you model the specifics of which activities are executed, in which order, and under which conditions. Exception handling is expressly included. Since the sequence diagram is so important, let us look at its core elements in more detail. Figure 2.3 shows a simple sequence diagram. You can infer from the arrows the order in which the individual steps are performed and you can see where the sequence flow is split following a decision.

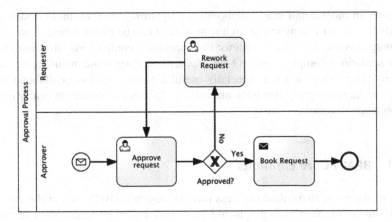

Fig. 2.3 Simple sequence diagram

One feature that distinguishes BPMN from other process notations is the option of modeling the interaction between two or more processes based on message exchange. It uses collaboration diagrams to do this. I also make intensive use of them in this book, since process-driven applications rely heavily on interaction with their environment, and collaboration diagrams are an excellent way to clearly visualize the communication between processes. Figure 2.4 illustrates this with a simple collaboration diagram. You can clearly recognize the message flows between the two processes, represented by dashed connecting arrows with an envelope decorator.

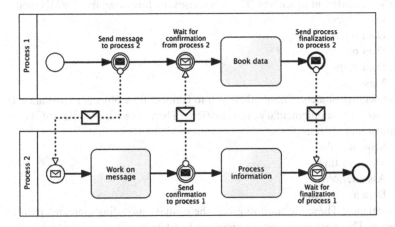

Fig. 2.4 Simple collaboration diagram

The last two diagram types in the list, choreography diagrams and conversation diagrams, do not have any relevance for this book. Choreography diagrams represent the time and logical sequence of the message flows exchanged between processes in more detail than collaboration diagrams. However, these details are superfluous to our discussion of architectures and can be omitted here. Conversation diagrams are overview diagrams; they provide a compact visualization of an entire scenario in complex process landscapes, particularly those including external partners. These diagrams are especially useful for cross-company collaborations; however, the scenarios in this book are not of sufficient complexity to justify using conversation diagrams.

2.4.1 BPMN Core Elements

Process diagrams, also called business process diagrams (BPD), are at the core of BPMN modeling. They are a graphical representation of what needs to be executed, in what sequence, when, and under what specific conditions; they must also include particular exception situations and how they are to be handled. BPMN has five core element categories for implementing the properties of BPDs (see also Fig. 2.5 for a graphical depiction of these elements):

1. Flow objects: These are the main graphical elements of BPMN and define the behavior of a process. There are three separate types of flow objects:
   • Activity (displayed as a rectangle with rounded corners), can be further subdivided into tasks and subprocesses
   • Gateway (displayed as a diamond)
   • Event (displayed as a circle)
2. Data: This is information that is either processed within a process or exchanged between different processes. This comprises the following five BPMN elements:
   • Data object
   • Data input
   • Data output
   • Data store
   • Message
3. Connecting objects: These allow you to connect flow objects to one another, or connect to supplementary information. There are four different types of connecting object:
   • Sequence flow
   • Message flow
   • Association
   • Data association
4. Swimlanes: These are used to group the primary modeling elements mentioned above. There are two types of grouping in BPMN:
   • Pools
   • (Swim-) Lanes
5. Artifacts: These are used to provide additional information about the process. The current set of artifacts includes two elements:
   • Group
   • Text annotation

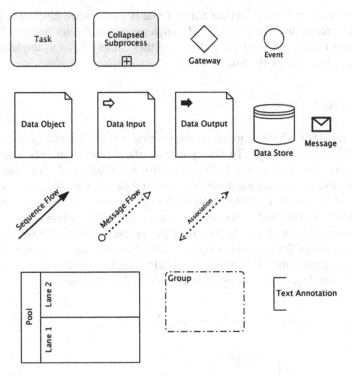

Fig. 2.5 BPMN core elements

For more details, see the table in the Appendix A.1 (Table A.1: OMG 2011, p. 59ff), which summarizes the core elements and their main properties.

2.4.1.1 Semantics of Process Models

Before I go into more detail about events, gateways, and activities, I would like to explain an important concept for describing the semantics of process models. The specification employs the concept of a token or marker, which journeys through the process model like a counter in a board game. Information technology students will be familiar with this concept from Petri nets. At the start of a process, a token is generated on the start event and travels from there along the modeled sequence flow to the various activities, gateways, and events. For example, if the token arrives at an activity, the activity is activated for processing and the token remains on the activity until the relevant task has been completed. At gateways, the token branches and can, depending on the gateway type, even multiply, so that several paths can be executed in parallel. Likewise, at gateways that merge different process paths, tokens are merged and passed as one token, so that their number is reduced again. As already mentioned, the actual behavior of the token is determined by the gateway type. Finally, the tokens arrive at the end events, where they are destroyed. If there are no more tokens, the process is finished.

Tokens are merely a theoretical concept that is useful when discussing process behavior. Companies that offer BPMN implementation do not actually have to include the concept in their program code; they simply have to implement the semantics illustrated by the tokens.

2.4.1.2 Events

BPMN provides a whole range of events, making it well equipped to respond to a host of different situations. To help you understand process models with events better, I have included a table in the Appendix A.2 (Table A.2) that summarizes how to use events in models and how to interpret their functionality. I have used the example of a message event to illustrate the various cases. A message event is a special form of event and is displayed as an envelope (✉) within a circle, which generally symbolizes an event. The envelope represents the trigger for the event, namely a message. Just as an envelope characterizes a message as an event trigger, a clock (🕓) represents a timer event. In all, BPMN 2.0 has no less than 13 different types of event. Figure 2.6 summarizes the options for messages.

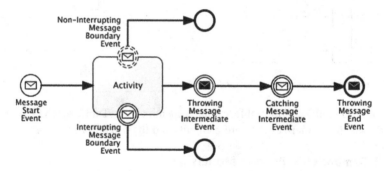

Fig. 2.6 Uses of events

You can combine the various uses of events shown in Fig. 2.6 to model a wide range of error situations, as will be explained later in the book (Sects. 4.1.3 and 5.4). Note the visual differences between a start event (circle with a single thin line), an intermediate event (circle with a double thin line), and an end event (circle with a single thick line); and those between sending/throwing (black symbol = event triggered), receiving/catching (white symbol = waiting for event to happen), non-interrupting boundary (circle with a double dashed line on the border of an activity), and interrupting boundary events (circle with a double line on the border of an activity). The various event types will be explained as necessary, depending on the context.

2.4.1.3 Gateways

Events enable differentiated handling of extraordinary process situations and are an important part of the notation. Gateways are equally important; these are used to split and merge process flows. BPMN has five different gateways that can be used within processes, and two that can be used at the start of processes. The table in the appendix explains the differences (Appendix A.3, Table A.3). Figure 2.7 shows the visual representations of the different gateways.

Fig. 2.7 Gateways

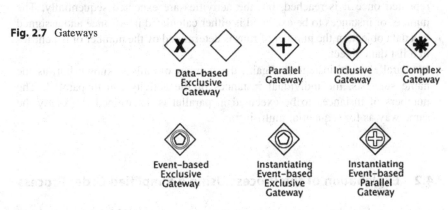

2.4.1.4 Activities

Activities can be divided into tasks (atomic activities) and subprocesses (non-atomic activities). Tasks can be subdivided further. Figure 2.8 shows the task types available in BPMN. They are distinguished by different markers in the upper left corner of the activity. Again, for a detailed description and properties, see the Appendix A.4 (Table A.4).

Fig. 2.8 Task types

You can also give activities (individual tasks and also subprocesses) certain markers to visualize their execution behavior. We distinguish three main markers:

- ↻: Standard loop—This is always used when it is not known how often the activity should be repeated once it is reached. The frequency of execution is not determined until runtime. A completion condition, which is defined at design time, defines the end of the loop. Each time the activity is completed, this condition is checked. If the completion condition is not met, a new instance of the activity is generated; if the completion condition is met, the normal process sequence flow continues.
- ☰: Sequential multi-instance—It is known how often the activity must be repeated once it is reached, but the activities are executed sequentially. The number of instances to be executed is either calculated in advance and assigned to a data object, or the number of runs is determined by the number of list entries in a list data object.
- |||: Parallel multi-instance—Again, the number of calls is known but, as the name suggests, the individual instances of the activity run in parallel. The numbers of instances to be executed in parallel is determined in exactly the same way as for sequential multi-instance.

2.4.2 Explanation of the Process Using a Simplified Order Process

Now that you have been introduced to the main aspects of BPMN, I would like to illustrate its execution by using a simple process. I will use a simplified order process as my example, displayed below in Fig. 2.9.

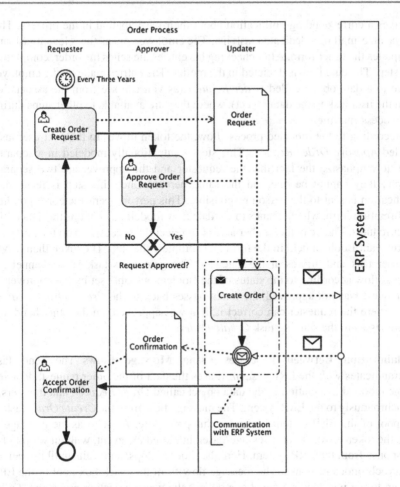

Fig. 2.9 Simplified order process modeled with BPMN 2.0

The figure shows two pools: The left pool represents the order process itself, the right pool represents an ERP (Enterprise Resource Planning) system where the order data is stored. The *Order Process* pool of the process-driven application contains all the process details. It is therefore referred to as a white box pool, as opposed to the pool of the ERP system, which contains no sequence flows and is therefore called a black box pool. The order process consists of three lanes, which represent the process roles involved: the requester and the approver as user roles, and the updater to represent a system call.

Process in Detail The process is started by a timer start event. You can see that the process is started automatically every 3 years, for example, because old laptops need to be replaced. Once the process is started, a token is placed on the user task *Create Order Request*. This task needs to be executed; the employee responsible receives a corresponding notification about their participation in the process. This can be an e-mail or a dedicated task list. The employee opens the relevant task and completes the order form. After checking his entries, he sends the order, completing this step. The data flow is depicted in the model: The entries made by the employee move to a data object called *Order Request* (as you can see from the association from the user task to the data object), where they are available to other steps during the process runtime.

According to the modeled process flow, the token moves to the next user task, labeled *Approve Order Request*. This step is intentionally modeled in a separate lane, to emphasize the fact that the requester and the approver are two separate people; they cannot be one and the same person. Once this step is reached, a notification is sent to the person responsible. This person opens the corresponding confirmation form, which, thanks to the data flow modeling, contains the data of the order request. They can then either accept or reject the request. To do this, they set the relevant Boolean field in the form and complete the step. The token then leaves the user task and arrives at the gateway. The gateway's task is to channel the process flow according to the status of the Boolean variable set by the approver. If the request was not approved, the token passes back to the *Create Order Request* step, where the requester can correct it. If it was approved, on the other hand, the token passes to the sending task *Create Order*.

Collaboration Between Processes Using Message Flows The send task communicates with the ERP system. It uses the data of the order request, depicted by the inbound association of the data object called *Order Request*, and transfers it asynchronously to the ERP system. The message flow from the *Create Order* task to the pool of the ERP system illustrates this procedure. As soon as the message is sent, the token moves to the message-based intermediate event, without waiting for a response from the ERP system. Here the process stops, and waits until it receives an asynchronous response. The message flow from the black box pool of the ERP system to the intermediate event symbolizes the communication procedure. Order confirmation data is transferred and saved in a new data object called *Order Confirmation*. The intermediate message event is connected to the data object by means of an association. As soon as the message is received, the token leaves the intermediate event and moves to the user task *Accept Order Confirmation*.

This task informs the requester that the order has been placed successfully. The requester displays the order confirmation data and completes the activity. The token arrives at the end event, where it is destroyed. Now that there are no active tokens remaining in the process model, the process can be completed.

The BPMN element *Group* is also used in the process model; it contains the send task as well as the message-based intermediate event, and is labeled *Communication with ERP System*. This shows clearly how you can use groups to emphasize which artifacts belong together. Groups, however, do not influence the execution of the process model in any way; they are simply for documentation purposes.

This process model is not complete; it cannot be and it should not be. For example, the requester has no option to exit the *Create Order Request* and *Approve*

Order Request cycle. There is also no option to react to errors in the order confirmation. No provision is made for handling communication errors or monitoring message receipt. Basically, we have modeled the "happy path", comprising the steps that represent the normal flow of processes from a business perspective. Error situations are omitted intentionally. Business experts usually create process models at this level. As we will see, these are then fine-tuned until we have an executable model. However, this introductory example is perfectly adequate for our needs at this stage, that is, to understand the main aspects of BPMN: how the various elements are used and their meaning during execution. This book looks at other BPMN models as well; these will reveal the details of the notation. The next section uses the notation to represent typical examples of process-driven applications.

2.5   Example Processes for Process-Driven Applications

I want to use this section to present a few examples of processes that are typical in process-driven applications. This will give you a feeling for how these processes can handle typical problem areas. Each of the examples involves a number of different process participants and requires access to different services, which are provided by existing systems. As such, they exhibit all the properties that characterize a composite. As you will see from the references, the examples date from a time when SAP was promoting composite applications, but they have lost none of their relevance in the meantime. Note that I have chosen just one example process for each area of usage discussed. A complete process-driven application, on the other hand, would usually contain a multitude of collaborating processes. Furthermore, only the business processes are depicted. I have intentionally left out the service contract and the service contract implementation layer, as this section deals purely with the business applications. A complete implementation would require a service contract for the service tasks executed in the process models and the services used in the user interfaces, and would have to be implemented technically in the service contract implementation layer. We will address these details in later chapters.

The next few pages contain processes for the following scenarios...

- Creating new master data (based on Malek and Dimitrova 2008)
- Handling problems during large-scale projects (based on Stiehl and Deng 2008)
- Resource planning of shift employees (based on Hill and Dimitrova 2008)
- Damage reports in the public sector (based on SAP 2010a)

2.5.1   Master Data Processing

This example is based on a case familiar to most companies who work on the Internet: A company wants to establish a good business relationship with new

customers; to do this, it needs their master data. It is crucial for today's companies
to integrate new customers into their business network immediately. They need to
build mutual trust and simplify future business dealings. Companies can generate
additional sales potential by creating customer profiles and offering other products
based on a customer's purchasing behavior. The customer is notified about the
company's upcoming new products and services, which results in increased customer satisfaction and customer loyalty. Customer loyalty is critical to success,
especially during an economic downturn. Moreover, competition is fierce for
Internet business; customers have few qualms about changing providers and
often do.

Master data plays a key role in this. So how can we make the most efficient use
of it? After all, it is not possible to process each individual request manually. A new
process should automate the procedure where appropriate. This is a typical example
that belongs to the category of request confirmation processes (see the sequence
diagram in Fig. 2.10).

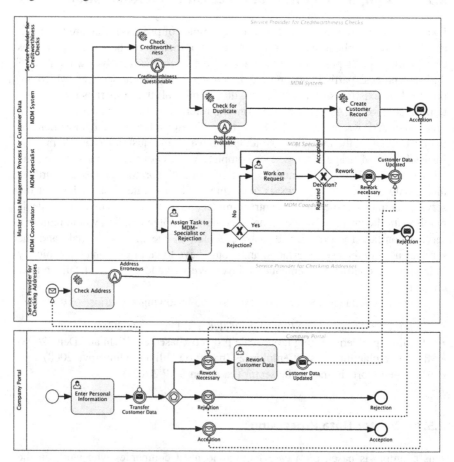

Fig. 2.10 Master data processing as a BPMN diagram (from Malek and Dimitrova 2008)

The customer enters his personal information in a company portal. When the input form is sent, the process is instantiated in the company. First, services (which can be from various different providers) verify the data. This can include classical plausibility checks such as checking the postal code or whether a street exists in a town, or a check for duplicates in the existing master data management system (MDM system). If these checks are completed successfully, other aspects such as creditworthiness are checked. Here as well, services are available from service providers. If a customer passes all the checks, he is added to the master data management system and receives a mail to this effect. If, however, the customer is already in the system or does not pass the checks satisfactorily, manual processing is required. A company will generally have several master data specialists who receive the customer data that needs checking from a coordinator. Depending on what these specialists decide, the customer is either added to the master data, rejected, or is given the option of amending his data. Whatever the decision, the customer is informed of the outcome by e-mail.

This example clearly shows the collaboration between the customer and the company, and the collaboration between coordinators and specialists. The initial objective is to automate the process as far as possible; company employees are only involved if exceptional situations arise. This pattern is often used for processes of this type. It also shows how existing functions are reused by calling a service. In practice, this scenario has proved to be one of the most attractive for companies. It is a classic example for companies new to the world of process-driven applications.

At this point, I would like to point out a particular feature of the model: In Fig. 2.10 you can see that the three service tasks *Check Address*, *Check Creditworthiness*, and *Check for Duplicate* all have escalation boundary events. I like to use escalation events to illustrate business problems. Without them, I would have to use exclusive gateways after each service task to ensure that the return of the service call is evaluated and split accordingly. Using escalation events makes the model more compact and you can see at a glance which business problems might occur. However, this is my own preference and does not imply that using gateways would be in any way incorrect.

2.5.2 Troubleshooting in Project Management

In large projects, it is common for problems to arise or for the original parameters (for example, target, scope, or design) to change. This can have negative implications for scheduling and resources. Once these threats have been identified (a challenge in itself), the next question is how to tackle the problems and at what level. Failing to deal with these situations, or not having a suitable process in place to support troubleshooting when changes or problems arise, are among the main reasons for project failure. Other consequences could be your project going over budget before it has even got off the ground, or having to repeatedly postpone going live or releasing a new product. The process depicted below (see Fig. 2.11) addresses these issues.

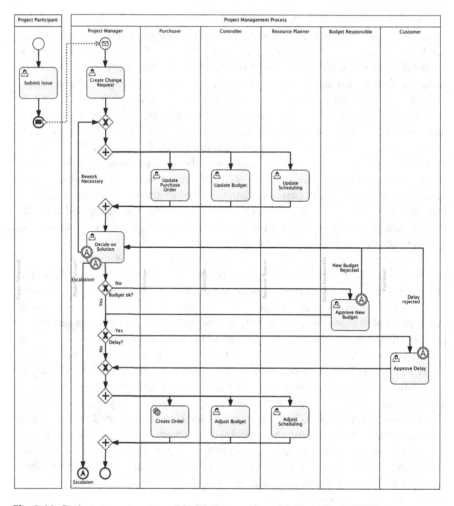

Fig. 2.11 Project management as a BPMN diagram (from Stiehl and Deng 2008)

This process enables companies to identify emerging problems at an early stage, to document them in detail, and at the same time, to bring in experts to evaluate the implications on time and budget. These evaluations then determine how the process continues. If you use a troubleshooting process, you eliminate the risk of changes to project parameters, or problems, going undetected, which could jeopardize the whole project. The process is based on the following principles:

- Problems/changes are entered in a dedicated form by project participants; this is forwarded automatically to the project manager, who creates a change request
- The status and progress of troubleshooting is monitored
- Tasks are assigned to the relevant experts, such as controllers or resource planners

- The effects of possible solutions on costs and scheduling are evaluated
- The customer is involved in clarifying the problem
- The budget and scheduling are updated, as are purchase order documents
- Confirmation from the customer is requested automatically in the event of missed deadlines or cost overruns

I do not claim that the process illustrated in Fig. 2.11 is complete. It is merely intended to show how process-driven applications can be used to handle these tasks. The striking thing about this solution is its user-centricity. It involves no less than seven different roles with many interactive user tasks. The number of activities that can be handled without human involvement is relatively low in this case; the primary role of the composite is as a coordinator, ensuring that tasks are processed in a structured and efficient way.

2.5.3   Resource Planning for Shift Workers

Our third example deals with resource planning for shift workers when unforeseen events arise. Companies have long searched for a solution to optimize the use of shift workers. Especially in economically difficult times, companies are looking for ways to optimize shift planning while retaining the flexibility to cope with unexpected situations. On the one hand, they want to reduce costs by avoiding additional shifts. On the other hand, they cannot risk not having enough workers to cover peak times, as this could endanger production or service quality. Flexible working time planning can help solve this problem, especially shift work. This model is suited to restaurants, hotel chains, or manufacturing plants, which all need to provide high-quality products or services to satisfy customers. To achieve these goals, a company needs highly motivated employees, and these employees want control over their working hours. Companies negotiate contracts with their employees that set out their working hours for particular days.

This scenario has two different groups of shift workers: the first group works in regular shifts at set times, the second group forms a pool that the employer uses as and when required. The second group provides a buffer that the company can use at any time to deal with unexpected events. The company can make use of the pool at peak times or when unforeseen events mean that they need staff at short notice. Let us look at the procedure for requesting replacements. Usually, a resource planner is responsible for this task when such a situation arises. However, it is somewhat unrealistic to expect that a resource planner will be available round the clock to be notified of staff shortages, for example, due to illness. Notices of absence can be received at any time, even outside normal working hours. Employees need to be able to inform their employer at any time that they will be absent, even if this is in the early hours, in the evening, or at weekends. It is even more of a problem if resource planners are responsible for a large number of shift workers. They cannot be expected to be able to monitor and manage the entire resource planning. The only way to solve this problem is to automate the resource planning procedure almost completely. Figure 2.12 shows how this could be implemented.

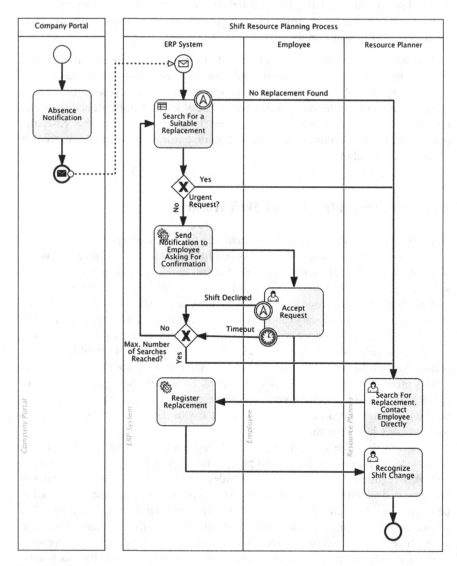

Fig. 2.12 Shift work as a BPMN diagram (from Hill and Dimitrova 2008)

To illustrate the procedure, let us use a notification of absence as an example. The worker in question has entered a notification of absence on the company portal and sent it. This triggers the shift resource planning process. There is an automatic search for a suitable replacement, based on business rules. Once a possible replacement is found, this employee receives an automatic notification, for example, via SMS or on a paging device or beeper as used by the emergency services. The employee who has been contacted now has various options:

- He accepts the shift: The problem is solved, the replacement is registered in the system, and the resource planner is informed of the change, which he sees the next time he is at work.
- He declines the shift: The process for automatic assignment is repeated.
- He does not react: Once a specific waiting time has passed, the automatic assignment is reactivated.

The resource planner is only involved explicitly in the process if the automatic assignment cannot find a replacement, if a particularly critical situation arises, or if a configured maximum number of alternatives has been exhausted.

This example shows once again how a high level of automation can improve efficiency in a company. We also once more see a pattern where personnel are only involved in exceptional situations.

2.5.4   Damage Reports in the Public Sector

The last example I will present is from the area of self-service scenarios in the public sector. Here in particular, there is a lot of scope for automation scenarios. The damage report scenario addresses several common grievances. In the public sector, there are usually no established processes for unexpected maintenance work (for example, a fallen tree blocking a road, defects in public buildings). Rather, internal personnel decide on an ad hoc basis how to proceed. If there is a sudden increase in these extraordinary events, this can easily result in an overload. The lack of automation means that the overall costs for solving the problem are high. Besides the process-relevant aspects, it is important to also consider that members of the public might have difficulties finding the right contact person, are thus unlikely to find a quick solution to their problem, and will be left feeling very dissatisfied with the process.

Therefore, the central objective of this example is to ensure clearly defined processes to address the weaknesses mentioned above. Members of the public are more involved in the process, there is more cost-saving potential as a result of process automation, the quality of the solution is improved due to the use of external specialist companies, and the employees can concentrate on their own tasks, such as monitoring and performing standard maintenance work. Figure 2.13 shows the main steps of the process.

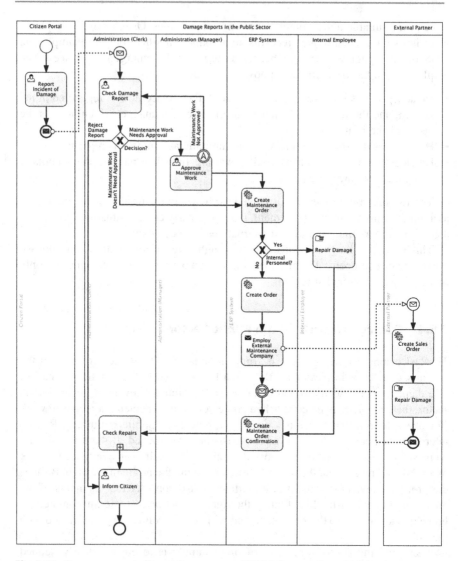

Fig. 2.13 Damage report in the public sector as a BPMN diagram (from SAP 2010a)

The process is triggered when a member of the public reports an incident of damage. This report can easily be submitted as a form on the Internet as part of a citizen portal. Once notification of the damage has been sent (for example, a report that a seesaw is broken at a children's playground, including a photo of the damage), an administrator in the maintenance department will be informed of the problem. Once the administrator has checked the damage report, rules can be used to determine automatically whether approval from a manager is necessary (for example, if the estimated repair costs will exceed a certain amount). Rules can also be used to determine automatically whether the repairs are carried out by internal personnel or whether it is necessary to use an external specialist firm. Depending on how the rules channel the process flow, additional participants are involved. For example, once an administrator has the approval of their manager, they can use a business-to-business integration to employ an external maintenance company to repair the damage. Once the repairs are complete, the invoice is automatically sent to the municipal authority in question. Finally, the administrator checks that the repairs have been carried out satisfactorily and approves payment of the invoice. In the very last step, the administrator informs the member of the public who triggered the process that the damage has been repaired.

This example shows once again the integrative nature of process-driven applications: not only does the scenario extend across various different roles in different departments in public authorities; external partners and suppliers are also involved in the process. If this solution is to be used as a product in other municipal districts as well, a sustainable architecture for composite applications becomes even more significant. The next chapter addresses this topic in more detail.

Architecture of Process-Driven Applications

3

In Chap. 2 we discussed the properties of process-driven applications in great detail, and you should by now have a clear idea of what sets them apart from other application types. In this chapter we will focus our attention on how to actually go about implementing the architecture and its properties. To start with, let us consider the questions you might ask if you decide to go ahead and develop a process-driven application: Where should I start? I want to implement new business processes: Should I use these as my starting point and basis for decisions and for working out the requirements of the process-driven application? Or, do I start with the services that already exist in the system landscape and combine these to build new processes? You probably already have a good idea of how to answer these questions but, as you will see in this chapter, there are certain factors that need to be taken into account when developing process-driven applications (independence from back-end systems, for example), and these will influence how you proceed. In the method I present here, we determine what the main elements of the composite are and combine these in accordance with a specification. It will become clear that in process-driven applications a differentiation needs to be made between business and technical processes; although they are loosely coupled as regards their interaction, they should be strictly separate in their implementation. We will look at the role loose coupling plays and find out which functions are represented in which layer. The chapter concludes with a discussion of the importance of repositories to process-driven applications.

One comment before we start: In the top-down method presented here, we start with a preliminary (and somewhat abstract) sketch of the architecture and gradually fill in the details to arrive at our process-driven application. As a result, some of your questions may still be unanswered at the end of this chapter, but rest assured, these will be addressed later in the book, where we will implement an actual composite and focus on the technical details.

We have a lot of ground to cover, so let's begin.

V. Stiehl, *Process-Driven Applications with BPMN*, DOI 10.1007/978-3-319-07218-0_3,   43
© Springer International Publishing Switzerland 2014

3.1   Methodical Approach: Top-Down

Faced with the task of developing process-driven applications, developers will want to know if there is a particular method they should follow. Looking at the literature (SOA publications being a useful source of information, thanks to SOA's similarities with process-driven applications), the recommendation would seem to be a combination of the top-down and the bottom-up approach (for example, Josuttis 2007; Bloomberg and Schmelzer 2006). With a top-down approach, you break down a problem into smaller and smaller elements until you have identified the core components of the application, for example, business objects and basic services (this is called decomposition).

With the bottom-up approach, you do exactly the opposite: you build new processes using the existing services of the applications that are to be integrated (this is called composition). The following quote from Bloomberg and Schmelzer (2006), also in Josuttis (2007), is particularly interesting in this respect:

> *In SOA, the approach should be both top-down (process decomposition) and bottom-up (using existing functions as services and composing these into processes). If you only use the top-down approach, this will likely result in services that are difficult or complicated to implement from a technical point of view. If you only use the bottom-up approach, this can result in services that are surplus to requirements or, even worse, do not fulfill the business needs.*

Nicolai Josuttis expresses this in his brochure about the SOA Manifesto (Josuttis 2010) as a list of SOA stages (p. 4/5):

> *In practice, the SOA environment has various stages:*
>
> *   *In the first stage, services are introduced, that is, business-led, autarkic interfaces that encapsulate implementation details and provide IT services.*
> *   *In the second stage, these services are used to realize distributed functions in large systems or system landscapes. (...)*
> *   *In the third stage, more varied services are used to realize entire business processes. (...)*
> *   *In practice, there is often a fourth stage as well: enterprise architecture management.*

He summarizes this as follows (p. 5):

> *In practice, the term SOA is used for all of these stages. It is a point of contention, however, whether business processes and architecture management are actually part of SOA, or simply a useful addition.*

These statements demonstrate how little value is placed on business processes and that the focus is firmly on services (it would seem that the label *service orientation* is quite justified). However, to me, this still implies a bottom-up approach. So, how should we deal with such statements in the context of process-driven applications? In my opinion, this is where SOA differs most from the approach I describe in this book, which is why I use the term *process-driven methodology* right from the start. In Chap. 2 I mentioned that one of the features of composite applications is their high degree of independence from back-end systems, which rules out the bottom-up approach. Instead, architects should design their process-driven applications top-down, omitting all details of the IT landscape. I put it like this:

Note
"For every decision you have to make about the process-driven application, simply imagine that you don't know anything about the system landscape in which your solution will run."

At first this may seem rather radical and unrealistic, but think back to our original objective: to develop a specific type of application with very special properties, as discussed in Chap. 2. We do not want a project solution where we have to know and plan around the system landscape from an early stage; we want to produce a solution that is more like a product, with the potential to be used in other environments as well. Of course, the fact can't be ignored that process-driven applications do have to deal with concrete system landscapes, and it may be necessary to include specifics about the involved back-end systems for want of a better alternative (this is discussed in more detail in Sect. 3.2.6). In this case though, the service contract implementation layer can be used to include the dependencies of specific systems in the process-driven application. The above note is more of a mental nudge to help refocus your thinking away from the IT landscape and more towards finding the solution to the business problem at hand. This prevents the solution from becoming overly dependent on application functions, their interfaces, and the data types used.

Business Processes as a Starting Point   Process-driven applications are driven by the business functionality that is required, and our starting point is the process or processes that need to be implemented. To emphasize this point and to differentiate the resulting applications and architecture from SOA, I use the terms *process-driven application* and *process-driven architecture* (or PDA for short). This puts the emphasis squarely on the business processes, and it is from the sequences of individual process activities within these processes that we determine the components that make up a composite, displayed in Fig. 2.2.

- Processes
- User interfaces
- Business objects
- Services

You define these components for the particular composite that you are implementing, where the processes solve a specific business problem. Initially, you should design your process flows to deliver an optimal solution for the company, without making compromises or allowances for existing landscapes or functions. You need to identify the process roles in the processes; based on these, you then design the user interfaces that will best support each role in its respective function in the process. These interfaces should provide the information and functions (for example, searches and input helps) that the end user needs to be able to work as efficiently as possible. This includes features to assist the user with data input, and charts and diagrams to help the user make decisions.

Data and Services The next step is to derive from the processes exactly what data the composite will work with, and we can then compile the individual attributes and fields into business objects. But remember: Only include what is absolutely necessary. The systems in the IT landscape may well have complex structures for business objects such as customer, product, or order, with a host of attributes, but process-driven applications will generally only use a fraction of this data. There is really no need to burden the composite with this complexity; keep it as minimal as possible.

You should define the required services solely from a business perspective as well. It doesn't matter if a service is required within a user interface or called from a process step, the focus must be on the business function that the service provides. In this respect, process-driven applications are fundamentally different from conventional SOA-based applications, where existing services are usually called directly from the end application. In process-driven applications you create new definitions for all outgoing external calls; these make up the service contract. The interfaces reflect the business requirements of the composite, that is, its processes determine which input and output parameters are included. If, for example, you have a new process for creating orders that requires only the product number and the quantity, the public interface of this service only needs these two pieces of information as input parameters—no more, no less. The interface may well need to be changed later during implementation, but for the moment, the primary task is to express the business requirements. For this reason, a composite does not simply import an existing interface and add process steps or user interfaces to implement the calls; instead, new interfaces are defined, thus abstracting the required functionality. At the beginning of this section I mentioned that a risk of the top-down approach is that you may embark on developing services that are technically difficult or complicated to implement, but in practice this has proved to be less of a problem than feared. Because the business and technical processes are separated, and because the communication between them is asynchronous, it is possible to have a time delay between the caller and the called, in particular for changing services (write, delete, update), which allows you to implement even complex functions.

Business Process Model = Executable Process Model? The question is: If a business department produces a BPMN model with little or no consideration of if or how it can be executed, can it actually be executed in this form (or with only very minimal changes)? Current opinion is fairly unanimous, with comments such as "*A BPMN model is either executable or it can be understood by the business team—it can't be both*" or "*Considering the time and money invested in the business model, it should stay as it is. To develop an executable process, we recommend creating a new BPMN model, whose only connection with the business model is to show which* *executable processes need to be changed if there are changes on the business side. Do not create a new version of the business model just to make it executable."*

What should we make of these statements? First, let us consider who exactly BPMN models are intended for. During the lifecycle of a process, there are various different consumers or "customers" of process models: process owners, process managers, process participants, process analysts, and process engineers (see also Freund and Rücker 2012), each with a different perspective on processes, different requirements as regards the process model, and, of course, each with a different understanding of BPMN. It is impossible to make any general statements as these perspectives often overlap, and the methods for representing the processes can range from a simple overview or sketch (which doesn't even have to use BPMN) to a very detailed and informative BPMN model. If BPMN models are used at a strategic level, then these are usually too high-level to be useful as a template for executable processes. In this instance I would agree with the above comments. However, if a company wants to not only document its processes, but also, ideally, to use the same model to execute them, then this is a different matter. The more important executability is as a factor, the more detailed the business model must be, and in this case the business model would be created by a process analyst with a sound knowledge of BPMN and capable of modeling, accurately and consistently, business process flows in BPMN. It is this type of model that we will focus our attention on.

I would also suggest that the above comments stem from a misunderstanding: that the developer has to take the business model produced by the business team and develop it so that it becomes executable, combining business and technical processes into one model. I would certainly agree that this approach does not work, but if we follow the process-driven application approach and strive to keep business processes and technical processes separate, then another picture emerges. The objective here is to keep the business processes as they are, as originally devised by the business departments. Of course, some compromise will be necessary to execute the model at a later point in time, but I remain convinced that close cooperation between business and IT experts can result in a *common model* for the business process, one that can be both understood by the business departments and can be executed. In any case, the technical process is in the remit of the IT department and contains technical details (such as retries in the event of errors, or service call splits to optimize performance) that do not belong in the business model. I therefore do not see the need for separate executable and non-executable business models. We can avoid the model mismatch that results from separating the business processes, and this is certainly something to strive for, not least because it also encourages cooperation between the involved parties to achieve a common goal.

Of course, this aspect can be viewed another way: What happens if we do separate what is executable on the business side and what is not? Who is responsible for maintaining and managing these pairs for every single process? Will the original core process actually be recognizable in its executable form? Surely the administration and maintenance effort is the same as, if not more than, that of designing a common model? Who will make sure that the executable variant actually does what the business department intended? Does this approach not merely add to the burden we have had all along: the discrepancy between what the business departments ideally want from a process and how this can be implemented? Now that we have finally found a common language in BPMN that can bridge this gap, I think we should seize its potential. It should be clear to both parties what they can gain by working together, by closing the gaps in their knowledge, and by establishing a solid foundation on which to create sound business processes that meet the requirements of both worlds.

As already stated, the only way to determine the details of processes, user interfaces, business objects, and services is for business and IT departments to work closely together, and the next section investigates what information is necessary to do this.

3.2   Specification of Process-Driven Applications

If you plan to implement new business processes as a process-driven application (comprising both the business and the technical side), and want to find out more about how to get the information you will need, there is a wealth of publications available. Therefore, this section concentrates on just those aspects that are relevant to process-driven applications. Also, there are already some very detailed methodologies available for process management on the business side, in particular *Enterprise BPM* by Dirk Slama and Ralph Nelius (Slama and Nelius 2011). The authors have developed an integrated BPM project methodology (IBPM), which uses many aspects of BPMN and provides exactly the information that is needed for implementation. I borrow directly from Slama and Nelius' conclusions, and use the information to create a suitable implementation architecture.

The specification of process-driven applications is something I have addressed in earlier publications (Stiehl 2006; Rauscher and Stiehl 2008), although at that time I was still working under the assumption that the available services would be accessed directly from the composite. This method is no longer common practice, as explained in the previous section. Not only does it create dependencies, which should be avoided at all costs; it also has a number of issues that actually increase complexity. Nevertheless, these earlier publications contain some important ideas that I would like to reiterate here, as they do contribute to our discussion of process-driven applications.

This section is essentially an overview of the data and requirements that have to be factored into a composite application to ensure its later implementation. This task falls to the experts in the business departments, perhaps with help from colleagues in IT. A composite is business-led, which means that most of the required information can only be provided by the business experts. The following sections make up a checklist that can be used as a guide when creating a specification. Note however, that this checklist only includes composite-relevant aspects; it makes no claim to provide a complete software specification. It is, however, well suited to agile methods.

When creating a specification for a composite, the various stakeholders may describe their requirements verbally, as sentences. This means that requirements that are in essence similar, or even identical, are expressed completely differently stylistically by the different groups. In their book *Requirements Engineering Fundamentals* (Pohl and Rupp 2011), the authors explain how using requirement templates can minimize the scope for misinterpretation, and thus reduce project risk. A requirement template consists of sentence patterns, as shown in Fig. 3.1.

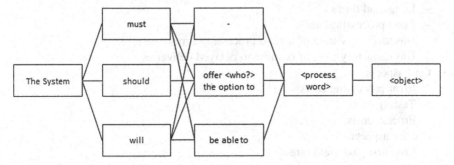

Fig. 3.1 Example of a requirement template (from Pohl and Rupp 2011)

It is a good idea to use patterns like this when specifying process-driven applications as well; they leave little room for misinterpretation and result in common consistent descriptions. Compiling the individual aspects into a table makes it easier to create the specification and gives you a better overview. In an earlier publication (Stiehl 2006) I defined a comprehensive set of tables for composite applications; these are very helpful when dealing with the specification aspects mentioned below.

You can supplement informal descriptions with graphics, for example, the OMG Systems Modeling Language (SysML 2010), which is recommended for depicting relations between individual requirements and for linking the requirements to other model elements, such as test cases to verify the requirements. This makes cross-dependencies and relationships that would be lost in verbal descriptions visible.

The method for specifying process-driven applications follows the top-down approach outlined in the previous section, and has six main steps:

1. General information about the process-driven application
2. Process information
3. Exception/event handling
4. Business objects
5. User interfaces
6. Services

3.2.1 General Information About the Process-Driven Application

First of all, the business department must understand the objective of the process-driven application. As a rule, you should use composites if you want to eliminate existing weaknesses, strengthen competitive advantage, or move into new business areas, and these objectives are generally consistent with the strategy set out by executive management. Management must be able to understand what the problem is and why a new solution is needed. Ideally, you need to show how non-existent, inefficient, or faulty processes are affecting the current situation, and back this up with the relevant figures, for example:

- Time aspects
  - Long lead times
  - Long processing times
  - Unsatisfactory ratio of lead to processing times
  - Unsatisfactory ratio of on-time to delayed deliveries
- Cost aspects
  - Error processing costs
  - Testing costs
  - Process costs
- Quality aspects
  - Low first pass yield rate
  - High error rate
  - High return rate due to quality defects
  - Material waste

You can then go on to present the solution concept and explain how it would address these issues and keep future problems at bay. In some cases, it may even be possible to use process simulators to support the proposal for a process-driven application, and cost-benefit analyses are certainly indispensable at this stage. Management needs to be convinced by the idea, they need to believe that the new solution will bring improvements, for example, increased efficiency, flexibility, and quality; reduced costs and error rates; increased throughput and customer satisfaction. And however you plan to bring about these improvements, there must be a monetary value attached to them; this is the key to getting management on board.

It is important to continue to document these aspects over the course of the project so that it is possible to check, at any time, whether it is achieving what it set out to do. It can also be helpful to go back to the original objectives whenever decisions need to be made during the project. Ultimately, this information is used to justify the very existence of a process-driven application and the effort that goes into compiling and evaluating it should reflect this.

3.2.2 Process Information

This part of the specification lists all the processes that are involved in the process-driven application, gives a brief description of their functions, explains how they contribute to achieving the objectives of the composite, and then characterizes each individual process in detail. The following information needs to be compiled for each process:

- General process information
- Involved process roles
- Visualization of the process flow
- Detailed information about the process steps
- Description of the data flow within the processes (process context)

The individual aspects are discussed in more detail below, with helpful pointers to help you produce your own specification.

3.2.2.1 General Process Information

General process information means the starting conditions and timetable of a process. The following questions need to be considered:

- Under what conditions will the process start?
  - Time
    - The process starts at a particular time (for example, once on December 24 at 14:00, or regularly each Wednesday at 06:00).
    - The process starts after a particular time interval (for example, once in exactly 7 h, or regularly every 6 h).
    - The process starts in relation to another time (for example, 1 month before December 24).
  - Conditions
    - The process starts once one or more conditions are met, for example, a warehouse is restocked with a particular product once stock levels go below a predefined threshold value.
  - Messages
    - The process waits for a particular message to arrive.
  - Events
    - Events have an important role, especially in exception situations. An event is triggered when an extraordinary situation arises that requires special handling, for example, a late delivery, a machine failure, an accident, or similar.
  Of course, the start can depend on more than one of the conditions mentioned above; this should be noted accordingly.
- Are there any time constraints for the process?
  Does the process have to be completed within a particular time? If yes, what happens if it exceeds this deadline? Who needs to be informed and what follow-up activities need to be initiated?
- General process roles

Who can monitor the process to get an idea of its progress status? Who can forward activities to a substitute, for example, if the person usually responsible is on vacation? Who can take on unprocessed activities themselves? And who is not authorized to monitor the process, distribute activities, or process them themselves? Answering these questions helps us clarify typical process roles such as administrators, potential task owners, and excluded task owners.

3.2.2.2 Involved Process Roles

The involved process roles define who is responsible for performing which activities during the process. All you need is a simple list of process roles and a description of the functions the roles perform within the process. At runtime, users and groups from the company's user management solution are assigned to these roles. Although this presents a challenge, the complex task of assigning users to process roles in workflow management systems within company organizations is outside the scope of this book and is not discussed in more detail here. For more information, I would recommend Zur Mühlen (2004), which also contains an overview of other literature available on the subject.

3.2.2.3 Visualization of the Process Flow

In process-driven applications especially, the visualization of the process flow is of great importance as this is the means of communication between the business experts and the architects tasked with implementing the process requirements. Again, we will use BPMN for the process modeling. The process model must show what has to be performed, when, and under what conditions. The specification does not have to model all the details (this is outside the remit of a business department), but the business experts should provide at least the following information:

1. The sequence flow of the process steps for the *happy path*, that is, the normal process flow if no errors occur. In BPMN, this is done using sequence diagrams.
2. Typing of activities as either fully automated or requiring end-user interaction. BPMN has user and service tasks for this purpose.
3. Assignment of roles to user tasks. In BPMN, this is done using pools and (swim) lanes.
4. Handling of business exceptions. In BPMN, you have either events or a range of end states at your disposal, which are then evaluated using gateways. Note that the model should only include business exceptions such as delays, quality defects, or cost overruns. Technical exceptions such as connection problems, database failures, or incorrect data formats can be ignored at this stage. This keeps the BPMN model manageable.

BPMN is indeed very powerful, perhaps even overwhelming, so it is no wonder that many authors want to see a reduction in the number of BPMN elements for modeling at the business level. Freund and Rücker (2012) and also Silver (2011) recommend reducing the BPMN artifacts used on the business side to an absolute minimum. Bruce Silver proposes the following BPMN constructs for business departments:

- Pools and (swim)lanes
- User and service tasks
- Subprocesses (both collapsed and expanded)
- Start events (untyped, timer event, message event)
- End events (untyped, message event, terminating event)
- Exclusive and parallel gateways
- Sequence flows and message flows
- Data objects, data stores, and messages
- Annotations
- Link events for continuing process models onto another page

He also recommends a step-by-step method for modeling business processes, with the model becoming successively more detailed at each level:

- Level 1: Descriptive modeling
- Level 2: Analytical modeling
- Level 3: Executable modeling

Each level has its own recommended set of BPMN constructs. The current version of the BPMN specification (OMG 2011) also splits the modeling process into levels called process modeling conformance classes.

Level 1 creates a simple representation of the process flow using the most basic BPMN artifacts (which we are familiar with from classic flow diagrams) to model typical activity sequences and to assign process roles to these activities. The resulting models may be simple, but this ensures that they can be communicated to all project participants and that even non-BPMN specialists can quickly understand and apply them. This level meets most of the requirements important in the specification of a process-driven application, and is primarily the responsibility of BPM consultants and process managers in the business departments.

Level 2 uses the more complex and powerful BPMN elements, which allow detailed process modeling, including exception and event handling. However, it remains business-oriented and the resulting process models are not yet executable (although they can be used in simulations to analyze process performance). These models represent the business view of the process that will be executed later in a BPM system (BPMS: Business Process Management System). They do not yet contain the technical details that are required for execution. Level 2 is usually the responsibility of company architects and analysts or dedicated process analysts.

Level 3 supplements the model from level 2 with the technical details that enable the model to actually be executed in a process engine. This is one of the main features that sets BPMN apart from other modeling notations such as event-driven process chains (EPCs) or the activity diagrams of the Unified Modeling Language (UML): it is based on a controlling process engine. In this context, Bruce Silver points out that BPMN is part of a higher OMG objective: a model-driven architecture (MDA) in which executable systems are controlled by graphical models and not by code. Level 3 is clearly the responsibility of developers.

A very interesting aspect of Silver's model is hierarchical expansion, whereby you start with a rough end-to-end process model, then fine-tune it using the subprocesses supported in BPMN, nesting them hierarchically one within the other. This produces more manageable models: they can be viewed at the level of detail you require, that is, you can look at the model from the views of the various different roles, be it a process manager on the business side, a process analyst, or a developer. *One* process model meets all the requirements. With tools that allow navigation along the hierarchy, this method simplifies process analysis, construction, and implementation.

Another advantage of nesting subprocesses hierarchically is that parts of processes can be reused in other scenarios. A subprocess encapsulates a well-defined, self-contained business function as a component, or, in an SOA environment, a service. BPMN thus forces the componentization of processes and subprocesses and makes you think in terms of reusable units. To fully exploit the advantages offered by this method, you should apply it during the specification phase.

The level of detail that is required in the specification of process-driven applications is comparable to that of level 1, so let's take a closer look. We find much in common with the recommendations made already. Silver favours the following five steps:

- Step 1: Define the scope of the process: What function does the process provide?
- Step 2: Create a top-level model for the "happy path"
- Step 3: Supplement the top-level model with paths for handling exceptions
- Step 4: Extend the model by adding subprocesses to visualize further details at the child level
- Step 5 (optional): Add message flows to external pools

Using multiple pools (step 5) requires advanced BPMN knowledge, and there may not be someone with this level of expertise at the company. For this reason, in their "Real-life BPMN" book (Freund and Rücker 2012) the authors advise against using multiple pools, claiming that this is too complicated for business departments. Personally, I support using multiple pools, because I think this is the only suitable way to visualize the collaboration between the various parties, and this is an important factor when dealing with end-to-end processes in process-driven applications. Ultimately, the company must decide for itself which method it wants to use. The number of constructs used should definitely be reduced, but this decision must be taken by each company individually. Whatever the decision, the end result is a representation of the processes of the process-driven application in the form of BPMN models, which we can then use as the basis for the following sections.

3.2.2.4 Detailed Information About the Process Steps

We now have to work out the details for the process steps that we described in the previous section. We need to determine what functionality is provided, how, and by whom. The following checklist helps you identify the information required for the implementation; use it for every process step:

- Description of the business background of the step: What contribution does it make to the overall process? What business logic is executed? What data is processed? Which actions are performed on the data (read, write, delete)? Does the step use services? If so, what business functionality does the service provide, and what data is required from the perspective of the process-driven application?
- Is the step interactive or automated? If it is interactive, which entries need to be made?
- Does the step have to be performed more than once? If so, is the number of executions known or can the step only be completed if it meets a condition? If the number of executions is known, can the steps be processed in parallel or do they have to adhere to a strict sequence?
- Could exception situations arise during the activity that would require special handling? What are these exceptions?
- In the case of interactive steps, which process role does this task have? Are there any time constraints? In this case, it is important to define a time by which the activity must have started and a time by which it must have finished. You also have to define what will happen if these deadlines are missed: Is there a separate escalation path, and if so, should the activity be interrupted or not?
- Which statuses does the process step return? Each status requires a corresponding reaction and this needs to be reflected in the process flow.

3.2.2.5 Description of the Data Flow Within the Process (Process Context)

All kinds of information and data are collected and handled during process execution, and it is not only the logical sequence of process steps that you need to consider when dealing with processes, but also the data flow between the individual tasks. The specification of a process-driven application must specify explicitly which data is available to the individual activities during the process. It is important to take the temporary nature of this data into account: Once the process instance has finished, this process data (also referred to as the process context) is irretrievably lost. If you want the data to be retained beyond the process instance, you must define this explicitly in the specification and separate it clearly from the process context data. You can represent the data in the specification by using class diagrams, for example, where the attributes required by the data flow are grouped into objects. You must also include any relationships to other objects; this is discussed in more detail in Sect. 3.2.4 (Business Objects).

3.2.3   Exception Handling

It is crucial to include any business exceptions that may arise during execution of the process. This forces the business departments to also consider potential error scenarios. Many of the models currently available deal almost exclusively with the "happy path", even though it is usually the errors that occur in process models that generate the most work. This part of the specification defines how to handle *business* exceptions only. You have to specify the circumstances in which exceptions may arise during a particular activity, and the appropriate reaction. In automated steps (service tasks in BPMN), you also have to specify whether the call is repeated and if so, how often and at which intervals. You also need to bear in mind that the entire process could terminate, and there must be a solution for this eventuality as well, to determine how to proceed and who to inform.

If you follow the hierarchical approach, as suggested in the previous section, you also have to consider how to communicate exceptions from a subprocess to the parent process instance by using BPMN events. If exceptions occur in subprocesses, you need to pay particular attention to how this status is communicated to the parent process so that it can react appropriately. There are three options:

– The error is indicated by an error status in the subprocess. In BPMN, you can use a none end event and add a text describing the end status. This text can then be evaluated by a gateway in the parent process. This is illustrated in Fig. 3.2.

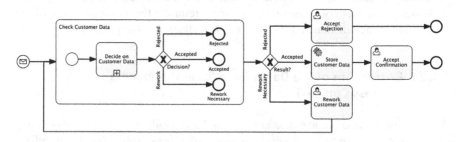

Fig. 3.2 Communication between subprocess and parent process using none end event

– An event is thrown. Since we are dealing with business exceptions, you can use the escalation event in BPMN. The parent process catches this event with a catching escalation boundary event attached to the subprocess and follows the modeled sequence flow. This is displayed in Fig. 3.3.

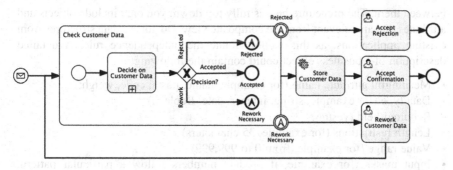

Fig. 3.3 Communication between subprocess and parent process using escalation end event

– A variable is set in the process context of the parent process. This is only possible if the subprocess is embedded in the parent process, not called as a separate process. Figure 3.4 shows how the variable is set in the subprocess using explicit service tasks and is then evaluated in the parent process at an exclusive gateway.

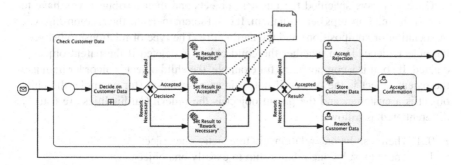

Fig. 3.4 Communication between subprocess and parent process using process variable

I would recommend the second of these three alternatives, as it enables you to depict different error cases clearly, and react accordingly. The model stays compact and there is a clear distinction between the normal sequence flow and the sequence flow for handling exceptions.

3.2.4   Business Objects

Process-driven applications work with a particular set of data, which can be grouped into business objects such as customer, order, or supplier. In process-driven applications, business objects are not usually used in isolation, but in relation to other objects. Accordingly, when specifying business objects, you need to not only specify the attributes of the individual objects but also the relationships between them. The procedure here is fully top-down; you only include objects and attributes that are relevant from the composite view. Do not use data structures from existing applications, as this would violate the independence rule. A detailed description of a business object could contain the following:

- Meaningful attribute name (for example, name, postal code, weight)
- Data type (for example, string, integer, date, Boolean)
- Required field (yes/no)
- Length restrictions (for example, 35 characters)
- Value range (for example, from 0 to 999,999)
- Input masks (for example, if product numbers follow a particular pattern, predefined symbols are used in the masks to control data entry)
- Storage location of the fields (this is a technical issue and should be defined in cooperation with IT experts). What are the composite's expectations as regards the persistence of the individual attributes: local (within the process-driven application) or remote (in an existing system in the IT landscape)?
- Dependencies on and relationships with other fields (for example, if field xyz contains the value abc, field uvw must lie within a particular range)

Once you have specified the business objects and their attributes, you have to specify the relationships between them. It is sufficient to define the relationship type (association or composition) and the cardinality. The type of relationship between the objects depends on whether the child object is deleted if the parent object is deleted. If so, it is a composition (for example, the child object is an order item and the parent object is the order); if not, it is an association (for example, the child object is a customer and the parent object is the order). Cardinalities are usually differentiated as follows:

- 0..1: There can be one relationship to exactly one object.
- 1..1: There must be one relationship to exactly one object.
- 0..n: There can be one relationship to several objects (n can have a upper limit if the particular business instance requires it; otherwise n stands for an infinite number).
- 1..n: There must be at least one relationship to an object.

    m..n relationships are defined by two 0..n or 1..n relationships in the objects in question. To ensure your business objects are easy to understand, it is advisable to use some non-functional requirements, for example, information about the expected number of objects, the frequency of access at runtime, or the primary type of usage (read, write, search). These details are helpful later when you need to decide which technology to use during implementation.

3.2.5   User Interfaces

User interfaces are very important in process-driven applications given their collaborative nature, and even at this early phase of development, the input screens
have to be adapted to the requirements of the end users and their roles. If you
involve users during the development of user interface prototypes, this will improve
the level of acceptance later on when the interface goes live. It can also reduce costs
in the long run, as problems are identified early on and can be remedied without
excessive effort or expense.

Our objective is to support end users as best we can in their process roles, by
providing and presenting all the data they require for their tasks in a user-friendly
way. At the same time, the screens must make the users as efficient as possible; they
should be able to access the information they need with a minimum of keystrokes
and clicks. Regular review circles with users can identify further areas of improvement for the interfaces. Once you are happy with your interface, it can be included
in the specification as a screenshot. The next step is to associate each screen field
with the relevant data. To do this, you reference the business objects that have been
defined, so that important information such as data type, required fields, and input
restrictions (such as value ranges or field masks) is provided automatically. You
also need to add other properties such as visual representations of the data (for
example, charts, bar charts, pie charts, or curves), and you must assign user
interface components such as radio buttons, checkboxes, dropdown lists, calendars,
and trees to individual fields. Finally, you have to define whether the fields are read-
only or if they can be modified.

You can make the user's life easier and save them time by including input helps
in the screen, particularly if there are complex relationships between fields. If you
intend to provide input helps for certain fields or field groups, you have to clarify
how the values they contain are determined. Often, the entries are not determined
until runtime by service calls, in which case you have to reference the service calls
explicitly in the specification, and describe the functions they provide (the next
section explains this in more detail). The values for input helps are sometimes
hardwired into the code because of performance reasons, for example, for static
lists. I would generally advise using rule-based solutions, where decisions can be
provided as decision tables. This combines two advantages: first, they remain
maintainable, even outside the program code, and second, they have little effect
on performance. If the decision logic is sufficiently general to be applicable
elsewhere, the rule set can also be provided as a service.

Field checks are also usually performed using services; a link to the relevant
service is sufficient. Rule-based approaches are another alternative; in this case, you
have to specify the rules for the field check explicitly.

It is generally a good idea to list the possible permitted entries for fields. This
makes it easier for architects to implement the requirements and avoids queries.

3.2.6   Services

Reusable services form the basis of any process-driven application. We have made frequent mention of them already in this chapter; we've looked at how they can be used when compiling detailed information about the process steps, and in the definition of user interfaces. Services have two functions in a composite:

- Providing *new* business logic that is developed specifically for the composite in the absence of any other alternative; this logic is provided as a service.
- Encapsulation and abstraction of *existing* business functions in the form of the service contract

Irrespective of how the service is used, what is important is how the interface looks in the specification. The interface *must be defined from the perspective of the process-driven application* and must be purely business-led. We have made a conscious decision not to use existing interfaces of services from application systems such as ERP or SRM solutions (especially for the interfaces of the service contract, which is the external representation of our process-driven application) since this would create dependencies, which we want to avoid. This is a fundamental difference from approaches that recommend using back-end services directly, for example, because providers have predefined services available or because specialized SOA competence centers within companies have developed reusable services. I think that this point is very important, not least because it is often misunderstood and neglected, even in SOA publications. Therefore, I would like you to think about the following two sentences, which you can use to determine whether your service contract interfaces are well-formed and whether they are truly independent of external interfaces. The sentences relate to the second of the two functions mentioned above, that is, you want your interface to use existing business functionality and you need to abstract this in your application:

> **Notes on Independence of Service Contract Interfaces from the Services of Back-End Systems**
> Your service contract interface is independent if a change (adding/changing fields with no change to the business functionality) to the service interface of the back-end system *does not have any effect* on the service contract interfaces of your process-driven application.
>
> If a change to the service contract interface of your process-driven application is required, then this is *motivated exclusively by a business change in your application*.

You can achieve this by using the service contract implementation layer. You will often be faced with decisions about how far to let what happens in the back-end system affect the service contract and thus the process-driven application. For example, if a new optional field is added to the back-end system, this has no effect on our composite because it does not use the field anyway. But if a field is removed from the interface in the old system, you have to determine whether the composite has needed this field up to now or not. If so, you must ensure that the field can still be made available to the process-driven application. Since the backend is obviously no longer responsible for the administration of this field, this task falls to the service contract implementation layer, where an additional persistence of this field has to be provided. The composite itself remains unchanged. Things get critical as soon as a new required field is added to the back-end interface, or an optional field is changed into a required field. At this point, the business functionality is no longer the same, since a new business service is now offered that was not available before. But even here, you do not have to throw in the towel and simply add the field to the service contract. In many cases, the fields can be derived from information that is already available, for example, by using rules or existing services. If, for example, "Gender" is now a required field for customer data, you do not necessarily have to add it to the composite and extend the service contract; instead, you can use a *nameToGender* service to determine the gender automatically from the name (look on the Internet; you'll be surprised at how many of these services are available).

Another interesting example is the use of cardinalities when defining the relationships between data objects (see Sect. 3.2.4). What should you do if the specification of object 1 (for example, an order) stipulates a 1..n relationship to object 2 (for example, a customer address), which is stored completely externally, but the backend sets an upper limit for object 2, which means it can only save a limited number of objects (for example, a maximum of 5 customer addresses)? One option is to include this upper limit in the object definition in the process-driven application, so that it is only possible to process up to the number of objects specified by the backend. Alternatively, any objects above this limit could simply be saved in the service contract implementation layer, and the composite does not have to be aware of this issue at all.

Of course, not all cases will be this easy to solve, and I don't want to create the impression that changes to objects and interfaces must be avoided at all costs. However, if possible, you should try to maintain independence from back-end fields and back-end restrictions in the service contract. Try to think of alternatives that you can realize in the service contract implementation layer instead. You can introduce interactive steps as a way to get additional information, for example, you could send end users an interactive form as a PDF (Portable Document Format), which they have to fill out with any missing information before their request can be processed. Dialog steps do not necessarily have to be in the process-driven application; depending on the use case, it might make more sense to put these activities in the service contract implementation layer.

You specify services for use in process-driven applications as follows:

– Assign a meaningful service name using naming conventions that make the business function of the service clear from its name. Usually, verbs are combined with nouns, for example, the service `createProject` or `calculateFunding`.

- List all input and output parameters of the service, including the data types to be used. Ideally, you can reference attributes of business objects that have already been specified, so that you have not only the data type, but restrictions and value ranges as well. Once again: Only include those fields that are necessary to provide the business functionality. Anything else is superfluous and should be eliminated.
- Give a short description of the business functionality or logic to be provided. This defines the semantics of the service.
- Indicate whether the required business functionality is provided by an external implementation, or is a composite-specific service that has yet to be developed. If the interface is for a service that is provided externally, the interface definition also defines the service contract from Fig. 2.2 between the process-driven application and the external world. This decision needs to be made together with the business application experts. You need to find out which standard functions can be expected from external applications and which functions require new logic to be developed for the composite.
- If you are going to develop a new service, you need to define how it will handle access conflicts for changes such as updates or deletions. If there is a write conflict, should the most recent call overwrite all previous changes or should the service indicate the existence of a conflict by an exception, as is usual with optimistic lock procedures? Naming conventions can be helpful here. SAP uses the `change` and `update` prefixes in the definition of its enterprise services as follows: The `changeCustomer` service makes a change without recognizing a conflict, whereas `updateCustomer` recognizes if there is a conflict and indicates this with an exception. In the latter case, a reaction may be required from the caller, and this also has to be specified.
- Services do not throw exceptions only for conflicts, but to indicate other extraordinary situations during its execution as well. Since exceptions have already been specified, they can be referenced in the corresponding section of the specification. These cross-references also help you identify and fill any gaps in the list of exceptions.
- Especially when specifying services that are provided externally, you must not forget to specify non-functional requirements, the quality-of-service attributes (QoS). This can include information about the expected load in terms of call volume (for example, number of calls per time unit), security aspects, availability, and time aspects. The last item is particularly important; it includes information such as the time limit in which the service must/should be completed, what proportion of calls should be made within a specified time (for example, 90 % of calls should be less than 1 s), and how to react if the stipulations are not met. If the time overrun is critical, should all running activities be stopped and an error returned to the caller as an exception, or should the calls that have already been triggered continue while a technical administrator or expert is informed?

– Ideally, assign the individual service operations to the business object that they process. For example, you can assign the operations `createOrder`, `updateOrder`, and `cancelOrder` to the *Order* business object. This gives you *one* service for the *Order* object with three service operations. This bundling of service operations into one service has proved successful in the SOA world. The external representation of the process-driven application (that is, the service contract) can comprise several services, with each service being made up of one or more service operations.

A specification created in this way forms a sound basis for the subsequent implementation of the process-driven application. What is striking about this procedure is its consistent top-down approach: from the business requirements alone we derive the processes and the detailed process sequences, and then the user interfaces, the data to be processed, and the services to be used. The data types used are also an important aspect. So far, all we have said on this subject is that data types from existing back-end systems should not be reused, because this creates dependencies on these systems. So, what other option do we have? The following section looks at the available alternative.

3.2.7 Importance of the Canonical Data Model

One of the central principles running through the development of process-driven applications is to avoid the dependencies that can result if external services are used directly. If you have imported interfaces from an application that is then replaced at some later date, you need to adapt your solution to the modified system landscape, and the effort involved extends throughout the entire process-driven application; not just on the service side, but the user interfaces and processes as well. This affects the flexibility of the composite, impairing its ability to react swiftly to changing conditions. Things get even more difficult if different data types from various different applications are reused in the composite, as this makes incompatibilities between the data types unavoidable. The following are typical examples:

– A customer object from application A uses separate fields for first name and last name, but the customer object from application B combines these into one field.
– You have to switch between different data types, for example, strings and integers. If there are different value ranges as well, finding a solution can prove to be complex and time-consuming.
– A value mapping is necessary. For example, one application provides content 1 to identify the form of address "Mrs" and content 2 for the form of address "Mr", whereas another application uses the actual texts.

The composite developer knows that data type transformations should be avoided in a composite, but is confronted with a situation where there seems to be no way around this. The solution is to use a canonical data model, and this should be included in the specification of the process-driven application. A canonical data model is a universal cross-system data model that is completely independent of the applications to be integrated. These models are nothing new (see, for example, Hohpe and Woolf 2004) but they can now be used not only in integration scenarios but in the process-driven application itself. This enables loose coupling at the data-type level, resulting in a harmonized data type system within our composite application and no need for transformations. We have encountered data types several times already in the specification of process-driven applications:

- In the definition of the process context
- In the definition of data for user interaction
- In the description of service interfaces
- In the definition of business objects

It is advisable to use the canonical data model for all of the above, as it then stretches across the whole composite application. It is particularly important to use the canonical data model when describing service interfaces whose business logic is provided by external systems and that therefore represent the service contracts from Fig. 2.2. The service contracts can then be implemented in a variety of ways in the service contract implementation layer, for example, mapping within an Enterprise Service Bus (ESB). If the same canonical data model is used at this level as well, this reduces the transformation effort even further. ESB solutions are already widespread in large companies and it is standard procedure to use canonical data models for integration at the ESB level. Since process-driven applications are completely new applications, it is advisable to reuse the data model already defined at the ESB level. Gregor Hohpe and Bobby Woolf (Hohpe and Woolf 2004) explain just how useful the canonical data model is at the ESB level in terms of the number of mappings you would otherwise have to define between the various data formats. This model is also particularly helpful if you have an ever increasing number of applications to integrate. In bidirectional point-to-point connections where n systems have to be connected with m systems, you need n * m * 2 mapping definitions. If n systems have to be connected to each other, you need to define n * (n−1) mappings. The curve increases quadratically. If we introduce a canonical data model, this has the following effect: Where n systems communicate with m other systems, (n+m) * 2 mappings are required; where n systems are connected to each other, n * 2 mappings are required. There is a linear progression. There are other advantages as well:

- Services that are based on the canonical data model do not need to know the data type dialects of their communication partners. This is in line with the objectives of process-driven applications, where the partners are not known until the installation in a system landscape. The service consumer (the composite) is completely detached from the internal data dialect of the service provider.
- Changes to the internal data model of the service implementation do not have any effect on the service consumer.

- The transformation overhead decreases as the number of systems increases.
- There is a clear division of responsibilities: The data types are clearly assigned to the systems, and therefore to the domains and the roles responsible for them.
- A canonical data model helps reduce misunderstandings, since the business and the technical side are talking about one and the same domain object.

There are, however, some disadvantages. Creating the canonical data model can be a problem in itself, as differences in opinions and expectations can make it difficult to agree on a common model (see Sect. 3.2.8). You can use standards as a guideline, especially when defining basic data types. The SAP world, for example, uses global data types (GDT), which are based on the CCTS standard (CCTS: Core Component Technical Specification, a UN/CEFACT standard—see also UN/CEFACT 2003). GDTs are defined uniformly across SAP and represent business-led data models. SAP's enterprise services (well-defined, self-contained business functions that are provided as Web services) are all based on global data types. You may be concerned that basing your own model on GDTs will create some kind of dependency on SAP solutions, which is just what you are trying to avoid by using the canonical data model, but this is not the case. Firstly, you should not be using the complex data structures in your process-driven application anyway (remember: keep to the minimum), and secondly, the basic types are completely independent from SAP, so there is no reason not to use them in your solutions. The GDTs are simply a guide; they show you what data structures can look like for various business objects, but how you define your own data structures is up to you.

GDTs may not be the ideal solution for every company, but they do provide a useful template for defining your own model. Another alternative is to use a sector-specific data model, such as S.W.I.F.T. (Society for Worldwide Interbank Financial Telecommunication), which is used in the banking sector. OAGIS (Open Applications Group Integration Specification—see also OAGIS 2009) from the Open Applications Group (OAGi) is a cross-sector standard that is also very helpful as a starting point for creating your own data model.

Purely technically speaking, there is some additional transformation effort required during message transfer if you use a data model other than the data model used in the ESB in the composite: Although the total number of mapping definitions is reduced (see above), the number of mappings (that is, the actual number of mapping calls) that are executed during runtime increases. After all, each message that leaves a process-driven application has to be transformed to the data format of the ESB and then to the data format of the target application; the return path is just as complicated. It is clear why the recommendation is to use a single format at the process-driven application *and* at the ESB level. Each transformation takes time; this accumulates and leads to delays. Therefore, this method is not recommended for high-load scenarios. In this case, the only alternative is direct transformations from the source format to the target format. For process-driven applications, which are designed specifically for highly heterogeneous environments, the struggle to reconcile ease-of-use, improved maintainability, and increased flexibility with reduced performance and increased complexity is par for the course. Generally, the good outweighs the bad, so the focus should be on maintainability and increased flexibility. However, the performance aspect is critical, and if your architecture cannot fulfil the performance requirements, you will have to look for alternatives, even if this means straying from the architectural principles, as customers simply will not tolerate overly long response times. But before you reject the entire architecture, you should look for alternatives that can provide improvements within the existing framework. In particular, think about parallelization (horizontal scaling) possibilities, which are well suited to stateless activities like the mapping mentioned above. Modern multicore machines parallelize these services and improve performance as a result.

3.2.8   Cooperation Between Business and IT Experts

The specification of a process-driven application involves many people in various different roles. What we don't want to happen is this: The business team shuts itself away, works out a new solution without any outside involvement, and then presents this to the IT department with a simple "Implement this, please". This may be an exaggeration, but you understand my point. This approach has never worked and it never will. The key point to understand is that representatives of the business departments, IT specialists, architects, and developers are all in the same boat. They have a common goal: to implement the company's strategy and its business processes as quickly as possible. Therefore, all the participants should have the opportunity to be involved from the start; if each role is represented from the very beginning of the project, this fosters a better working relationship between teams and prevents misunderstandings. Of course, each role has its strengths and its involvement will focus on certain stages of the project: Business processes will be driven mainly by the business departments, with the IT team having little influence on their definition, but the closer we get to the service contract implementation layer, the more input the IT faction will have. Beyond the service contract implementation layer, it is predominantly the IT experts that will take care of the actual implementation, but even here, a good working relationship with the business experts is a must.

Process-driven applications throw up a few special questions of their own. In the previous section we looked at the canonical data model. Who defines this model and what is the extent of its validity? There is no one-size-fits-all answer to this question; in fact, you do not want the scope of the "global" data type system to be too wide, because the number of parties that would have to be involved would mean interminable discussions and extensive coordination effort. To start with, it is sufficient to find a data model that fits the scope of the planned process-driven application, and this is a challenge in itself, since this usually involves processes from a range of different systems. The data model must be valid for the business domain that is covered by the business processes of a process-driven application. The data model is also reflected in the interfaces of the service contract and thus directly affects IT; only through equal involvement of business and IT departments can we arrive at a successful finished model. It is an advantage to have the same data model as in the ESB, as mentioned earlier, but we cannot assume that this will always be possible. At the very least, we should aim to define a harmonized data model for at least the area of validity (=domain) of the process-driven application, including the service contracts. The service contracts are driven by the business department (after all, the interfaces need to reflect the business requirements), but the fine-tuning is down to the IT department, who usually make various additions, for example...

- ...fields for correlation between processes
- ...complete objects containing the old status of a previously read object in the event of optimistic locking.

These fields are purely IT-driven and cannot be provided by the business departments. However, as we saw in the example from Sect. 3.2.6, where the back-end systems required particular fields, the service contract interface sometimes has to take certain factors into account and may have to include business fields that are not actually necessary for the execution of the process-driven application. Such fields should only be included in the service contract in exceptional cases; consider the alternatives also mentioned in Sect. 3.2.6. The implementation of the service contracts is the task of the IT departments, with the expert help of the business departments.

This brings us to the end of our discussion of the roles that are involved in the specification of composites. I have focused intentionally on the aspects specific to the development of process-driven applications. You can find more general discussions in the specialist literature.

3.3 Introduction to the Basic Architecture of Process-Driven Applications

Now that I have summarized the main challenges facing process-driven applications, I will move on to look in more detail at their basic architecture. First, I will reiterate what I perceive to be the main problems with current implementations, and then discuss the long-term consequences of using these methods.

3.3.1 Evolution of a Business Model into an Executable Process

Let's use our trusty order example again. We will start with a simple process model, defined in purely business terms, as illustrated in Fig. 3.5.

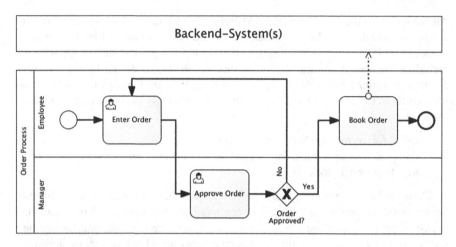

Fig. 3.5 Order process—starting point

Although I use a commercial example in this case, the scenario can be applied to any business area, as is true for all the statements in this book. I use the terms *business expert* and *business functionality* in their widest sense; they are not restricted to any particular commercial, technical, or specialist area.

So, back to our BPMN model: The **business expert** uses the model to express how, ideally, the order process will look. An employee enters an order interactively (hence the user task) in a form. The order must then be approved by a manager. If the manager rejects the order proposal, the employee must amend it. If the manager approves it, the order is placed. The business expert is not interested in the technical details of how exactly the order is placed; therefore, he uses an untyped task with a message flow to the *Back-end Systems* pool to visualize that the order procedure involves one or more back-end systems. So far, so good.

At this point, a **process analyst** takes over and fine-tunes the process. He is familiar with the systems involved and can consult with the business experts to identify the data required for the implementation. He is also aware that there is more to the process than simply placing the order in an ERP system. The data also has to be transferred to other internal systems in the company, using service calls, for marketing and statistical purposes. Once the process analyst is finished, we can see that the model looks slightly different:

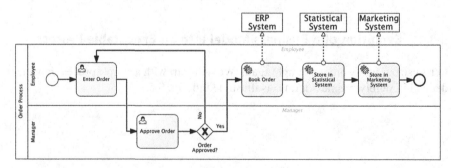

Fig. 3.6 Order process after processing by process analyst

All that is left to do is bring the process model to life! We have used the BPMN notation throughout, which can be executed immediately, so we are close to producing the first executable solution of the process, assuming that the application interfaces and services have been assigned to the user and service tasks. The final modifications are made by the **developer**, who knows how to address the individual systems. For example, communication with the ERP system is in the form of asynchronous message exchange, which means that we need a monitoring element to check whether the ERP system responds within a particular time, and we need to decide what should happen if this time limit is exceeded. The developer consults with the process analyst and the business expert and together they decide that an ERP expert would have to be involved in this case, to place the order manually. Also, the marketing system needs to know exactly which product was ordered. This information is stored in various clients of the system, according to product number. Figure 3.7 shows the finished model:

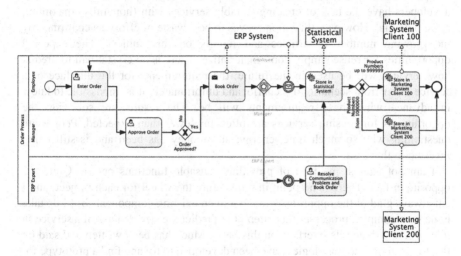

Fig. 3.7 Order process after processing by developer

So, with the help of SOA and BPMN, we have assigned the user interfaces and existing services to the relevant tasks in the model, and we can now execute it using a process engine. Our model is finished, is it not? Well, in theory yes, but let's be honest, can we really be happy with the end result? The business experts would hardly recognize their original process in among all the technical details. And is our model really flexible? Can the process be used, for example, in other regions that our company operates in? Other regions will very probably use different systems, so we will have to make all kinds of adaptions; the model would practically have to be developed again from scratch. The sobering truth is that we have let ourselves be dazzled by SOA's and BPM's promises:

SOA provides the services; "all" you need to do is orchestrate them as befits your requirements. This is where executable BPMN comes into its own: It allows you to string services into execution sequences. Add some interactive steps, and processes can be executed exactly as intended in their original design.

In reality, things are not quite so simple, and these promises are more of a hindrance than a help when it comes to implementation. The business models, such as the one shown in Fig. 3.5, suggest that once the process reaches the *Book Order* task, all you need is a service call to the target system and the solution will be complete. Even with the extra modifications that result in the process model in Fig. 3.7, you would still expect the last step to be fairly straightforward; surely it can't be that difficult to quickly integrate a few services? After all, the providers of the back-end systems have made the effort to ensure that the ERP systems are fit for use in an SOA, that is, they provide the required functions as well-encapsulated (Web) services. And it is not just the providers that provide (Web) services; some companies even have their own SOA competence centers, where architects and developers have the task of creating suitable services with (hopefully) maximum reuse potential. However, this often proves to be a waste of effort, as confirmed by the growing number of articles and reports on this subject. The expected opportunities for reuse simply don't materialize. There is no crystal ball to predict how services will be used in the future; the requirements for the interface of a service differ from scenario to scenario, and unfortunately it is impossible to know in advance what these requirements will be. The results are sobering: the opportunities for reusing services are often far fewer than expected. People are questioning why so much time, energy, and money has been and is still being invested in this area.

I am not against the idea of providing reusable functions per se. Quite the opposite in fact: There is no point in reinventing the wheel for each project, and I am always glad of the opportunity to tap into an existing component. But I do take issue with complex processes that attempt to predict the size and use of a service *in advance*, and define its interface on this basis. Much has been written and said on this topic; entire methodologies have been developed to try and find a prototype for services to ensure a high degree of reusability. Reusability has become the be-all and end-all, and takes precedence over (almost) all other factors. We need to move away from this way of thinking. There is no such thing as a *one-size-fits-all* model for services or service interfaces. It might be the case that a business functionality is already available in the involved systems; this could be something that has evolved over time and the technology to access it may be exclusive to a particular company. Thanks to the introduction of software for integrating systems, these interfaces can now be used at any time in an SOA. Let us look at SAP systems as an example. There have long been mechanisms available for integrating SAP systems for synchronous and asynchronous communication, namely RFCs (remote function calls) for synchronous connections and IDoc (Intermediate Document) for asynchronous connections. Over the years, these proprietary technologies have proved their worth in a range of projects, and are now so robust, reliable, scalable, and well-performing that you might well question the wisdom of switching to Web services to call exactly the same functionality. In my opinion, your time could be much better spent. The same applies to non-SAP systems: Use the best protocol available for connecting your systems, one that has been tried and tested over time. Generally, any good middleware will support these technologies, so connecting the back-end systems should not pose a problem. Instead, focus your efforts on maintaining agility at the application development level.

This brings us to another central principle of the approach proposed in this book and its resulting architecture, namely, that we should distance ourselves from the idea of a service blueprint or perfect interface. We should put flexibility and independence from the existing IT landscape far above the reusability of service interfaces in our list of priorities. As already mentioned, I too welcome reusability, but I would place the emphasis on the reusability of business *functions* rather than *interfaces*. This produces an architecture whose objective is to keep the business process as close as possible to the original model produced by the business department; this architecture benefits from the executability of BPMN, but without any impact on the flexibility of the system as a whole. This approach removes all the technical process details to a separate layer: the service contract implementation layer. Figure 3.8 shows what happens if we apply this principle to the model from Fig. 3.7:

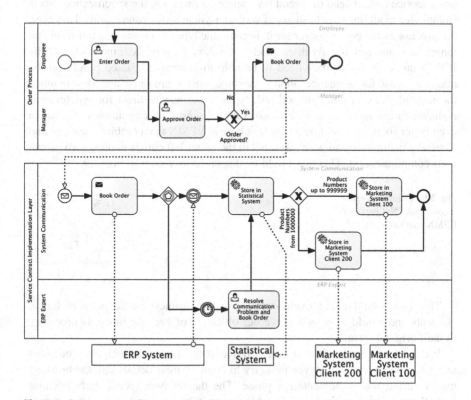

Fig. 3.8 Order process after separation of layers

The following chapters of this book are all based on this principle. You can see from the model how the core processes that are so critical to the success of the company are not obscured by the technical details because these are put into a separate layer. The valuable business process stays intact and, most importantly, remains under the control of the business department. However, the process can be easily adapted for use in other regions; you simply need to adapt the service contract implementation layer. Of course, this adaptation does involve some effort, but applying this approach will be of benefit to you in the long term, as it releases you from the complex web of connections between back-end systems. Business and technical processes can be developed and modified independently, but remain connected by the service contract. This architecture also helps you keep the business processes in their original form as conceived by the business departments.

We do stumble across a problem, however, if the business process has to wait asynchronously for a response from the technical process. In this case we need a message-based intermediate event or a receive task after the send task *Book Order* in the business process. It is doubtful that the business department could model this sufficiently, so we once again have a situation where technical steps complicate the business process. This intermediate event is not business led; it is required simply to communicate with the service contract implementation layer. Of course, you could use a service task instead of a send task, since according to the specification this is suitable for modeling synchronous as well as asynchronous connections. However, our process would be the poorer for it, because the type of communication would no longer be visualized directly in the model. We should always bear the readers of the BPMN model in mind; they need to be able to understand, based purely on the diagram, what the sequence and/or message flow represents, and this requires meaningful and easily-understood task types. I use *service tasks* for synchronous communication and *send* or *receive tasks* for asynchronous communication, but an even better solution would be a new task type in BPMN that combines sending and receiving in one step and with a symbol in the upper left corner to depict asynchronous communication. This task could be displayed as shown in Fig. 3.9.

Fig. 3.9 Combined send/ receive task (Not part of the BPMN standard)

This task would avoid overcomplicating the business model with technical elements and would help us achieve our objective of keeping business processes in their original form.

We can learn another lesson here: Do not let the various participants (business experts, process analysts, developers) try to cram all their details into the business model during the implementation phase. The danger here (particularly because BPMN can be used to model executable processes) is that you start with a simple model and then make it more and more complicated, as shown in the figures (Figs. 3.5, 3.6, and 3.7). I can only advise you to resist this temptation. Do not reject the well-established principles of information technology; componentize and reuse where appropriate. Let me demonstrate this by using two figures. Figure 3.10 shows a model as a business department might design it, and also as recommended by Bruce Silver to represent collaborations between different business processes. Note the message-based intermediate event in *Business Process 1*, here receiving the confirmation of execution from *Business Process 2*. I criticized the use of such events earlier, but in this case it makes sense; it represents the coordination between the two business processes, and thus has a business motivation, so you could expect a business department to employ it:

Fig. 3.10 Business collaboration diagram

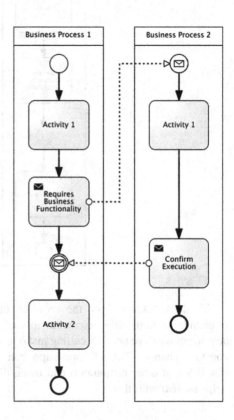

The figure shows a process where an existing business functionality is required after *Activity 1*. In our example, this is provided by another business process that *Business Process 1* collaborates with. The BPMN collaboration diagram models this business scenario very clearly, and the models that you receive from your business departments will be similar to this. Look at other examples in the BPMN literature; the models are all comparable. From a business perspective, everything is in order, and in theory we could implement and execute the model exactly as it is without a problem. *But wait!* According to our definition of a process-driven application, we want to be able to reuse successful processes and maintain their flexibility. To ensure that this is the case for *Business Process 1*, we need to remove its dependence on *Business Process 2*, by adding the service contract implementation layer, as shown in Fig. 3.11.

Fig. 3.11 Business collaboration diagram with service contract implementation layer

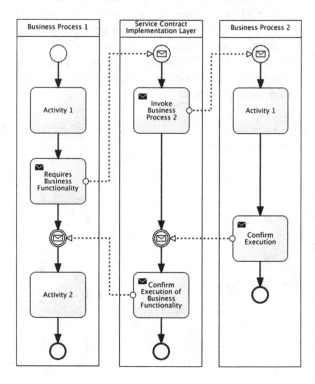

We do not know how the required business functionality will need to be implemented in different environments in the future. At the moment we may be able to get what we need by calling just one system, but an IT landscape is subject to constant change. The IT landscape can look very different in other regions (for ISVs, at other customers) and using different layers as depicted in Fig. 3.11 helps us deal with this.

3.3.2 Advantages and Disadvantages of a Process-Driven Architecture

The criticism leveled at this approach is that it is more complex; more communication is required between the layers, and this can also affect performance. This is a fair point, but if companies want to or have to implement their end-to-end business processes in a heterogeneous environment, I don't see how they can free themselves from a constrictive web of system connections and maintain and improve their capacity for innovation unless they rethink their architecture. I do warn against applying this architecture indiscriminately; it should only be used for process-driven applications that meet the criteria set out at the beginning of the book. I do not want to play down the issue of *complexity*; it should of course be taken very seriously and factored into all decisions for or against process-driven applications. Ultimately, this architecture will have to run and be monitored in productive situations; swift intervention will be vital if errors occur, and of course this is going to be more difficult in distributed applications. You need to think about the whole development process: application design, its development, the people/roles involved, testing, debugging in distributed IT landscapes, software distribution, and so on. Unfortunately, our proposed approach doesn't make this any simpler, but you can take some comfort in the fact that manufacturers of technology infrastructures have recognized these difficulties and stepped up to the challenge. They provide solutions that enable modeling and execution of business processes, business rules, and system/application integrations, which makes tackling the design, development, and operation of distributed scenarios a much less daunting prospect. There is some initial implementation effort, but overall this is far outweighed by the benefits. Furthermore, we can count on there being further improvements to the tooling environment in the future, making process-driven applications an even more attractive option.

To summarize: Once the business process *is implemented*, it never communicates *directly* with other systems; instead, it uses the service contract implementation layer, which decouples the technical details. The two business processes in Fig. 3.11 communicate *indirectly* with each other.

Granted, a process-driven architecture does have some obvious disadvantages, as mentioned above: increased complexity, impaired performance, and considerable initial development effort. On the plus side though, we can count the following benefits:

– One single BPMN model for both sides: business and IT
– Increased flexibility
– Alignment of business and implementation requirements in a single BPMN model is important
  • If business processes need to be adapted
  • If there are changes to the system landscape
– Quicker and more cost-effective further development of the application
– Lower maintenance costs
– Improved portability
– Business and technical processes can be further developed separately; this is a welcome improvement for many organizations, as it allows them to concentrate on their respective subject areas (separation of concerns).
– Better overview of end-to-end processes when using ESBs, since all communication goes through the ESB.
– Simplified process models for both the business and the technical side, improving the clarity of each individual process

Hence, it is advisable to use process-driven applications in the following cases:

– Alignment of business and implementation requirements in a single BPMN model is important.
– Independence from the system landscape is critical.
– More than one system needs to be integrated.
– The system landscape is not stable.
– The solution is complex and justifies the effort involved.
– The solution will provide a competitive advantage.
– The processes in the solution are expected to change frequently.
– The processes in the solution will be used in other organizational units, areas, regions, or other subsidiaries or companies.

However, if none of these statements apply to your development project, it is certainly worth considering alternatives to the process-driven architecture approach.

3.3.3 Separation of Business Processes and Technical Processes

At this point, I would like to revisit the issue of separation of business and technical processes, to bring together the basic concepts of the architecture of a process-driven application and to look at some more details. I refer once again to the diagram of a process-driven application (Fig. 3.12).

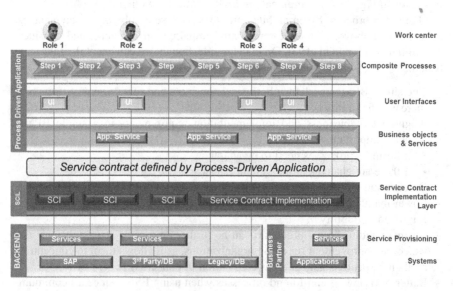

Fig. 3.12 Diagram of a process-driven application

What is immediately obvious here, and indeed characteristic of a process-driven application, is the complete separation of the actual application (labelled as *Process-Driven Application* in the top part of the figure) and the service contract and its implementation in the service contract implementation layer. The information collected in Sect. 3.2 is used exclusively to address the process-driven application. Processes, user interfaces, business objects, and services are all defined by this stage. Let us look at two important points.

1. The interaction of the process-driven application and the externally-facing service contract
2. The actual implementation of the service contract

In Fig. 3.12, it is clear that all communication between the process-driven application and the back-end systems running in the system landscape passes through the service contract implementation layer. The process-driven application itself provides those business functions that give the company an advantage over its competitors; the service contract implementation layer implements the external services required by the composite and contains all the technical details. This includes, for example, the physical connections to the back-end systems, support for various protocols, mapping between different data types, and error handling at the technical level.

This total, uncompromising separation is of fundamental importance to process-driven applications, as it ensures that the composite is completely decoupled from the backend: Calls are never made directly to an actual system in a process-driven application. The composite communicates exclusively with the service contract implementation layer, using the service contract defined from the perspective of the process-driven application. This ensures abstraction from the actual systems; dependencies, if any, between the process-driven application and the back-end system are minimal. As a result, the various lifecycles of these two worlds are largely independent. The innovative solutions fostered by process-driven applications can be driven forward more quickly, and with shorter cycles. The core applications in the older systems, on the other hand, stay stable for a much longer period of time. This is welcome news to those responsible for running IT landscapes within companies, whose goal it is to minimize changes to the core processes that bear the load of the day-to-day business and have to handle millions of transactions in a short space of time. This goal is also supported by the non-invasive nature of the process-driven application: Thanks to the service contract implementation layer, the services provided by the back-end systems are used as originally intended by the provider. The back-end systems are not changed in any way, which also complies with the software-as-a-service (SaaS) approach, where standard functions are outsourced to service providers, which means that changes to the back-end systems are not possible anyway. If, upon closer inspection, any functional disparity is identified between the expectations of the composite and the functionality provided by the backend, this too must be implemented in the service contract implementation layer.

It is clear that we should strive for a loose coupling between the process-driven application and the back-end systems providing the services. Data-type dependence, for example, is just *one* dimension we need to consider in the spectrum of loosely coupled systems. The following section addresses this and other aspects.

3.3.4 Loose Coupling

Loose coupling is one of the most important aspects to consider not only in the construction of process-driven applications, but when designing any large distributed heterogeneous system, as it is crucial to reduce dependencies in both cases. We need to distinguish between the various dimensions of dependency. The following table, originally introduced in Krafzig et al. (2004) and expanded upon in Josuttis (2007), lists the possible forms of loose coupling:

Table 3.1 Forms of loose coupling (from Josuttis 2007)

	Tight coupling	Loose coupling
Physical connection	Point-to-point	Via mediation
Communication style	Synchronous	Asynchronous
Data model	Complex common types	Only simple common types
Type system	Strong	Weak
Binding	Static	Dynamic
Platform specifics	Strong and/or many	Weak and/or few
Interaction pattern	Navigate using complex object trees	Data-centric autonomous messages
Transaction security	2PC (two-phase commit)	Compensation
Control of business logic	Central control	Distributed control
Versioning	Explicit upgrades	Implicit upgrades

Nicolai Josuttis and Dirk Krafzig et al. discuss the aspects mentioned above in detail in the context of a service-oriented architecture, but I would like to concentrate on their implications for the architecture of process-driven applications.

3.3.4.1 Physical Connection

This point addresses the question of whether process-driven applications should be physically connected to their communication partners. Do they actually need to know the physical network addresses of their partners or should an intermediary be used? According to the definition of process-driven applications, a direct physical connection is prohibited because this results in a direct dependency on technical details such as the IP address or the protocol to be used. According to the architecture recommendations in Fig. 3.12, these details belong in the service contract implementation layer. So, mediation is used, as proposed in the loose coupling table. This does not necessarily have to be in the form of message-oriented middleware (MOM) or an ESB; deciding to use a process-driven application does not mean that you are obliged to install an appropriate messaging product. You can use a lightweight solution such as Java SE, Java EE, C#, or any other programming language you like, as long as the service contract meets the requirements of the composite.

3.3.4.2 Communication Style

Please note that the styles of communication discussed in this section relate only to the external communication between the process-driven application and its service contract implementation layer. This communication can be synchronous or asynchronous; synchronous in this context means that the sender waits for a response from the receiver before continuing processing. In the literature, this type of communication is also referred to as a request-reply or request-response message exchange pattern (MEP). It is important to understand that both the outgoing and the incoming message are processed in the sender call. A synchronous interface definition in WSDL (Web Services Description Language) therefore includes both input and output parameters.

In asynchronous communication the sender dispatches a message without waiting explicitly for a response from the receiver. Accordingly, the interface definition in WSDL contains input parameters only. This distinction is important because it is also possible to use two asynchronous messages to construct an asynchronous request-response message exchange pattern. As you will see, this pattern plays an important role in the interaction between the process-driven application and the service contract implementation layer.

In process-driven applications, synchronous or asynchronous calls can be used for the external communication with the mediation layer, depending on the usage case: Synchronous communication is preferable for read calls from user interfaces, whereas write calls are generally asynchronous. A special pattern is used for the write procedure; this is discussed in detail in Sect. 3.3.5.3. The motivation for using synchronous read calls from user interfaces can be found in the response times: End users simply will not tolerate long response times. The system must react to user requests as quickly as possible. Since asynchronous communication creates additional effort/overhead (for example, assigning the response to the request, establishing the context at the time the message was sent, saving the message content of the request and of the corresponding response during processing in ESB, and so on), which increases latency times, this type of communication is not suitable where rapid response times are required. There are of course some exceptions, but this is far from ideal. Even if you do use synchronous calls, this does not automatically guarantee short response times. The service contract of the composite only defines which data it requires from the implementation layer. The implementation layer may have to call several systems to compile this information for a particular IT landscape, and if this is the case, the sheer number of backends involved can lead to delays. The only solution in situations such as this is to replicate the data in the service contract implementation layer. Here, additional measures are necessary to ensure that the different data sets in the backend and the service contract implementation layer are kept synchronized. MDM (Master Data Management) solutions have proved to be useful in such situations.

In the chapter on the specification of process-driven applications, we learned that service calls can originate from user interfaces, but also from process steps. For the latter, you can use a non-blocking (asynchronous) method, since there is no end user waiting for a response, and this gives you more flexibility in error handling. You do need to factor in the effort required to implement an asynchronous solution, as it will take longer (and therefore cost more) than a synchronous solution.

These considerations do not apply to external write operations from the process-driven application. If possible, these operations should not originate from user interfaces. The reason for this can be found in the criteria for a process-driven application: Since we do not know the exact details of the IT landscape in which the application will be used, we also do not know the reaction times. Therefore, write access should originate from a process step, using the asynchronous method. Section 3.3.5.3 goes into this in more detail.

To summarize, we can make the following recommendations for communication between the process-driven application and its service contract implementation layer:

– Use synchronous communication for read access from user interfaces
– Use asynchronous communication for write operations from process steps
– Use synchronous or asynchronous communication for read access from process steps, depending on the situation and the effort required
– Avoid write operations from user interfaces

3.3.4.3 Data Model/Type System

In Sect. 3.2.7 we looked in detail at the data model and type systems that are used in process-driven applications, and concluded that it is important to use a canonical data model within a composite and also to define the service contract. This does not necessarily mean that you are limited to only the most simple common data types, resulting in a relatively weak type check (see Table 3.1). If you reuse established standards (such as CCTS, GDT, S.W.I.F.T., and so on), you can design data models with business-specific data types and a stable definition, but that also guarantee the abstraction from back-end systems that is so important to process-driven applications. What you should avoid is reusing existing data types from legacy systems in composites, as this leads to dependencies.

3.3.4.4 Binding

Binding addresses the question of when symbols and calls are assigned to their implementations: compile time, start time, or runtime? For process-driven applications we are only interested in the connection of the service contract to the implementation layer. A concrete implementation must be available for each interface of the service contract for the target landscape in question. Therefore, the connection between the service contract and the implementation is determined statically; it is not established dynamically at runtime. However, the connections can be changed at any time during runtime, because each potential interface can have several implementations, depending on how the system landscape changes.

3.3.4.5 Platform Specifics

Process-driven applications do not themselves use any of the platform specifics of the systems that are to be integrated, as these belong in the service contract implementation layer, which encapsulates the technical details. You should, however, exploit any particular features of the target platform that can help optimize how the target system is used, for example, by improving performance or reliability.

3.3.4.6 Interaction Pattern

The interaction pattern addresses the complexity of the service signature, for example, whether an interface can be deeply nested, whether it supports enumeration types, or whether value ranges can be used for particular interface fields. If the signature is optimized, you can program against the interfaces to take advantage of this additional information, and prevent errors early on. For example, if enumeration types are used, the possible values for a field are displayed on the user interface, which prevents the user from making incorrect entries. Likewise, value ranges can be verified upon entry. This results in a much more robust application that is less susceptible to errors in its communication behavior because possible error sources are eliminated early on. Be aware, however, that if you define the possible values for a field in the form of enumeration types, your data model is then more likely to need modification later on because it will have to be adapted each time a new value is introduced. This makes maintenance more difficult, but you can improve matters by using rules, which enable business experts to make changes at runtime.

If the signature optimizations mentioned above are derived directly from connected systems, we are once again faced with an increased level of dependency, but thanks to the service contract implementation layer, which abstracts these details, process-driven applications do not have this problem. From the conclusions drawn in our discussion of the canonical data model (that is, that you should use one and the same data model for the process-driven application and the interface to the service contract implementation layer), we can derive that the use of complex structures must be explicitly allowed in the communication between these two parties. This means that the composite can be developed at a more abstract level, and you can make life easier for end users by creating more user-friendly interfaces. You can also exploit platform-specific advantages in the connections between the implementation layer and the connected systems.

3.3.4.7 Transaction Security

Ensuring transaction security in loosely coupled environments is a particular challenge for the architecture of process-driven applications. The classic two-phase commit protocol (2PC for short) is unsuitable for use in a distributed service landscape for several reasons: it involves significant programming effort, it provides a central resource manager, and requires that all involved systems support the same transaction protocol. Also, the systems involved must be constantly online for 2PC to function, and process-driven applications do not meet this requirement. Composites are used in heterogeneous environments where system downtimes are unavoidable, whether planned (for regular software updates or hardware mainte-nance) or unplanned (due to errors such as network problems or system crashes). The only solution is compensation, whereby you provide services that can roll back the business effects of a service that has already been executed and is committed from a transaction perspective. You must always consider a compensating solution when planning changing services. This is dealt with in more detail later on (Sect. 4.1.5).

The implications for process-driven applications are as follows: The application cannot determine in advance how long a change operation will take, so it makes asynchronous write calls from the process layer to the service contract implemen-tation layer in the form of a background step. It does not wait actively for a confirmation, but instead puts itself into a wait state after making the call. The implementation layer can now set about procuring the required business function-ality, without the pressure of having to meet particular response times, since there is no user actively waiting at a user interface in the composite. The service contract implementation layer calls the back-end systems and, if errors occur, can initiate the necessary activities. These could be compensating calls, but it could also simply be a matter of notifying administrators (for technical problems) or business experts (for business errors) so that they can take the necessary measures. This is just a rough outline of how to deal with the issue; Sects. 4.1.3 (Exception Handling) and 4.1.5 (Transactions and Compensation) go into possible solutions in more detail.

3.3.4.8 Control of Business Logic

To control business logic, either you coordinate the process flow from a central unit (for example, a process engine) or the involved systems coordinate themselves by sending messages (for example, if the status of a business object changes). In the latter case, this can be done using point-to-point connections (P2P) or publish/subscribe methods. Where you have loose coupling, the decentralized procedure is more robust; using a central process engine can lead to bottlenecks at runtime and increase dependencies.

In process-driven applications, we have a clear picture in this respect: The business flows are implemented within the application in the form of process models, which are then executed by a process engine. The transfer from the composite to the service contract implementation layer represents the transition from the business to the technical side. The technical process is implemented as an executable model as well. In this regard, process-driven applications can be considered to be tightly coupled, that is, to the execution engine. This has the advantage that the process flow is obvious from the model, which makes it easier to analyze any errors that may occur. In the decentralized scenario, there is no such context information, which makes troubleshooting more difficult.

3.3.4.9 Versioning

One of the main features of process-driven applications is that they are not dependent on any particular system version. We have placed particular emphasis on creating a business-led definition of the service contract using a canonical data model, because we want to be able to develop the individual solutions further, but at different times. Composite applications tend to have short development cycles, whereas legacy systems typically need to be changed less frequently. This means that our composites are loosely coupled to the versions of the connected back-end systems. This is achieved by abstraction, using the service contract implementation layer, which takes care of any adaptations necessitated by version changes. The process-driven application itself is barely affected.

If we look at loose coupling from the SOA perspective (as summarized in Table 3.1) and from the process-driven application perspective, we see that there are several differences, and we start to appreciate how multidimensional this issue is. A composite development has to address all the criteria we have discussed. The service contract implementation layer assumes the main burden of abstraction, but demonstrates that the price of loose coupling (at any level) is increased complexity. On the whole, though, the pros outweigh the cons, and only by using this type of architecture can you hope to acquire the flexibility and agility required to adapt to changing business requirements and evolving system landscapes, to implement management strategy quickly and effectively, and to ensure business-IT alignment.

We have discussed various aspects of loose coupling above; what I'd like to do now is investigate if there is any way to actually measure loose coupling, to enable you to determine how dependent your application is. At the outset I stated that loose coupling means fewer dependencies. Table 3.1 lists the criteria that you can use to determine the degree of loose coupling in your application. For each point, you need to consider what the impact on the process-driven application will be if this criteria changes in one of the connected systems. If it would be necessary to make changes in the composite, then the application exhibits tight coupling in this respect; if not, the coupling is loose. To illustrate this point, let us take the criterion "Physical Connection" as an example. We need to answer the following question: If the physical target address or the transmission protocol changes, what effect does this have on the business application? By answering this question, you can identify potential problem areas and work to address them. Your objective should be to reduce the level of dependency and thus keep the number of assumptions about the involved systems to a minimum.

Throughout this book, I advise you to keep your application architecture as independent as possible from the IT landscape. Whether it is actually possible to achieve a completely independent architecture depends on the project parameters, but you should strive to reduce dependencies as far as possible in your situation. In my view, the biggest problems are that too many of the services that are provided by back-end systems are called directly from the end application (the thinking being: "We've invested so much time and money in this application, we might as well use it!") and that there is too much reliance on information provided by back-end systems ("I need the information in my application. There is no alternative"). In my opinion this is far too simplistic. It is possible to design independent architectures if you commit from the very start of the project to keeping dependencies to an absolute minimum. In most projects, independence is not deemed to be a key issue and so is simply ignored while the solution is being developed. There needs to be a mindshift so that independence is taken into account; this is currently not the case.

Here again it is interesting to consult the SOA Manifesto (see SOA Manifesto (Erl et al. 2009) and the comments on the manifesto by Nicolai Josuttis (see Josuttis 2010)), where one of the 14 principles states the following (Josuttis 2010, p. 26):

> Reduce implicit dependencies and publish all external dependencies to increase robustness and reduce the impact of change.

Once again, the importance of reducing dependencies is emphasized and defined as a central factor in the architecture of applications that span several systems or even entire system landscapes.

3.3.5 Task Distribution and Interaction Between the Process-Driven Application and the Service Contract Implementation Layer

Let us now take a closer look at the two layers, that is, the "process-driven application" and the "service contract implementation layer", and examine the task distribution and the interaction between them.

3.3.5.1 Process-Driven Application (Business Composition): Focus on User-Centric Processes

Based on what we have already learned, we can summarize the following about the architecture of process-driven applications (see also Fig. 3.12).

- Process-driven applications follow a layer model consisting of the business processes, the user interfaces used in the processes, and the business objects and services relevant for the composite.
- Process-driven applications work exclusively with a canonical data model, across all layers.

- Process-driven applications define the external business functions required by means of a service contract (expressed, for example, with WSDL), which is also based on the canonical data model used, and requires a clearly defined business functionality. I use the term *service contract* whenever I am referring to this external representation of the process-driven application.
- Processes, user interfaces, and services communicate with back-end systems exclusively through the service contract (by way of the service contract implementation layer). Every single call from a process-driven application goes through this layer.

The specifics of the processes, interfaces, business objects, and services that are used are determined purely by the business requirements. What we have is a *business composition* with a focus on user-centric processes (human-centric processes). Accordingly, the user interfaces are role-specific: They support the users involved in their particular function and process situation, and provide context-sensitive information. The user interfaces are not generic, they are specific interfaces tailored to a specific role and situation.

The term *composition* emphasizes that a functionality is provided by reusing existing business functions in the form of services (expressed by the service contract) within the processes. It follows that a *business composition* provides a business functionality by composing user interfaces and services into new solutions.

This concept of business composition is also applied to the business object and service layer. Here as well, the services and the business objects are tailored solely to the new processes; their details are determined by the business requirements. In the case of business objects, this means reducing the attributes to just those fields that are absolutely necessary in the processes; the services provide functions tailored exactly to the processes.

The objects and services throw up a new issue that was not relevant in the other layers, namely the separation of internal and external business objects, and the separation of functions provided internally and those provided externally.

When designing a process-driven application, you have to make a clear distinction between objects that are completely new and therefore not represented in any of the connected systems, and objects whose values are filled from the backends. These two object types must be kept completely separate because they have different persistence mechanisms: For new objects, persistence must be within the process-driven application itself (that is, process-driven applications always have their own local persistence for new application-specific data). For example, let us imagine we are developing a new composite to handle and process innovative product ideas (see the SAP solution SAP xApp Product Definition—SAP 2002c), and are defining the business object *Idea*. We are very unlikely to find this in any standard application; therefore, this object must be saved in the process-driven application itself.

If, on the other hand, we reuse objects from systems that are provided externally, these do not require a local persistence. The object data is read using the service contract, which contains exactly those fields that are essential for the process-driven application. We then provide the actual data to the composite in the form of transient objects (for example, in Java or C#). It may well be that the externally-provided data does not entirely meet the business requirements of the composite. In this case, the additional information that we require is new and specific to the composite, so has to be saved in a separate, locally-persisted object. For example, we could read general customer data from a CRM (Customer Relationship Management) system to the object CustomerCore, but save any other additional data that the composite requires separately, in a locally-persisted object called CustomerExtension. There is a 1:1 relationship between these two objects. However, it is only possible to separate these two object types explicitly if we are aware of the division at design time (see Sect. 3.2.4 about the specification of objects within process-driven applications). If external applications express through the service contract of the process-driven application that they cannot in fact provide the fields they are supposed to because they do not persist or manage them, the required functionality must be included in the service contract implementation layer. Section 3.3.5.2 explains exactly how to do this.

Depending on the usage case and the performance requirements, you can use caching to save externally-provided data locally, to avoid having to run frequent imports. This method is particularly suitable for master data, which is usually fairly stable. Transactional data is somewhat more problematic because the data for each object can change very frequently. In this situation, you have to decide on a case-by-case basis which method is most suitable. If you decide that caching the object data is your best option, you must consider whether you need data synchronization. You can use classic caching algorithms in these situations.

It is a similar story for services: Here too, we differentiate between new and external, reused business logic. The new logic is encapsulated in separate, composite-specific services and made available to higher layers using standardized interfaces. Whether or not the logic can be reused at a later point in time in other solutions is not the priority here. Therefore, we can ignore the governance aspects from SOA development (another distinctive feature of process-driven applications). The services should be implemented solely in line with the requirements of the composite. You do, however, have to consider criteria such as the extent to which the function is self-contained, the level of granularity, and whether or not the service is stateless. These factors all influence the possible reusability of a service later on.

With regard to the calls themselves, you should select the most performance-efficient variant, as the services are used locally within the process-driven application. SOAP access using HTTP should be avoided for communication within the composite; local method calls in the respective programming language are preferable.

The business functions that need to be provided externally (from the point of view of the process-driven application) are defined using the service contract, which can be based, for example, on the WSDL standard, and also uses the canonical data model. It does not matter whether you use WSDL or an alternative (for example, OData); what does matter is *that* the contract is made at all. Again, when it comes to the services of the service contract, reusability is not our main concern. They are specific to the process-driven application. The following relationships apply:

- A process-driven application has **exactly one** service contract (1:1).
- A service contract has **at least one** service (1:n).
- A service has **at least one** service operation (1:n).
- Depending on the target landscapes in which the process-driven application will operate, there can be **several** implementations for each service contract. There is a 1:1 relationship between the implementation and the system landscape. This relationship does not depend on how many installations of the process-driven application there are; if you need another installation in exactly the same IT landscape, it is possible to reuse the existing implementation.

Since the process-driven application and the service contract implementation layer are both controlled by the software provider (and so both come from the same source), these interfaces can include more complex data structures and higher-value data types. If the interface will be used to transfer whole objects that are already used within the composite, it is possible to use the data structure associated with the object directly within the contract. This method is useful if you want the software user to be able to extend the composite, without modification, at a later point in time. In this context, "without modification" means that the following criteria are met when a customer extends the software:

1. The original source code does not have to be adapted for the extension.
2. The extension made by the customer remains active even if the original solution is updated. The customer extension is re-integrated automatically after the software update import.

Extension points, predefined by the software manufacturer, are usually used to realize these requirements. They reference interfaces, which are called from the original software when the extension point is activated. Chapter 6 goes into more detail about how this extension concept can be applied to process-driven applications, and the role that objects play.

For a process-driven application, it is advisable to use development environments that enable integrated development of the following:

- Processes
- User interfaces
- Business logic
- Persistence

Highly-integrated development suites have long been used in the Java environment in particular, the leading providers being Oracle, IBM, and SAP. Microsoft also offers an environment of this type, based on C#. These suites now support model-driven development; it is possible to create an application almost entirely in a model-driven way. Processes are modeled with BPMN, the user interfaces are constructed using WYSIWYG (What You See Is What You Get) editors, and the data displayed on the interfaces is implemented using graphically created class diagrams. Even for services, at least the interfaces can be modeled. If the service is a composed service that aggregates the results of other services and returns them as a whole, this logic can be realized by modeling the data flow between the service calls and without having to write source code. The actual codework is reduced significantly; it is only necessary for new business logic and to handle special cases and exceptions that the modeling tools would have difficulty coping with. Therefore, development environments should provide APIs for cases where the standard functionality is not sufficient. All in all, the developer can work more efficiently, the implementation time (and thus cost) is reduced, and quality improves significantly.

A process-driven application has many different artifacts, and the tools and frameworks that are necessary to create them have to interact seamlessly at development time and at runtime. A best-of-breed strategy is not necessarily the best option, because on top of the actual implementation of the process-driven application, you would also have the extra effort of integrating the various tools and runtime environments, which can differ in any of the following ways:

- Programming models (not aligned with each other)
- Error handling mechanisms
- Data models
- Troubleshooting tools (no common logging)
- Security concepts
- Internationalization concepts
- Administration
- Monitoring
- Configuration concepts
- User management
- Lifecycle behavior in the components created with the tools
- Support for tools/frameworks from the provider

Ultimately, the best-of-breed strategy does not give developers an overall view of their process-driven application. Even the leading providers cannot always provide an overview showing all dependencies between the developed components. Figure 3.13 shows how such an overview might look.

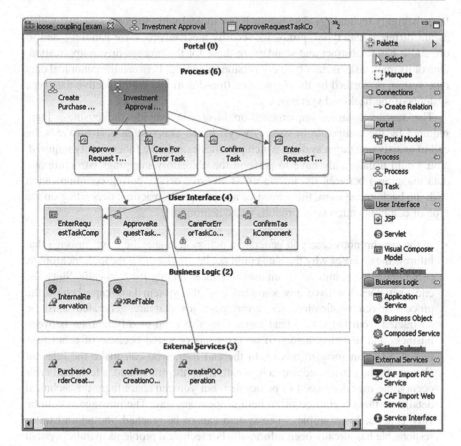

Fig. 3.13 Composite Designer perspective of SAP NetWeaver Developer Studio

This figure shows a screenshot of SAP's Composite Designer perspective, which visualizes all artifacts of a process-driven application including its dependencies. You can clearly see the layers of the application, just like we have discussed in this book.

There is nothing to prevent you using best-of-breed solutions to implement the approaches we present here (both the architecture and its implementation are independent of the tools used), but if you do, I would urge you to use the list above as a checklist so that you can identify any differences that would require additional solutions.

3.3.5.2 Service Contract Implementation Layer (Technical Composition): Focus on Integration-Centric Processes

In the service contract implementation layer, the business-led service contract defined by the process-driven application must be implemented against the existing system landscape. In contrast to the process-driven application, the implementation layer is highly technology-dependent: It has to deal with different systems, which means different data types, protocols, security mechanisms, error handling, and so on, and it has to abstract and standardize these for the process-driven application. One of its main tasks is data-type conversion (mapping) between the canonical data type system prescribed by the application (top-down) and the respective data type systems of the back-end systems.

The service contract implementation layer can provide the business logic required by the composite in various ways. In the simplest case, it forwards the call to exactly one target system, which provides exactly the functionality required. You would usually only have to perform the obligatory mappings (structure and data mappings) between the interfaces. If an error occurs during communication with the back-end system, there must be an appropriate reaction, depending on the type of communication (synchronous or asynchronous):

- In the synchronous case you generate a non-system-specific error message that informs the end user why the data could not be provided. To recap: Synchronous communication is initiated from user interfaces mainly for read calls. Since the end user does not have any knowledge of the system landscape behind the process-driven application, the error messages that are generated must be abstracted from the actual landscape. You also need to differentiate between business and technical errors. If an error has occurred because of a business reason, you can forward this on to the end user, who can make the relevant changes to the entries and start a new call. If, on the other hand, a technical error occurs, the user does need to be notified, but you can spare them the technical details, as these would be of no help to them anyway. The message should be very generic, for example, "The system cannot be reached; the administrator responsible has already been informed". For technical problems, parallel system messages should be sent to administrators or business departments, depending on the cause of the error, who can deal with the problem.
- The situation is very different for the asynchronous case. The end user is not actively waiting for a response. The user interaction with the process-driven application is complete, the business process has closed the dialog, and the data is sent asynchronously in an automatic process step to the service contract implementation layer to be updated. Once the data has been sent, the business process goes into standby and waits to be reactivated by the implementation layer. Any errors that occur must be solved by other mechanisms, because the contact with the end user is lost due to the loose coupling of the implementation. The advantage is obvious: If end user activities are totally decoupled from the actual update in the implementation layer, this provides a time buffer. It is no longer of utmost importance to respond within a matter of seconds, as was the case in the synchronous scenario. Any errors can be handled in a more consid-ered fashion. However, there still has to be a distinction in the asynchronous case between technical and business errors. In the event of technical errors such as network failures, system crashes, or downtimes as a result of upgrades or maintenance work, corresponding messages are sent to the administrators

responsible for the affected systems, who can turn their attention to the problem straight away. Because the problem is of a technical nature, the assumption in asynchronous communication is that the problem can always be resolved as far as the process-driven application is concerned. Once the technical prerequisites are met once more, the service call can be triggered again, and the business functionality is restored.

Business errors are handled differently. Here again, the end user cannot be notified immediately that corrections are necessary, due to the loose coupling. Instead, the business experts must be notified of the situation by e-mail or, in urgent cases, by SMS. They can then decide to either correct the error themselves, if they have the necessary experience and expertise, or get in touch with the end user to find a solution. If none of these options are successful, an error message can be sent to the waiting business process in the process-driven application. You must consider this error message in the definition of the service contract, so that appropriate reactions can be incorporated into the process flow at the process-driven application level.

If more than one system is involved, the implementation of the service contract becomes more complex. In write operations, we have a transaction problem to deal with, on top of the problems already mentioned. We are still working on the assumption that the business functionality can be provided in full by calls to the system landscape, and that it is not necessary to incorporate any additional services into the implementation layer. Now we have to clarify whether the write calls can be executed within one transaction or not. If the calls must be executed within one logical unit of work, we have to account for transaction rollback and model this explicitly in the technical processes with the help of compensating services. Section 5.4 looks at possible error handling patterns in more detail.

Things get even more complicated if the required business logic can no longer be provided by the back-end applications, for example, new fields are required that are not in the backends, or whole business functions are missing. In these cases, the logic can be implemented in the service contract implementation layer. To understand why, think back to the rules we defined earlier relating to the responsibilities between the two layers. The service contract and the services to be provided are defined during the specification phase and the process-driven application relies on this. Accordingly, the implementation layer must provide this service in full. In some circumstances, it has to implement its own persistence for missing fields, or implement completely new logic, but whatever the requirements are, they must not be implemented in any of the end applications (the back-end systems), as this would violate another important requirement: non-invasiveness. The only remaining option is implementation in the implementation layer itself, which is actually a very sensible solution, as it ensures encapsulation at a central location, and this makes for much easier maintenance than if the requirements were strewn across numerous different systems.

To summarize: The service contract implementation layer covers complex, integration-centric processes and at the same time encapsulates all technical communication aspects. Therefore, I call this layer *technical composition*, which, unlike user-centric business composition, focuses on the processes that establish the connection between the back-end applications that you want to integrate. Similar to a *business composition*, a *technical composition* provides a service by *composing* existing functions.

Since *processes* are the focus of both layers, we can use the same procedures and notations for both layers during implementation. This is expanded upon in Chap. 4, which deals with the actual implementation of a process-driven application and the service contract implementation layer.

When it comes to the implementation itself, there are of course various different technologies available. Whichever you use, the single most important thing is that the finished service contract fulfils exactly what was defined in the specification. It is advisable to use modern suites to implement asynchronous calls, as these suites are able to meet the high demands of non-functional criteria such as reliability, security, robustness, scalability, and performance. Examples are ESB implementations or MOMs (Message Oriented Middleware). Modern solutions also make it much easier to model asynchronous flows, either using BPEL or the more modern BPMN. You will know by now that I personally favor BPMN for the implementation of both process types (business and technical).

For synchronous calls, you can choose from a much wider spectrum of technologies. Be it programming languages such as Java, C#, C++, or ABAP, or scripting solutions such as Ruby, Python, or Scala; they all support the implementation of WSDL interfaces and are therefore suitable for implementing business logic using synchronous calls, as long as the functionality can be provided using Web services. However, since the service contract implementation layer operates in a business-critical environment, it is crucial to consider the non-functional criteria when making your selection, which will rule out some options. I do not recommend one particular solution over the other; the primary consideration for a process-driven application is compliance with the service contract, and this can be achieved by a range of different technologies.

In this and the previous sections, we discussed just the core tasks of the process-driven application and the service contract implementation layer. The following sections look at other properties that are provided by one side or the other, or through collaboration. Each section explains the function and who provides it. By now, we are familiar with the concept of the separation of tasks between the two layers. This can be summarized as follows:

- Any business aspects that are not dependent on back-end systems belong in the process-driven application. Conversely, all system-specific business aspects must be assigned to the service contract implementation layer.
- The business services required by the process-driven application that need to be provided externally are formulated in service contracts.
- All technical aspects relating to the integration of the end applications belong in the service contract implementation layer.

- The process-driven application only ever communicates with the IT landscape by way of the service contract implementation layer. There is no alternative route.

This checklist can help you decide what to implement in which layer. The next section illustrates the collaboration between the two sides by way of a scenario example, and provides other information to help you make your decision.

3.3.5.3 Interaction Between the Process-Driven Application and the Service Contract Implementation Layer

How exactly do the *process-driven application* layer and the *service contract implementation layer* work together, taking transactional aspects into account? We can illustrate the process flow and the collaboration by looking at an actual scenario. In particular, we will revisit the discussion from Sect. 3.3.4.2 (Communication Style) on the implementation of synchronous communication for calls from user interfaces and asynchronous communication for write operations from process steps. Our example is a simplified order process. The corresponding BPMN diagram in Fig. 3.14 illustrates the process flow.

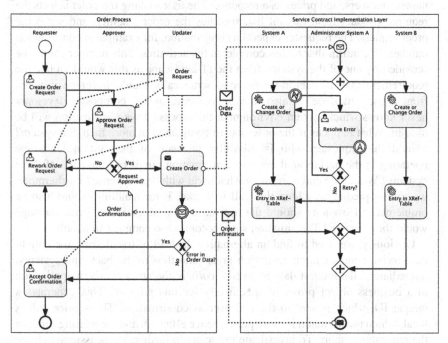

Fig. 3.14 Simplified order process as BPMN model

The model shows two pools: The one on the left represents the process-driven application and the one on the right represents the service contract implementation layer. The business order process itself is executed within the process-driven application; the technical process required is executed within the service contract implementation layer. As we learned in the previous section, we can use the same notation for processes of a business or technical nature. In this case, we are using BPMN. You can clearly see that each side has a different focus. The process-driven application is a user-centric application; this is evident from the number of user tasks within the BPMN model. The implementation layer on the other side is more integration-centric; all steps except one are automated service tasks. The process flow is structured as follows:

1. In the process-driven application, the business process starts with a user processing a request form for an order. Although the model does not show it explicitly, calls are made at this point from a user interface to the service contract implementation layer (the requester will surely want to search a catalog, which is usually already available in the company, to select which product to order). We therefore have to define an interface during the specification; this interface is based on the requirements of the application, which will be provided externally. In this simplified scenario, we will use a search as an example, where the product name and/or product number are search fields and are transferred to a search service. The process-driven application expects a list of products with product names, numbers, and prices as a response. The user making the order selects the required product from this hit list, specifies the order quantity, and sends the order request. The requester expects a confirmation, for example, a confirmation number, to confirm that he has completed his activities. This number cannot be provided by one of the systems from the IT landscape as this would violate the requirement that asynchronous external write calls should never be initiated from a user interface. It also makes no sense, as the composite developer never knows which system environment the process-driven application will be used in. What happens if the order has to be updated in more than one system? Should the requester, who is blissfully unaware of the system landscape operating in the background, receive confirmation numbers from each of these systems? Would the end user know what to do with this response? Furthermore, we cannot predict how long this call will take. Error handling would also be problematic: How long should the user have to wait, and what error message would they receive? The situation soon becomes too complex to handle.

   Obviously, we need to find an alternative. Instead of transferring the data to the service contract implementation layer (and thus to the back-end systems) immediately, the request data is saved *locally* in the process-driven application in a business object provided specifically for this purpose. This generates a unique ID, which is sent to the end user as confirmation. The service call is local, which means that it is more performance efficient, and the waiting time for the requester is short. To investigate the scenario further, let us assume that the internal number 4711 is generated when the order request data is saved locally. Saving the order request data and generating the internal number concludes the first process activity. As you can see from the process model, the process-internal data object *Order Request* is generated. This is the content of the process context, which we introduced in the chapter on the specification of process-driven applications. The data of the process context is available to all steps of the process at any time and is kept for as long as this process instance is active. Of course, this also means that the data of the process context cannot be accessed once the process has ended. The order request data is transferred to the implementation layer (to be updated) later by way of an asynchronous call. So, the requester finishes his step and in doing so initiates the approval of the order request by the role labeled *Approver* in the pool.

2. The approver simply has to check the data entered by the requester and approve or reject it. The data is transferred from the *Order Request* data object to the dialog step of the approver. This step does not have anything to add to our discussion of the collaboration between the process-driven application and the implementation layer. If the approver rejects the request, the requester has the opportunity to make corrections. The requester's user interface is filled with the information from the *Order Request* object, and the changes are sent back to the approver. Since the user may have to perform another search and save the data locally in this step too, the comments made for point 1 apply here as well.

If the request is approved, the data can be transferred to the service contract implementation layer to be updated in the IT landscape. This begins the asynchronous collaboration between the two layers, which is discussed in more detail below.

3. According to the model in Fig. 3.14, the send activity *Create Order* is performed within the process-driven application in the *Updater* lane. Send activities are used in BPMN to represent asynchronous communication steps with other processes. This is exactly what is expressed in the interaction between the process-driven application and the service contract implementation layer: We transfer a message to the *technical composition*, whereby the message content corresponds to the service contract between the composite and the implementation layer. The contract for this scenario, if using XSD (XML Schema Definition), could look like this:

```
<xsd:element name="createPurchaseOrderOperation">
    <xsd:complexType>
        <xsd:sequence>
            <xsd:element name="correlationID"
                         type="xsd:string"/>
            <xsd:element name="productID"
                         type="xsd:string"/>
            <xsd:element name="quantity"
                         type="xsd:decimal"/>
        </xsd:sequence>
    </xsd:complexType>
</xsd:element>
```

From the perspective of the process-driven application, the service contract simply transfers the selected product (productID field) and the order quantity (quantity field). However, the interface also has an additional field called correlationID, which is used later when the results are returned from the implementation layer to find the composite process instance that originally initiated the update request. This assignment is important because it is possible to process several instances of the order process in parallel, and there must be a way to assign the response correctly to the request. This is achieved by way of a unique identifier, in this example by the field marked correlationID. The content could be the order number generated locally in the application.

The model shows that the interface data is also filled with the content of the process context. Once the data has been transferred asynchronously to the implementation layer, the process in the process-driven application reaches the message intermediate event, where it waits for the order confirmation with the matching correlationID. In the literature, the pattern for correlating two processes with a unique ID is also referred to as a *correlation identifier* (see also Hohpe and Woolf 2004, p. 163).

An interesting variant of the illustrated process flow is where more activities are executed parallel to the wait procedure, as shown in Fig. 3.15.

Fig. 3.15 Waiting and executing other activities in parallel

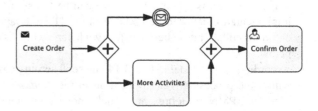

You can use the waiting time to execute other activities. Once the additional activities are complete and the order confirmation message has arrived (converging parallel gateway) the process can continue.

4. But what happens in the service contract implementation layer? Figure 3.14 only shows the sequence flow for this layer; I left out the data flow so as not to overload it.

   Once the order data has been received (message start event), the process flow splits at the parallel gateway to illustrate that two systems can be involved independently within the implementation layer to implement the business requirement *Create Order* on the composite side. In another system landscape the implementation could look completely different, and this is exactly what makes the collaboration between the composite and the implementation layer so flexible, and therefore so interesting. This clear and complete separation offers a wealth of options for implementing the requirements of your composite.

5. The order data is updated in system A and in system B using service tasks. An error situation is included in system A to show how this could be handled. In productive implementations, this error handling process would be included in system B as well, but this was left out in Fig. 3.14 to keep the model simple. The error handling itself is represented by the interrupting error boundary event

attached to the *Create or Change Order* service activity for system A. In this case the process follows the sequence flow from the error event: An administrator is informed about the error straight away and can decide whether to call the service causing the error again (*Retry?* gateway), or make the necessary corrections manually in the target system to resolve the error so that the process can continue straight to the next step. The administrator's decision determines which route the process flow takes. Of course, the error may not be of a technical nature and cannot be solved by an administrator. It may be a business issue, in which case someone from the business department needs to be involved. In this case as well, the person responsible would access the respective target system (in consultation with the requester, if necessary) to solve the problem. It is important that all errors, whether they are of a technical or business nature, are dealt with close to the back-end systems and are not simply passed on to the process-driven application. At this early stage, it is much more likely that the cause of the error can be found and resolved. We can summarize that both technical and system-specific business errors should be handled within the service contract implementation layer. *System-specific* in this context means that the error is related to a *particular target system*. However, if the error is *not specific to a particular target system*, it is a *system-neutral business error*, which must be returned to the process-driven application and handled there. This is indicated in the figure by the sequence flow leading from the interrupting escalation boundary event that is attached to the *Resolve Error* step. The administrator has an option in the dialog to use an escalation to indicate that the error is a system-neutral business error that he cannot handle, and to ensure that the error is dealt with appropriately. In this case, this means returning the error to the process-driven application. This makes sense, as errors of this type can only be solved within the composite.

6. For both system A and system B, once the order is created in the respective target system, the process flow reaches the *Entry in XRef Table* step. This is a cross-reference table that manages the references between the internal number of the order being used in the process-driven application and the respective order numbers in the target systems. A locally-persisted object is set up and used specifically for this purpose in the implementation layer.

The task of managing the cross-reference table clearly belongs to the service contract implementation layer, as the table contains technical details about the integrated end systems. These technical details are always outside the process-driven application and therefore belong in the implementation layer. Table 3.2 shows how the table looks for our example scenario. The order number being used in the process-driven application is taken from the `correlationID` field of the service contract; the order numbers in system A and system B are taken from the respective fields in the return parameters of the *Create or Change Order* service calls to the systems.

Table 3.2 Cross-reference table for example scenario

Order number in process-driven application	Order number in System A	Order number in System B
4711	815	4500002012

The cross-reference table is then used for all subsequent calls, irrespective of whether they are read or write calls. If, for example, the scenario has an order change process in addition to the order process, data from system A and system B will have to be read to enable changes to be made. Using our example data, if we want to change the composite order with the ID 4711, this requires access to the order data from system A with the number 815 and the order data from system B with the number 4500002012. Also, if you know the numbers in the back-end applications, you can see which object in the composite will be affected by any changes in the backends. This knowledge can be used to inform the composite of changes using events, and give the composite opportunity to react with appropriate measures. The entries must be kept in the table for as long as the corresponding business objects are not deleted. This is particularly important for archiving runs, which must include the process-driven application, the back-end systems, and the cross-reference table. If one of the back-end systems in the cross-reference table is replaced with an offering from a different provider, or is removed completely as a result of consolidation measures in the company, this must be updated in the table. In the event of a system consolidation, the column in question must be removed from the table. If a system is replaced, the identification number of the old system must be replaced with that of the new system. This is done as part of the data migration from the old to the new system.

The cross-reference table plays a central role in the collaboration between the process-driven application and the service contract implementation layer and is therefore an important part of the implementation layer. It is a crucial factor in achieving independence from back-end systems, since the process-driven application itself no longer needs to work with the primary keys of the legacy applications, but works with the new internal key instead.

7. Once the cross-reference table or tables have been updated, the waiting process is reactivated in the process-driven application. The parallel gateway first synchronizes both paths in the implementation layer. Only when both are ready does the process continue with the throwing end event. This message is also part of the service contract and could look like this:

```
<xsd:element name="confirmPurchaseOrderOperation">
    <xsd:complexType>
        <xsd:sequence>
            <xsd:element name="correlationID"
                         type="xsd:string"/>
            <xsd:element name="errorCode"
                         type="xsd:string"/>
```

```
                    <xsd:element name="errorMsg"
                                 type="xsd:decimal"/>
            </xsd:sequence>
        </xsd:complexType>
    </xsd:element>
```

You can see that none of the numbers generated by the integrated systems are returned to the process of the composite. There is no need for this information; the process-driven application does not make any assumptions about the system landscape anyway. correlationID ensures that the correct waiting process is identified. Once the data has been sent, the technical process ends.

8. The order confirmation data is loaded into the process context on the process-driven application side. We then have an exclusive gateway to react to any error messages in the implementation layer. This illustrates how a simple system-neutral business error is handled by the process-driven application; in contrast to technical and system-specific business error handling, this takes place within the implementation layer. If a system-neutral business error occurs, the requester has the opportunity to correct the data and submit it for approval again.

On the other hand, if the order was updated successfully in the systems, the data required for further processing is forwarded from the process context to the interface of the requester, who can display the order confirmation. Once the data is confirmed, the process can be ended.

Two-Layer Architecture This example scenario helps us understand the main aspects of the basic architecture of a process-driven application in its interaction with the service contract implementation layer, and shows how the tasks are distributed across the two layers. On this basis, we can now focus in on other details of the process-driven application and the implementation layer, not only to clarify the separation and task distribution between the two layers, but also to learn how to make the architecture more stable and robust for use in business-critical scenarios, while increasing its flexibility. In the next section, our first step is to elaborate the model by including an enterprise service bus (ESB) in the implementation of the service contract implementation layer. There are several reasons to do this. In the two-layer architecture shown in Fig. 3.14 (consisting of the process-driven application and the service contract implementation layer), the BPMN engine that executes the two layers would have to be able to connect directly to each of the involved back-end systems, and this is rather unlikely considering the large number of different systems and possible technical connection options. Furthermore, we would have to continually adapt the integration-centric process of the service contract implementation layer at the BPMN level every time the system landscape changed (system consolidations, introduction of new systems) or corrections were made to the interfaces to the systems. Last but not least, the integration-centric process is responsible for tasks such as receiver determination, interface determination, and mapping between the various interfaces, which are better served by an ESB. The following section explains how we can address all these problems by using an ESB.

3.3.5.4 Including an ESB in the Service Contract Implementation Layer

Tasks that are typically performed by an enterprise service bus (ESB), such as routing messages, transforming messages by mapping, and managing the technical connections to the systems involved, do not necessarily have to be modeled in the integration-centric process. ESBs are optimized for these types of tasks and relieve developers of many of the routine tasks in message communication in heterogeneous environments. A major advantage of ESBs is that you can configure integration scenarios rather than using traditional (and time-intensive) programming. ESBs are a great enhancement for the architecture of process-driven applications. So, what are the effects of using an ESB on process-driven applications and the service contract implementation layer? The process-driven application itself is not affected because the tasks taken on by the ESB that we mentioned above are all technical services. The service contract continues to provide its stable interface, and it is only necessary to separate tasks in the implementation layer. The implementation of the service contract shown in Fig. 3.14 is still vulnerable to additions or removals of target systems. Every time a back-end system is added, or removed as a result of consolidations, the process at the parallel gateway must be adapted accordingly. In this case as well, the tasks can be separated between the integration process and the ESB to increase stability, so that these changes do not have any impact on the integration process. This is shown in Fig. 3.16 on the following page.

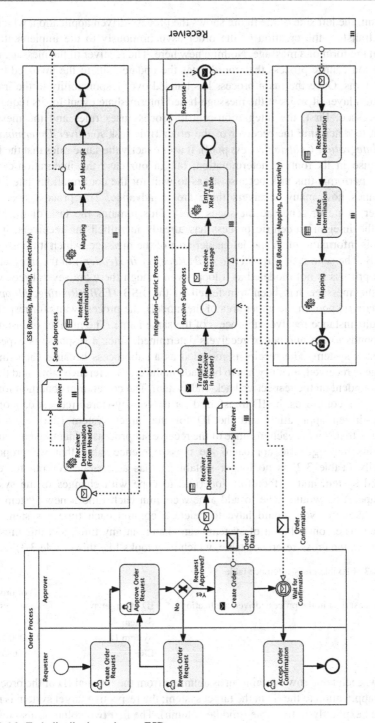

Fig. 3.16 Task distribution using an ESB

Again, the left side of the figure shows the process-driven application, which, as usual, transfers the creation of the order asynchronously to the implementation layer in the form of a message. Nothing new here. The receiver of the message is an integration-centric process that coordinates the update calls to the involved back-end systems. Once the main process has handed over responsibility to the implementation layer, it waits at the message-based intermediate event for its request to be processed. First, the integration-centric process uses rules and the message content to determine the receiver of the order (rule task *Receiver Determination* in the *Integration-Centric Process* pool). It uses exactly the same rules that the ESB would use in its routing determination, but in our case the integration-centric process performs this task because it has to wait for the confirmations later, so it determines how many receivers there are in advance. The process does *not*, however, route or send the messages itself. This remains the task of the ESB. Since the integration-centric process has already identified the receivers, it can store this information in a special header area of the message, which it transfers to the ESB. The send task (*Transfer to ESB (Receiver in Header)*) in the integration-centric process is not modeled as a loop, even though there are several receivers. Once the message has been transferred to the ESB (*ESB (Routing, Mapping, Connectivity)* pool in the upper area of the model), the process waits for responses in a multi-instance receive subprocess of the same name. The number of instances corresponds to the number of receivers determined, since a response is expected from each system. The receipt is modeled as a subprocess because each time a message is received, an entry has to be made in the cross-reference table, and this is also dependent on the respective back-end system. The correlation condition for the receive step comprises the ID transferred for the locally-stored request data of the process-driven application and the ID for the target system (the determined receiver). In this way, each instance of the receive subprocess is identified uniquely. With this new, generic approach, the cross-reference table that we proposed originally (Table 3.2) is no longer suitable; it has a separate column for each involved system and is therefore too rigid to cope with changes in the system landscape. You would have to add a new column each time a new system was added; likewise, you would have to delete a column each time a system was removed. The constellation of systems can change at any time, and this must be reflected in the cross-reference table, which now looks like this (Table 3.3).

Table 3.3 Flexible cross-reference table

ID of request data in the process-driven application	ID of target system	ID of order in target system
4711	System A	815
4711	System B	4500002012
4711	ERP	1GWL972

Now, each table row contains an assignment from the internal ID of the process-driven application to the ID in the target system; the respective target system is now included explicitly in the table (middle column). The first two columns also reflect the correlation condition for the receive step from Fig. 3.16 mentioned above. This table can deal with any change in the IT landscape and supports our drive for increased flexibility across the entire architecture.

Since the integration-centric process implements the service contract, and the data types used are based on the canonical data model, it is clear that the canonical data model will be used exclusively across the *entire integration-centric process*. The process does not have any contact at all with the proprietary data types of the back-end systems; this task falls to the ESB.

The ESB starts with the *Receiver Determination* service task; it takes the list of message receivers that have been determined by the integration-centric process. Based on the number of receivers found, a multi-instance subprocess is started, whose task it is to determine the correct interface for each receiver system, adapt the data to the target structures, and then send the data. This is where the ESB exhibits its strengths.

The receiver system, represented by the *Receiver* pool, processes the data and sends a response back to the ESB. The ESB uses the interface information of the received message as well as the sender data to determine the integration-centric process as the receiver. Before the data is transferred to the waiting process, a mapping step converts it to the canonical data model. The target interface has already been determined in the *Interface Determination* task. The integration-centric process updates the cross-reference table for each message received. Once the integration-centric process has received all the response messages in this way through the ESB, it can create the response message and pass this on to the process of the process-driven application, completing the cycle.

Error Handling We now need to think about what type of error handling is necessary and where it should take place. With our new distribution, errors are possible on all levels and we must make provision for error handling accordingly. Business errors are still handled in the order process. The stateful integration process will deal primarily with timeout situations, that is, where an expected response is not received within a predefined time period. In this case, an administrator is usually informed; the administrator looks into the problem and decides how to proceed, for example, by resending the message. Last but not least, the stateless integration process is responsible for all technical errors related to the direct communication with the involved back-end systems as well as mappings between the various interfaces. It is also responsible for situations where data content that the ESB needs for routing or data transformation is invalid. Here as well, an administrator will be involved to handle the error appropriately.

In all error situations, your general strategy should be to resolve errors as close as possible to their source, and not to inundate the business application with error messages that it (and the end user) are unable to deal with.

Sections 4.1.3 (Exception Handling) and 4.1.3.1 (Time Monitoring) explain how to model error, timeout, and exception situations with BPMN. Section 5.4 (Error Handling) contains a general discussion of error handling strategies.

Componentization When Using an ESB: Three-Layer Architecture We can see from the model that the tasks are clearly distributed; another componentization has taken place, in order to increase flexibility. I would strongly recommend using an ESB with process-driven applications: Not only does it round off the entire architecture perfectly, it also reduces the implementation time because complicated connections to third-party systems (and their technical connections, protocols, and data formats) are entrusted to the ESB and its tools, which are designed and optimized for this very purpose. If there are any changes in the system landscape, the integration-centric process does not need to be adapted; all communication with the back-end systems and their proprietary interfaces is dealt with by the ESB. Since any changes in the system constellation have to be reflected in the routing tables of the ESB, the integration-centric process benefits automatically from these adaptations because it accesses exactly this information from the ESB in the receiver determination. Working with data types is also relatively painless because the process from the process-driven application and the integration-centric process both work exclusively with the canonical data model. Transformations are only needed in the communication with the back-end systems, and these transformations are encapsulated in the ESB, making them easy to change and manage locally. We end up with a three-layer architecture, comprising the following:

1. Business process (*Order Process* pool)
2. Stateful integration process (*Integration-Centric Process* pool)
3. Stateless integration process (*ESB (Routing, Mapping, Connectivity)* pool)

You can see what an important role the ESB plays in the architecture. If you take a step back and look at the whole picture, you can appreciate how the ESB fits into the overall puzzle, how it can best be used, and how it can contribute to a sound application architecture.

> **Note**
> With its many advantages, the three-layer architecture is undoubtedly the architecture of choice for process-driven applications.

Simplifying the Architecture: Business Process Does Not Expect a Response Message I want to mention one last usage case before I conclude this chapter. If the business process from Fig. 3.16 does not expect a response from the involved systems, and the business requirements do not necessitate a cross-reference table, then you do not need to implement a stateful integration process. The data can be transferred directly from the end application to the ESB, which then ensures that the information is distributed correctly. This usage case is shown in Fig. 3.17; it simplifies the architecture without violating any of the prerequisites for process-driven applications.

Fig. 3.17 Task distribution when using an ESB without responses or cross-reference table

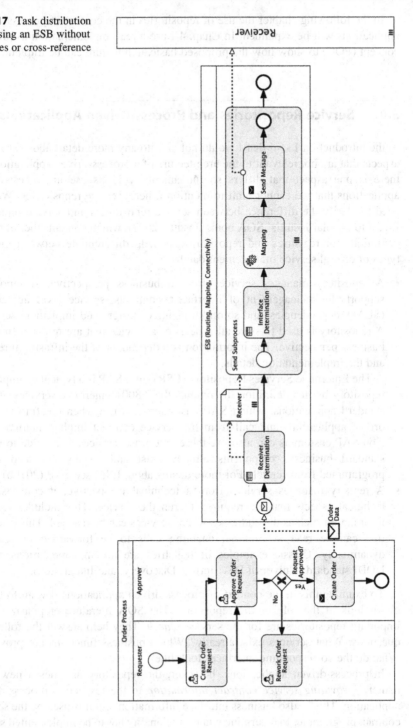

In the following chapter the use of repositories in the context of process-driven applications will be explained. In Chap. 4 I use a real implementation as proof of concept (POC) to show how the proposed basic architecture can be implemented.

3.4   Service Repositories and Process-Driven Applications

In the introduction I said that I would not go into any more detail about any SOA aspects that are not relevant to the architecture of a process-driven application, but there is one aspect that differs so fundamentally in its use in process-driven applications that we cannot omit to mention it here: service repositories. We also need to clarify the difference between service repositories and service registries. I refer to Nicolai Josuttis' SOA book (Josuttis 2007), which contains the following definitions for registries and repositories, to help differentiate between the two types of central service management database:

- A repository manages services from a business perspective. A repository supports the management of interfaces, contracts, service level agreements (SLAs), dependencies, and so on, to identify, design, and implement services. A repository is used to store all aspects of a service that are relevant from the business perspective. The information is independent of the infrastructure used and the implementation details.

  The Enterprise Services Repository (ESR) from SAP is a typical example of a repository by this definition. It contains the 2,800+ enterprise services of SAP standard applications, which SAP customers can use when creating process-driven applications and call from the service contract implementation layer. Non-SAP customers can also use these enterprise services as a guide to which standard business components already exist and so do not need to be programmed from scratch. For more details about ESR, see SAP (2010b).

- A registry manages services from a technical perspective; it comprises all technical aspects that are required to run the service. This includes runtime information such as the addresses where services can be reached. This information can be read at runtime, enabling calls to be forwarded or rerouted dynamically. Classic examples of registries are all implementations of the UDDI standard (Universal Description, Discovery, and Integration).

To examine this in the context of process-driven applications, I want to take a closer look at the role of the repository. The SOA literature emphasizes how important repositories are for the service *search*. They help answer the following questions: What services exist already? Which business functions are provided? What do the corresponding interfaces look like?

In process-driven applications, however, the repository assumes a new role, namely, *providing service contract information* to the respective process-driven application. This is also business interface information, but it is used by the service contract programmer to determine what functionality has to be implemented so that the process-driven application can run correctly. To do this, the programmer needs the business information that was mentioned above in the definition of a repository. The service contracts are business-led, so the service repository is exactly the right place for this data. Note that the interfaces of the service contract are not set up for reusability; they are designed for a specific process-driven application. This is another difference from how the content of the repository was used up to now, that is, to find reusable services.

Until now, service repositories were used to find services, but they can now also be used for the external representation of the process-driven application. Ultimately, the repository tells you which services a process-driven application expects to be implemented in the service contract implementation layer and which business services they provide. The contracts can vary depending on the version of the process-driven application, so version management for service contracts is essential within the repository. Modern repositories are well able to deal with version differences, and when a particular version of a process-driven application is introduced, the developer of the service contract implementation layer for a particular composite version is automatically presented with the corresponding service contract for implementation. The developer can then use the list of services that it contains as a guide during the implementation phase.

We now know that there are differences between SOA applications and process-driven applications as regards services, but there are some common features as well. Both application types require that services have certain attributes (I refer again to Josuttis 2007). Services in this context are what the process-driven application calls externally using the service contract implementation layer (consumer view), and not what is provided by the process-driven application (provider view):

- Self-contained: The services used in the service contract implementation layer are self-contained and therefore independent of other services and the general system status.
- Coarse-grained: The service comprises complex business flows and goes far beyond simple database operations. The enterprise services from SAP in the Enterprise Services Repository (SAP 2010b) show just how wide the range of services currently available to companies is.
- Visible/findable: A business function can only be reused if it is known to exist. Service repositories and registries are therefore very important for the findability of a service. Appendix B contains a few pointers for how to manage services so that you get a better hit rate in searches. For us, the business content is more important that the interface.
- Stateless: A service is stateless when a status does not have to be kept in the form of temporary local variables between two successive calls in the service implementation; they can be deleted after the service call. This status is different to the status that is manifested in a database, for example, after a service call. The service for creating an order is stateless because the temporary variables can

be deleted after the call. However, an order object is stored in the database; this can be accessed and changed by an order change service, which itself is stateless. Even stateless services will always have this type of status.

- Idempotent: A service is idempotent if it can be called several times with the same data, but the operation itself is guaranteed to be executed only once. Idempotence is particularly important in Web applications. If end users, having entered and sent their order data, do not receive an immediate confirmation on their screen that the data has been sent successfully, they are likely to press the send button again. Without idempotence, the current shopping cart would be ordered repeatedly. Idempotence enables you to recognize and handle such situations. This property is covered in more detail in Chap. 5 (*Advanced Concepts for Architecture Support in Process-Driven Applications*).

There are a few other minor differences between SOA and process-driven applications that we should mention. Process-driven applications do not insist that a service is implemented as a Web service. What is important is that the business function of a service is self-contained; how this is achieved technically, or how the interface is represented, is immaterial. Modern infrastructure products such as ESBs use adapters to enable protocol transformations; this means that you can integrate systems that are not yet technically able to handle Web services into your process-driven application. This applies to interfaces as well, if they are not yet available in WSDL. Here again, products are available that enable transformations. The SAP product family makes it possible to transform all business functions that are provided by the SAP-proprietary protocols and interfaces RFM (remote function module) and BAPI (business application programming interface) into WSDL descriptions by using a proxy generator, and makes them accessible using the SOAP protocol. This boosts the reuse potential of existing functions significantly compared with pure SOAP/WSDL-based services.

Another area where a difference is apparent is the importance of governance processes. In SOA the reusability of services is a central aspect, as therefore is the establishment of processes within the company to define the correct service granularity, the appearance of the service interfaces and the data types used, the creation of guidelines for creating services, the monitoring of service use, and maintenance of the service over its entire lifecycle. This is less important for process-driven applications. In this respect, composite applications are first and foremost service consumers. The internal services created during the composite's development are used mainly to implement the new business requirements within the process-driven application, and reusability is not a priority initially. If, however, there is a possibility to reuse a service at a later point in time, the governance processes established in the company can be applied, and the necessary changes can be implemented in the process-driven application by refactoring. To understand why governance is generally less important in process-driven applications than in SOA, we just need to consider how absolutely crucial composites and their rapid implementation are for a company. Composite applications, by definition, should support the innovative processes that give the company a competitive advantage. The quicker the solution is productive, the better it is for the company. Therefore, the implementation process should be kept as lean as possible, which conflicts somewhat with the long-winded SOA governance processes.

Implementing the Basic Architecture of Process-Driven Applications

4

Our next step is to put the concepts we covered in the last chapter into practice by developing an application that will demonstrate the main principles of the basic architecture of process-driven applications and their implementation. I want to focus particularly on the implementation of loose coupling and will use BPMN for both the process-driven application and the service contract implementation layer, so that we can look at the executability aspect.

So far, we have learnt that a complete process-driven application consists of processes, user interfaces, objects (including their persistence), and services. Our example application will implement all these elements. We also have to realize the interaction between the process-driven application and the service contract implementation layer; this is done using interfaces, expressed in the form of a contract, which too has to be implemented. However, before we make a start on developing the application, we will turn our attention back to BPMN, in particular its significance for the implementation of processes within the service contract implementation layer.

4.1 Significance of BPMN for the Implementation of the Service Contract Implementation Layer

In Sect. 2.4 (*The Role of BPMN (Business Process Model and Notation) for Process-Driven Applications - Basics*) we looked at the core elements of BPMN for modeling process-driven applications, focusing particularly on those elements used for business modeling. This chapter covers the more advanced BPMN concepts that are used in the service contract implementation layer. It is at this juncture that the new executability features in version 2.0 come into play; these render transformations into other executable languages such as BPEL unnecessary. I have intentionally avoided using such transformations in this book as I feel that the latest version of BPMN has everything you need to be able to accurately model and

V. Stiehl, *Process-Driven Applications with BPMN*, DOI 10.1007/978-3-319-07218-0_4,   111
© Springer International Publishing Switzerland 2014

execute even technical processes. BPMN has become a kind of graphical programming language, and as such, it has several concepts that we need to understand:

– Events
– Parallel processing
– Exception handling
– Transactions and compensation
– Collaborations and message exchange

4.1.1   Events

One of BPMN's great strengths is that it is event-oriented. As mentioned in Sect. 2.4.1.2 (Events), there are no less than 13 different event types. We have already met the message event (✉), which is activated when a message arrives, and the timer event (⏰). The following event types are also important for process-driven applications:

– Escalation event (**A**) to identify exceptional business situations
– Error event (**Ⱥ**) to display technical problems
– Cancel event (✖), used together with the compensation event (⏪), to perform transactions
– Signal event (△) for simultaneous communication inside and outside the process using publish/subscribe mechanisms
– Terminate event (●) to end the process immediately, irrespective of whether tokens are still in the process or not.
  The event types can be further differentiated by their characteristics:
– Position in the process: Events can be placed at different positions in the process flow, but not all positions are suitable for all event types. Events placed at the start of a process are referred to as start events, events at the end of the process as end events, and everything else as intermediate events.
– Use in the process flow: Events can be embedded directly in the normal sequence flow or attached to activities.
– Interrupting or non-interrupting: This distinction applies to boundary events, and tells the reader of the model whether an activity is interrupted or not when the event happens.
– Throwing or catching: This signifies whether the event is sent or received by the process.

Using events enables the modeler to display and react to extraordinary situations. The modeler has to decide how the process should react when certain events occur during the process flow, and can also use events to signalize that exceptions have occurred (usually when a process sequence deviates from the happy path). BPMN provides the tools for modeling event handling concisely yet accurately, and encourages the modeler to address potential error situations. Developers tend to view the programming of exception handling as a long-winded, tedious, and altogether unpleasant task, but this type of modeling not only makes exception handling a normal part of the process, it also saves a great deal of time, especially when dealing with executable process models. The event handling itself is deployed and monitored by the frameworks that are implementing BPMN.

We will continue to focus on events in the following sections, looking at other differentiating characteristics and how events are used in different environments.

4.1.2   Parallel Processing

Parallel processing is particularly important for process-driven applications. Activating parallel process paths optimizes process lead times and makes better use of computing resources, and BPMN supports this at various levels. Of all the BPMN elements we have discussed, the parallel gateway and the inclusive gateway are most relevant in this context.

The parallel gateway activates multiple paths without checking any conditions, resulting in a high degree of parallelization. Figure 4.1, for example, shows three systems that are supplied with data simultaneously in the form of messages.

Fig. 4.1 Parallel gateway

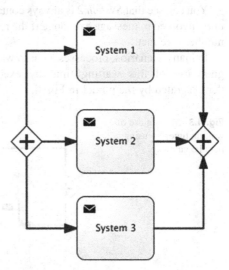

The benefit to the service contract implementation layer is that the parallel sequence flows are processed independently, which optimizes reaction times. Let us take the business function *Read Customer Data* as an example, which requires information from several systems. These systems can be called simultaneously, and once all the responses have arrived, the compiled information is sent back to the consumer of the function.

The inclusive gateway also allows parallel processing, but imposes conditions on the outgoing sequence flows. Nevertheless, there is a smart way to use inclusive gateways to model typical process situations: You specify a path without a condition in addition to the outgoing flows with conditions. This path is always activated, along with those whose conditions are fulfilled. This is shown in Fig. 4.2.

Fig. 4.2 Inclusive gateway with path without condition

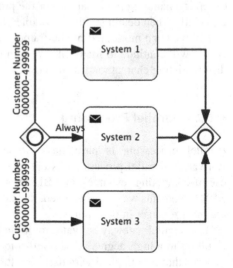

You can see that *System 2* is always contacted, whereas the other two systems are only involved in message exchange if the respective conditions relating to customer numbers are met.

In many scenarios, processes have to wait for messages to arrive. You can make good use of this waiting time by executing other activities in parallel, as demonstrated by the model in Fig. 4.3.

Fig. 4.3 Making use of waiting times by using a parallel gateway

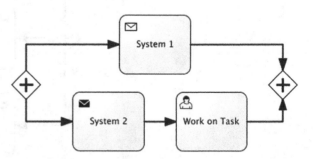

While the process waits for a message from *System 1*, a second system is contacted in parallel and a user task is completed. Both strands converge again at the next parallel gateway. Another way to model concurrency in BPMN is to use non-interrupting boundary events, and event subprocesses can also achieve similar results. Both options are discussed below.

Non-interrupting boundary events are a good choice if events occur during the processing of a task or a subprocess that do need to be handled, but are not so severe that it is necessary to interrupt processing. For example, a customer is booking a trip and adds the details of a new credit card (to be charged once the booking is complete) to the system. The customer has to provide this new information, but this is no reason to stop the booking process (see also OMG 2010b). Figure 4.4 shows a model using non-interrupting boundary events.

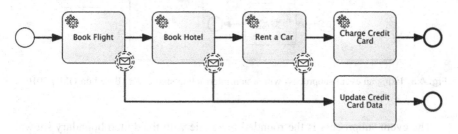

Fig. 4.4 Using non-interrupting events (Based on OMG 2010b, p. 28)

Because the message that the credit card details have been changed can arrive during processing of any of the three booking tasks, the non-interrupting event has to be bound to all three. An even more sophisticated method is to attach a non-interrupting boundary event to a subprocess containing the three tasks that make up the travel booking. The result is shown in Fig. 4.5.

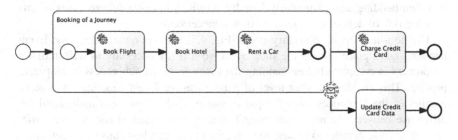

Fig. 4.5 Using non-interrupting boundary events on a subprocess (Based on OMG 2010b, p. 28)

Using a subprocess also defines the scope for which the event is valid. In our case, the event can only happen at some point during the processing of the three booking tasks because if the credit card has already been charged, there is no point in updating the details.

Figure 4.6 shows the same scenario, but this time it is realized with the new event subprocess from BPMN 2.0.

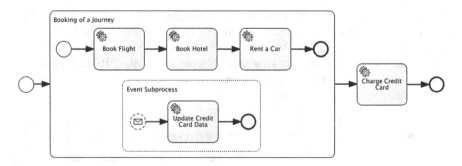

Fig. 4.6 Using an event subprocess with a non-interrupting start event (Based on OMG 2010b, p. 28)

The event subprocess is the rounded rectangle with the dotted boundary shown beneath the travel booking process. It is active for the duration of the surrounding subprocess and is activated by an incoming message. As the start event in the event subprocess is non-interrupting (indicated by the dashed boundary), the credit card data is updated in parallel with the execution of the booking sequence flow. The models in Figs. 4.5 and 4.6 are very similar, and at first glance do not appear to have any significant semantic differences, but they do behave very differently at runtime. If you use an event subprocess (Fig. 4.6) the subprocess for booking a journey is not completed until the event subprocess is completed, as implied by the fact that the event subprocess is embedded in the booking subprocess. Therefore, you should avoid embedding any particularly lengthy activities in event subprocesses as this runs the risk of delaying the process flow unnecessarily.

The non-interrupting boundary event (Fig. 4.5) behaves quite differently. Event handling takes place *outside* the subprocess, so it is not necessary to wait until the subprocess is complete before handing the token from the subprocess to its parent process. This enables a higher level of parallelization: Event handling takes place parallel to the subprocess and the parent process. Modelers must understand the difference between the non-interrupting boundary event method and the event sub-process method in order to be able to select the option that best suits their scenario.

All three methods enable you to represent concurrency clearly and compactly in BPMN-modeled processes.

There are certainly advantages to be gained by parallelization, but modelers must also bear in mind their responsibilities as regards data handling and access within the process. The individual tasks work with the data of a single process context; this means that the parallel branches will be competing for access to the process context, and you may have to take measures to prevent data being overwritten (for example, having separate areas in the process context).

4.1.3   Exception Handling

There is always potential for errors in tasks, subprocesses, and process flow sequences; a good notation will provide you with the right language tools to be able to react appropriately, and BPMN provides a range of constructs that help the modeler with this task. Let us look at a few examples. Figure 4.7 illustrates several different errors. From an exception handling perspective, the subprocess *Booking of a Journey* with the sequence *Send Booking Data* and *Receive Booking Confirmation* is viewed as a unit, where the following error situation could arise: The receiver of the booking data identifies an inconsistency and indicates this by means of an exception.

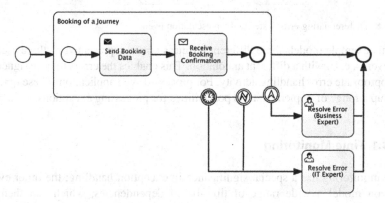

Fig. 4.7 Error handling using events

In BPMN, you could use the escalation event (**A**) in this case; I find this very useful for signaling business problems. For technical errors such as database problems or network connection issues, I would recommend using an error event (**N**). At the same time, the subprocess in the model is also being timed, and if the booking confirmation does not reach the receive step within a predefined time, the timer event (⏱) catches this and initiates error handling. By attaching the events to the subprocess, we also define the scope for error monitoring (in the above example, it applies to the duration of the subprocess). We could embed three event subprocesses in the booking subprocess instead, and this would have the same effect. The execution would be the same as when we attached boundary events to the subprocess, because the events are interrupting events, and so are not processed parallel to the subprocess, but as an alternative.

Another option is to attach events to a single task, in which case only the current task is monitored.

The choice of error handling options enables you to employ different strategies for different types of errors. This is particularly important as regards the interaction between a process-driven application and the service contract implementation layer; technical errors are handled in the implementation layer and business errors are passed to the composite.

BPMN lets you differentiate not only between various types of error, but also within one error type, as shown in Fig. 4.8.

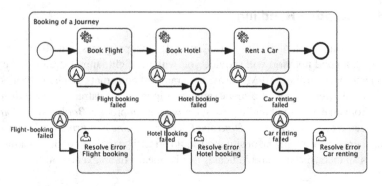

Fig. 4.8 Differentiating error states with an escalation event

This example models three different business errors, represented by three escalation events, each with a different annotation. This enables the errors to be assigned to
the appropriate error handling activity. For process-driven applications, these options
open up a range of implementation possibilities for processing exceptions.

4.1.3.1 Time Monitoring

Time monitoring has a special significance in exception handling; the timer event
lets you model a wide range of time-based dependencies, which can then be
executed using the appropriate runtime environments. I touched on this issue in
the chapter on the specification of process-driven applications, where I mentioned
that you can introduce a time element to the interfaces of the service contract, that
is, you can decide whether a service has to be executed within a certain time, and if
so, what will happen if this time limit is exceeded. The following examples
demonstrate the options that BPMN offers in this area.

The first example addresses a typical scenario in the service contract implementation layer: You want to monitor how long it takes for a response message to be
received. The process-driven application has sent a service request and is expecting
a response within a certain time. If the response does not arrive within this time, the
process is canceled and an error message is sent to the caller. Figure 4.9 shows the
BPMN model for this scenario.

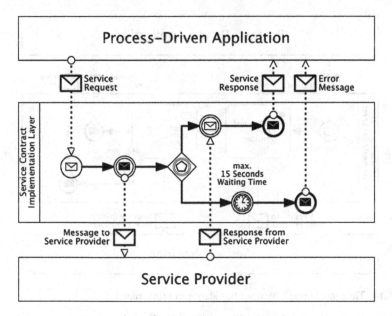

Fig. 4.9 Time monitoring of message receipt using an event-based gateway

The process-driven application sends a service request. The process is instantiated by the message start event and its first action is to send a message to the service provider (indicated by the throwing intermediate message event). The token instantiated by the process start reaches the event-based gateway, where it waits until one of the following events happens: the response message from the service provider arrives and the process follows the upper path, sending the result to the process-driven application, or the maximum waiting time of 15 s is reached and the process-driven application is informed of the situation by an error message. This model thus enables you to monitor a maximum response time of 15 s.

Using the event-based gateway to model time monitoring is a popular method for implementing this type of requirement, but it does have two disadvantages:

1. Only events can be monitored in this way, not activities (the sole exception being the receive task).
2. Whatever the event type, it is always interrupting.

You can solve the first problem by using boundary events. Figure 4.10 shows the same scenario as in Fig. 4.9, but modeled with activities and a timer boundary event.

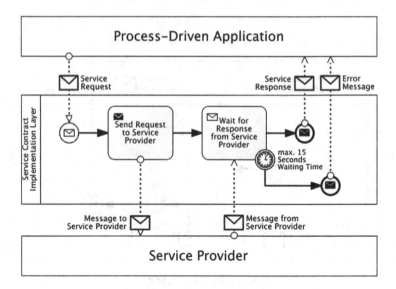

Fig. 4.10 Time monitoring with timer boundary event (interrupting)

Here, the receive task has an interrupting timer boundary event, showing that the task is being monitored. You can apply this method to any task, for example, a user task or a business rule task. This type of modeling also provides a solution to the second problem, as the interrupting timer event can be replaced by a non-interrupting event. For example, if you would like an administrator to be informed once the 15 s are up, so that the problem can be resolved while the process continues to wait for a response, you can model this as shown in Fig. 4.11.

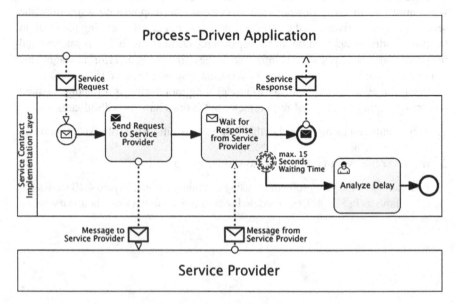

Fig. 4.11 Time monitoring with timer boundary event (non-interrupting)

It is clear from the figure that an administrator intervenes once the predefined time is up. And even though this sequence flow finishes at an end event, this does not mean that the process is finished. Because its path was triggered by a non-interrupting event, there is still a token at the receive task, and the process is therefore still active.

The combination of sequence flows with tasks and interrupting/non-interrupting boundary events gives modelers scope to cover all kinds of situations. Subprocesses are yet another option; these can be time-monitored as well. If the process is structured correctly, this scope can range from single tasks to sequences and even to entire processes. Figure 4.12 shows monitoring for a subprocess; this is the implementation of the requirement that a response must be received within 5 min. In this case, it is not sufficient to monitor a single step, as several activities have to be completed within this time.

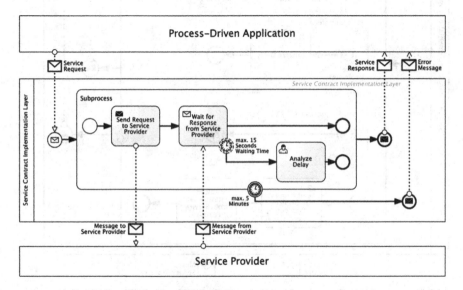

Fig. 4.12 Time monitoring of a subprocess

Here as well, we can see that the receive task is being monitored. In this case, the entire message handling is contained within a subprocess, to which an interrupting timer boundary event is attached. After 5 min, the event stops all communication and sends an error message to the process-driven application, informing it that the service call has failed.

The last variant for modeling time monitoring is to use event subprocesses, which we will illustrate using another example. Event subprocesses are activated during the runtime of a surrounding process or subprocess to handle events that may arise. They can be interrupting or non-interrupting. The BPMN model in Fig. 4.13 shows a cascaded time monitoring with a maximum of three possible timer events.

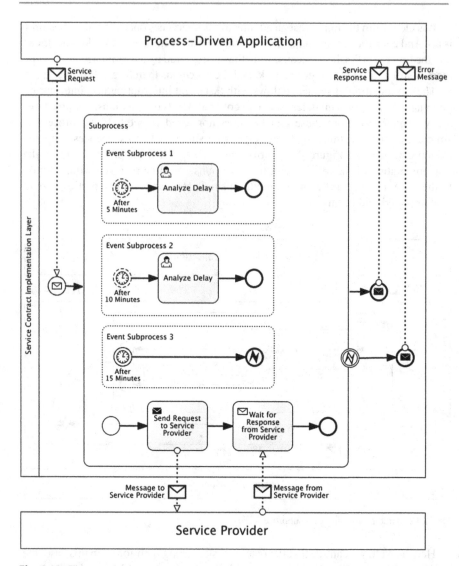

Fig. 4.13 Time monitoring using event subprocesses

The main subprocess handles message transfer to and from the service provider. If a message is not received within 5 min, the first non-interrupting timer start event is triggered, which starts *Event Subprocess 1* and informs an administrator of the problem. After another 5 min, *Event Subprocess 2* is started by another non-interrupting timer start event. If, after a total of 15 min, a message has still not arrived, *Event Subprocess 3* ends the communication with an interrupting start event. The error end event in *Event Subprocess 3* signalizes the error situation to the surrounding subprocess, which can react by sending an error message to the calling process-driven application.

These examples show how BPMN gives you the flexibility to handle a wide range of time-monitoring scenarios. We have also seen how these processes are relevant to our applications as regards the interaction with the service contract implementation layer.

4.1.4 Collaborations and Message Exchange

In the previous section we looked at process models with several pools: one pool representing the process-driven application, one the service contract implementation layer, and another the service provider. The message flows between the pools are represented by dashed arrows. In this way, we can illustrate the interaction between processes, and in BPMN, this is referred to as a *collaboration diagram*. A collaboration diagram is an excellent tool for modeling the interaction between the business and the technical process. BPMN provides different elements for the different types of communication between collaboration partners: You can model synchronous communication using service tasks, asynchronous communication using send and receive tasks, and publish/subscribe or broadcasting scenarios using signals, as shown in Figs. 4.14, 4.15, and 4.16, respectively.

Fig. 4.14 Synchronous communication using a service task

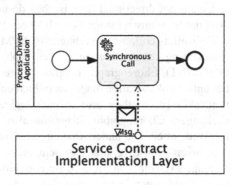

Fig. 4.15 Asynchronous communication using send and receive tasks

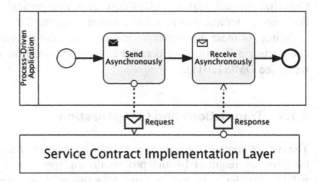

Fig. 4.16 Asynchronous
communication using signals

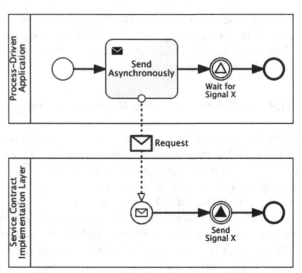

An important point here is that signals, unlike service tasks and send and receive tasks, are not directional (that is, they do not know their receivers), so the model does not have any message flows between throwing and catching signal events.

As well as collaboration diagrams, BPMN 2.0 has two other diagram types for representing communication: choreography and conversation diagrams (see also OMG 2011). Choreography diagrams represent the interaction between two pools, but unlike collaboration diagrams (which only show that some type of communication takes place) they also include logical relationships between the message exchanges. Choreography diagrams also show which messages are sent and received, when, and under what circumstances.

Conversation diagrams represent message exchanges in situations where the message exchanges are related by correlations. These are referred to as *logically related exchanges*. For example, there is a unique relationship between an order and the corresponding order confirmation in the form of the order number. Cancellations and delivery delays also relate to a particular order. These message flows can be represented in a conversation diagram.

Neither of these diagram types has any particular relevance for this book, so are not discussed in any more detail. For more information about the new diagram types, see OMG (2011).

4.1.5   Transactions and Compensation

The service contract implementation layer must ensure transactional integrity when the services required by the process-driven application are implemented, and BPMN provides a range of constructs for this purpose. The transaction subprocess in particular was designed for this very task; Fig. 4.17 shows how it works.

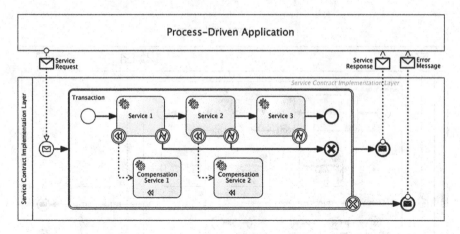

Fig. 4.17 Transaction subprocess

The process-driven application makes a service call to write data, which has to be updated in three systems. Unless all three write calls are successful, the transaction fails and any calls that have already been completed have to be rolled back by compensation. The three write calls are represented as synchronous service tasks within the transaction. Transaction subprocesses are displayed in BPMN with a double-lined boundary. You can see that all three calls have an interrupting error boundary event. If this event occurs, the flow within the transaction ends at the cancel end event (⊗). This end event activates the compensating sequence flows that are also attached to the service tasks. These are only executed, however, if the associated task was completed correctly. The compensations are called in reverse order, so if an error occurs in the last step (*Service 3*), first *Service 2* is rolled back, then *Service 1*. Once the compensations are complete, the interrupting cancel boundary event attached to the transaction is followed and an error message is sent to the process-driven application.

BPMN has five elements that interact in transactions:

1. Transaction or transaction subprocess: An activity containing the steps that are executed in a transaction.
2. Cancel end event: Reached within a transaction if an error occurs in one of the steps of the transaction; triggers the compensation.
3. Cancel boundary event: Bound to the transaction; defines the sequence flow to be followed immediately after compensation.
4. Compensation boundary event: Bound to tasks involved in a transaction; connected to the compensation task (see 5).
5. Compensation task: Displayed with a compensation marker (◀◀) and called during rollback processing. Its task is to compensate for business changes made during the normal process flow. Compensation boundary events and compensation tasks are connected by an association.

Rollback is not only possible during transaction processing; you can also roll back fully completed transactions, as shown in Fig. 4.18.

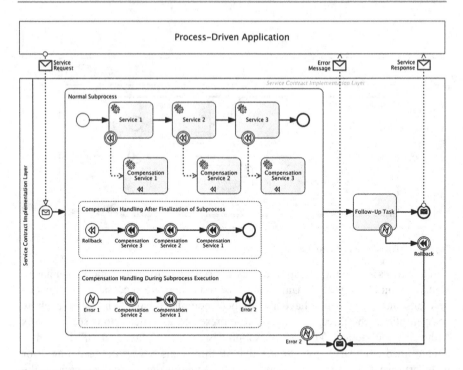

Fig. 4.18 Rollback of completed transactions

In this case the service tasks that make up the transaction are embedded in a normal subprocess. They are monitored by an event subprocess at execution time (shown in the figure as *Compensation Handling During Subprocess Execution* and triggered if an error occurs during execution of the subprocess). The compensation calls are modeled explicitly in this subprocess by throwing compensation intermediate events. To simplify matters, we assume that the called compensation tasks can determine for themselves whether compensation is necessary or not. If this were not the case, we would have to have an exclusive gateway before each compensation task to make sure that it is only called if the task was completed successfully. This would make the process model unnecessarily complicated. Once the event subprocess is complete, another error (*Error 2*) is triggered so that the surrounding main process can send an error message to the caller.

If there are no errors during the execution of the subprocess, we arrive at the *Follow-Up Task*. If this too is completed successfully, the main process can send the response message and is finished. If, however, an error occurs during its execution, the process follows the flow for the error boundary event, which leads to the throwing compensation event *Rollback*. This calls the compensation event subprocess *Compensation Handling After Finalization of Subprocess* (identified by the catching compensation start event) in the subprocess, effecting a rollback of all tasks that were completed in the subprocess. The subsequent throwing compensation intermediate events call the respective compensation tasks. Once all tasks have been rolled back, the main process can send an error message and is finished.

In this section we exclusively use BPMN to model transactions. Of course, it is not possible to solve every transaction problem with compensations, especially as this approach is fairly costly. Slama and Nelius take up this point in their book *Enterprise BPM* (Slama and Nelius 2011):

> In most projects, you will find that compensation mechanisms for resolving errors auto-
> matically are implemented rarely, if at all, due to the cost. (Slama and Nelius 2011, p. 234)

They go on to suggest more cost-effective alternatives such as analyzing logging entries (these can be standard system logs or project-specific business logs) as a bare-bones solution. Business logs have the advantage that they don't contain the multitudinous technical entries of system logs; they concentrate solely on business events. They can also have a dedicated recovery console for correcting transactional inconsistencies manually, which can certainly be useful in some cases, but you must weigh this up against the costs of developing such a console and consider whether the problems that it addresses occur so frequently as to justify this expenditure. Another option is to develop individual batch programs that process the data once and correct any issues. We'll leave this discussion there for now; other error handling strategies are discussed later in the book in Sect. 5.4 (Error Handling).

Once again, these examples demonstrate the diverse modeling possibilities that BPMN offers. These can be of particular benefit in the implementation of process-driven applications and their service contract implementation layers, and it is for this reason that I have chosen to use BPMN for both layers in our implementation. The procedure described in this book therefore differs somewhat from other approaches that use event-driven process chains (EPC) to model the business side and BPEL for the technical implementation.

4.2   Example Implementation of the Basic Architecture of a Process-Driven Application as Proof of Concept

In this chapter I present an example that demonstrates the actual implementation of a process-driven application, including the service contract implementation layer and an enterprise service bus. This implementation uses the latest version of the modeling and runtime environment SAP Process Orchestration (SAP PO), version 7.31. I must point out though that you are in no way bound to a specific software vendor for the implementation of the basic architecture of a process-driven application, nor are you required to use particular tools or servers. You can use any environment of your choice, be it Oracle, IBM, SAP, Microsoft, or Open Source, as the concepts I describe can be realized in any environment, even Assembler if you like (although this may be a little more difficult ☺).

I include a brief introduction to the development environment of SAP Process Orchestration before going on to explain the scenario that we will be implementing and the representation of the main implementation steps. We will then look at the runtime of the example, and finish with a summary of the main points learned from our implementation. This includes a detailed examination of the role of model-driven development. Loose coupling is a central pillar of the basic architecture, and we keep this as our focus while implementing the scenario using BPMN.

4.2.1　SAP Process Orchestration

SAP Process Orchestration (SAP PO) is a Java-based development and runtime environment for application development in distributed IT landscapes. It contains tools and runtime environments that were originally developed as separate solutions, but which have been aligned and brought together as SAP PO. The current version 7.31 of SAP PO contains the components displayed in Fig. 4.19:

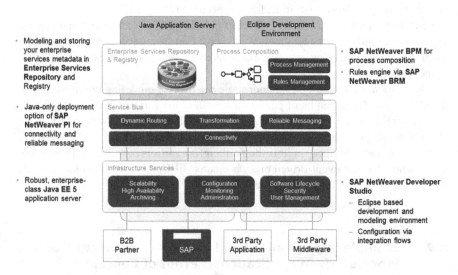

Fig. 4.19 Components of SAP Process Orchestration

The foundation of the stack is a Java EE 5-compatible certified application server. It supports common standards such as EJB 3.0, JSF 1.2, JSP 2.1, JMS 1.1, JPA, SDO 2.1, JMX 1.2, JAX-WS 2.0 etc. SAP PO also contains the development and modeling environment SAP NetWeaver Developer Studio (NWDS), which is based on the Eclipse framework and allows you to integrate Eclipse-compliant perspectives. SAP NetWeaver Developer Studio is closely related to SAP NetWeaver Development Infrastructure (NWDI), which is responsible for the software lifecycle management of the development components. Typical tasks are version management and transporting the components that belong to an application along the development landscape chain (development—integration—quality assurance—production).

SAP Process Orchestration combines three main products in one installation package

- SAP Business Process Management (SAP BPM)
- SAP Business Rules Management (SAP BRM)
- SAP Process Integration (SAP PI)

These three technologies have been combined with the objective of supporting companies throughout the whole process lifecycle and helping them to realize their specific requirements efficiently and effectively. It doesn't matter if the business processes use SAP or non-SAP systems, as the SAP PI component allows you to integrate any existing systems. SAP Process Orchestration covers the whole scope of application development: processes, rules, user interfaces, service development, and service management, with all frameworks running within a Java virtual machine, whereas you previously needed separate installations. Let's take a quick look at the properties of these three products that are especially relevant to the development of process-driven applications:

- SAP Process Integration constitutes the service-oriented foundation of SAP Process Orchestration, including an enterprise service bus (ESB) component for handling business-critical integration requirements. This allows SAP PO to act as an intermediary layer in heterogeneous system landscapes, whereby it can isolate the business processes from the involved backend systems, as described in this book. SAP PI, with its wide range of technological adapters, adapters for specific business applications, and industry-specific adapters, supports all common integration scenarios such as A2A (application-to-application) or B2B (business-to-business).
- SAP Business Process Management allows better alignment and collaboration within the SAP PO stack between the business side of a company and its IT department, by using a process-modelling environment based on the BPMN standard. The process engine of SAP BPM is used for user-centric and also for integration-centric processes as part of SAP PI. The result is a much better overview of the process landscape that you are operating in, including an evaluation of the most important process key figures.
- SAP Business Rules Management completes the picture; it allows you to add and adapt business rules for your processes to keep them in line with company strategy. One of its main advantages is the central management and maintenance of all business-critical rules by the business experts. These rules are subject to frequent change and if they can be maintained by the business departments themselves this gives you increased flexibility, helping you to realize business strategies more quickly, which in turn enables you to defend and strengthen your competitive advantage. Also, responsibilities are assigned to the appropriate people, and SAP BRM covers both Rete-based and sequential rule sets. This combination of processes and rules allows you to design very flexible yet stable architectures, which is of course a great benefit for process-driven applications. This is covered in a separate chapter (Sect. 5.7—More Flexibility by Combining Rules with Analytical Applications).

The SAP Process Orchestration package is a huge help to developers of process-driven applications. The tools were developed with the aim of lightening the load on application developers and to improve their productivity. As a result, all the tools apply model-driven approaches, which can be supplemented with Java code wherever modeling is no longer useful or possible. This combination enables you to increase both productivity and flexibility.

SAP Process Orchestration is geared towards providing support in the development of process-driven applications, and would appear predestined for implementing the composite basic architecture. I will now describe the scenario that we are going to implement and sketch out the main development steps in SAP PO.

4.2.2   Implementation Scenario: Simplified Order Process

We will take the example process from Sect. 3.3.5.3 and use it to demonstrate how to implement an order process. Figure 4.20 shows the process flow, simplified for the implementation.

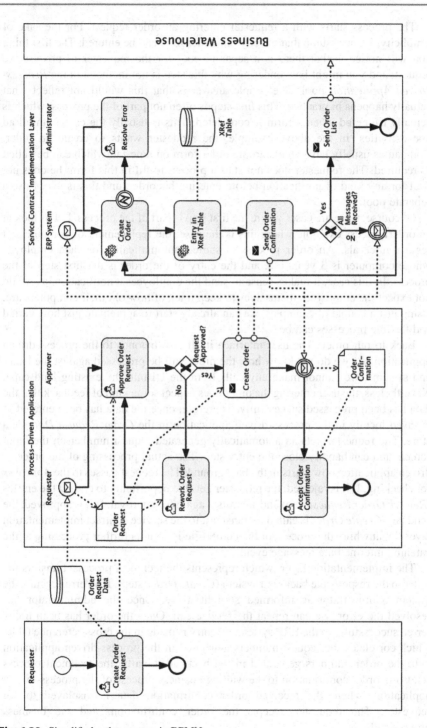

Fig. 4.20 Simplified order process in BPMN

The process starts with a requester entering an order request. For the sake of simplicity, let us assume that exactly one order item can be entered. The first thing you will notice is that there is a separate pool for the requester to process the request, and you might be wondering why this step is not included in the *Process-Driven Application* pool. The simple answer is that this would not reflect what actually happens in practice. This first step is often not part of the process, which is actually triggered when a form is completed. This is usually the case with all ad hoc activities. In the above example, the requester wants to create an order. Companies usually have an electronic order form on a portal, which can be called as required. The requester does not start a process to fill in this form; he does not wait for any kind of notification before entering his order, and this is why I use a separate pool.

Of course, there are cases where the first step is part of the process. Let us look at an order process example where this is the case: the replacement of computers at regular intervals. An order process is started automatically for each employee whose computer is 3 years old, and the entry of the order is the first step of the process. In this case, it makes sense to send the employees a notification, as we do not expect the employees themselves to keep track of how old their computers are. Using just a couple of examples, we can already start to appreciate just how varied and flexible processes can be.

Back to our order: The user interface itself also belongs to the process-driven application. As we do not know how the order will be processed against the back-end systems, we cannot make any calls from the UI into the existing landscape. Nevertheless, the user entering the order does expect some kind of feedback that the data has been processed successfully. Therefore, once the data has been entered, it is saved locally in the process-driven application in the *Order Request Data* data store. The requester gets an automatically generated request number on the input screen, and can happily close the entry step. The actual processing of the process-driven application now starts in the background. The request passes to the *Approver* for checking. If it is rejected, the requester gets the opportunity to correct the entries (*Rework Order Request* step) and submits it again for approval. If it is approved, the send task *Create Order* is called to transfer it to the service contract implementation layer. Meanwhile, the process of the composite interrupts further processing at the catching intermediate message event.

The implementation layer, which represents the technical process, transfers the order to the responsible back-end system (*Create Order* step). If an error occurs, the system administrator is informed straight away. Once the administrator has resolved the error, we can repeat the service call. Once the order has been transferred successfully to the ERP system, an entry is made in the cross-reference table, which correlates the request numbers generated in the process-driven application with the order numbers generated in the backend. Finally, the technical process sends the order confirmation to the waiting business process of the process-driven application, where the received order confirmation data is displayed to the requester. The requester accepts the order confirmation, and the business process ends.

If we look at our technical process, we can see that once the order confirmation has been sent (*Send Order Confirmation* step) the process flow reaches an exclusive gateway labelled *All Messages Received?*. Why is this extra query necessary? You will remember that the process-driven application never knows how orders will be processed. In our example we not only want to update the data in a backend; we also want to feed the data into a Business Warehouse. We might want to use the data for statistical purposes, for example, to find out how well-received this employee self-service for order entry is. The Business Warehouse requires that the transferred data is aggregated and bundled by product. The gateway determines whether the completion condition for collecting the messages is met. This completion condition can vary, depending on the scenario. It might require a particular number of messages to be received, a defined period of time to elapse (for example, 6 h), or a certain time to be reached (for example, 18:00). For our scenario we have specified that three messages must arrive. The exclusive gateway is followed by an intermediate message event, where the process waits for further messages to arrive. If the process receives a message and a correlation condition has ensured that the order is for the same product, it again follows the sequence *Create Order—Entry in XRef Table* and then *Send Order Confirmation*. Once all messages have been received, the process sends them in a bundle to the Business Warehouse (*Send Order List* step).

If you look at the message flows from the *Create Order* activity of the business process, you will see that they lead to the message-based start *and* intermediate events. This shows that one and the same interface is used for both event types. The process engine then has to decide whether to instantiate a new process each time a new message arrives, or whether the message can be assigned to an instance that is already running. This is determined by the correlation condition associated with the intermediate message event, which we will look at in more detail later.

4.2.3 Basic Development Steps

To give you an idea of what you need to do to execute a scenario like this, I will briefly discuss the main development steps when using SAP Process Orchestration.

4.2.3.1 Business Process and Technical Process

In line with the recommended top-down approach, the business process is at the start of the implementation, as shown in Fig. 4.20. SAP BPM, a component of SAP PO, provides an Eclipse plugin called *Process Composer* for BPMN modeling. This allows you to model the process graphically, resulting in the model shown in Fig. 4.21.

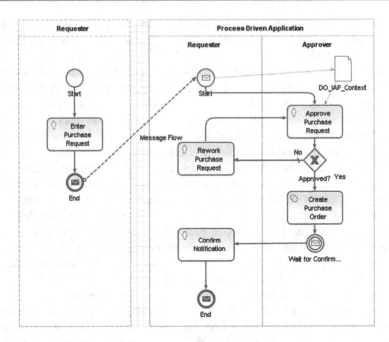

Fig. 4.21 Simplified order process modeled in Process Composer

If we compare this to Fig. 4.20 we can spot several differences. The current version of SAP BPM does not support the use of send tasks to explicitly represent asynchronous actions. SAP BPM does allow you to call services asynchronously, but synchronous and asynchronous calls are both represented by the service task (which still complies with the BPMN specification). Therefore, I have used the service task for the *Create Purchase Order* call.

The data handling also differs slightly from our original plan, because of how data objects are implemented in SAP BPM. The data objects in the process model represent the process context, that is, the data that is available to the individual process steps only during execution, after which it is no longer accessible. Simply providing a data object in the model is sufficient to be able to model the data flow in its entirety later on. The associations from the start event to the data object and from the data object to the *Approve Purchase Request* task do not have any semantic functions; they are purely for documentation purposes. The same applies to the message flow between the two pools. In Fig. 4.21, only the *Process-Driven Application* pool is executable, since in SAP BPM only one process of a process model can be executed. The other pools help to illustrate relationships and do not have any influence at runtime. They are displayed with a dashed pool border in the process model.

The implementation of the service contract implementation layer for our example is shown in Fig. 4.22:

Fig. 4.22 Service contract implementation layer implemented in Process Composer

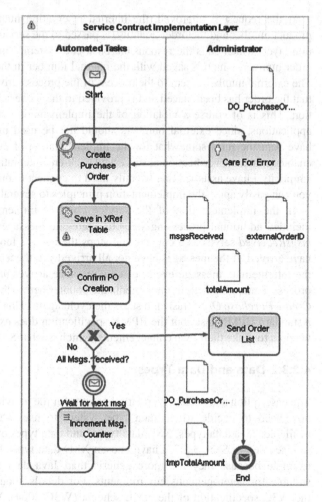

The only difference to Fig. 4.20 is the *Increment Msg. Counter* step after the message-based intermediate event; this simply increases the message counter.

The next step of our implementation is to define the data model that the whole scenario will operate with. According to our process model, the process flow starts with the creation of an order request. We don't want to make our example too complicated, so we will do without a product search. So, instead of selecting the required product from a hitlist, the requester enters the data about the product on a simple screen. This includes the product ID, the order quantity, the price, and any comments to explain to the approver why the order is necessary. Once the screen is confirmed, the data is first saved locally, in line with the implementation guidelines for process-driven applications, and an internal reservation number is generated.

The order data is then transferred to the approver for processing. The approver sees the input data and the total price as well, to help with the decision. The approver approves or rejects the request by selecting a checkbox, and can also add a comment to explain the decision.

If the request is approved, the internal reservation number, together with the product number and the order quantity, is passed to the service contract implementation layer, which calls the responsible back-end system. This produces an external order number, which is saved with the internal number in the cross-reference table. The external number is sent to the process of the process-driven application as proof that the order has been placed and is provided to the requester in the order confirmation. This is of course a violation of the implementation rules for process-driven applications, since external numbers should not be used in the application, but I have bent the rules somewhat for the implementation of our example scenario to enable immediate verification of successful back-end integration. Also, for the sake of simplicity I have assumed that we only need to connect to one back-end system, but you can easily apply the implementation principles to several systems.

In the implementation of the service contract implementation layer I have included additional processing steps to aggregate messages. An internal variable *msgsReceived* serves as a counter and stops the receive loop once three messages have arrived. If the messages have not all arrived yet, the technical process waits at the intermediate message event. Once a message arrives and releases the waiting process, a mapping activity increments the counter before the process returns to the *Create Purchase Order* task and starts the cycle again. This mapping activity is not a standard BPMN task, but the BPMN specification does expressly allow software vendors to make their own enhancements, which is what SAP has done in this case.

4.2.3.2 Data and Data Types

The description above has several implications for the individual data fields, and we now need to decide which data type system to use. There are many options available: Java data types, XSD data types, and data types of recognized standards, as discussed in Sect. 3.2.7. I have chosen XSD data types for our implementation example because they are more generic than Java data types and hence more suitable for heterogeneous environments. For details about XSD data types, see the W3C specification of the XML schema (W3C 2004). We can summarize the required fields including data types in XSD as follows:

```
<?xml version="1.0" encoding="UTF-8" standalone="no"?>
<schema
xmlns=http://www.w3.org/2001/XMLSchema
xmlns:tns= http://www.example.org/approvalprocess
                    elementFormDefault="qualified"
targetNamespace="http://www.example.org/approvalprocess">
<elementname="InvestmentApprovalProcess"
                type="tns:InvestmentApprovalProcess"/>
<complexType name="InvestmentApprovalProcess">
    <sequence>
    <element name="region" type="string"/>
    <element name="productID" type="string"/>
    <element name="quantity" type="decimal"/>
```

```
      <element name="price" type="decimal"/>
      <element name="totalAmount" type="decimal"/>
      <element name="comment" type="string"/>
      <element name="internalReservationID" type="string"/>
      <element name="externalOrderID" type="string"/>
      <element name="approved" type="boolean"/>
      </sequence>
    </complexType>
  </schema>
```

You will notice that the schema definition contains the element *region* as well as the other data already mentioned. This field contains the region that the order request comes from, and is used later on in a process extension, where the decision on whether to approve the order is made using rules based on the total sum and the region.

The data types used are self-explanatory, but what is worth mentioning is the choice of the `string` type for the identifiers *productID*, *externalOrderID*, and *internalReservationID*. For internal numbers, the developer can decide which data type a field should have, but this is not the case for external numbers. Binary representations can lead to difficulties in the communication between scenario participants (consider, for example, the manual search for messages). A representation that is easy to read and understand is far preferable, and this is assured if you use `string`. For the same reasons, `string` is also used for internal numbers.

4.2.3.3 Services

We need to look at the business requirements of the process-driven application in order to define the services and their interfaces:

- Between the start screen for the requester and the process-driven application
- Between the process-driven application and the respective service contract implementation layer (bidirectional)
- Between the service contract implementation layer and the Business Warehouse

We can identify four interfaces in total:

1. For asynchronous instantiation of the process-driven application from the request form of the requester, we need all the data that has been entered. Although we have persisted the data in a database, we transfer the data directly via the interface to the process for the purposes of this example to spare ourselves a database call.

```
<xsd:schema
 targetNamespace="http://www.example.org/
  start_IAP_Book_IF/">
  <xsd:element name="startProcess">
    <xsd:complexType>
      <xsd:sequence>
        <xsd:element name="region" type="xsd:string"/>
          <xsd:element name="productID"
                       type="xsd:string"/>
          <xsd:element name="quantity"
```

```
                                type="xsd:decimal"/>
              <xsd:element name="price" type="xsd:
              decimal"/>
              <xsd:element name="comment" type="xsd:
              string"/>
              <xsd:element name="internalReservationID"
                          type="xsd:string"/>
          </xsd:sequence>
        </xsd:complexType>
      </xsd:element>
    </xsd:schema>
```

2. For asynchronous instantiation of the technical process for updating the order data, the ordered product, the order quantity, the price, and the internal reservation number are transferred. The XSD representation looks like this:

```
    <xsd:schema xmlns=http://demo.vst.com
              xmlns:xsd=http://www.w3.org/2001/XMLSchema
              targetNamespace="http://demo.vst.com">
      <xsd:element name="PurchaseOrderMsg_MT"
        type="PurchaseOrderMsg_DT"/>
      <xsd:complexType name="PurchaseOrderMsg_DT">
          <xsd:sequence>
              <xsd:element name="purchaseOrder"
                          type="PurchaseOrder_DT"/>
              <xsd:element name="internalReservationID"
                          type="xsd:string"/>
          </xsd:sequence>
      </xsd:complexType>
      <xsd:complexType name="PurchaseOrder_DT">
          <xsd:sequence>
              <xsd:element name="productID"
                          type="xsd:string"/>
              <xsd:element name="quantity"
                          type="xsd:decimal"/>
              <xsd:element name="price"
                          type="xsd:decimal"/>
          </xsd:sequence>
      </xsd:complexType>
    </xsd:schema>
```

You can see that the actual order data is encapsulated in its own complex data type called PurchaseOrder_DT. The whole message is represented by the type PurchaseOrderMsg_DT, which also contains the field internalReservationID.

3. To confirm that the order data has been updated successfully, we need an asynchronous interface containing just the internal reservation number and the external order number created in the backend. The internal reservation number is

required for correlation with the process that initiated the write process. This
interface is represented in XSD as follows:

```
<xsd:schema xmlns=http://demo.vst.com
            xmlns:xsd=http://www.w3.org/2001/XMLSchema
            targetNamespace="http://demo.vst.com">
    <xsd:element name="PurchaseOrderConfirm_MT"
                 type="PurchaseOrderConfirm_DT"/>
    <xsd:complexType name="PurchaseOrderConfirm_DT">
        <xsd:sequence>
            <xsd:element name="internalReservationID"
                         type="xsd:string"/>
            <xsd:element name="externalOrderID"
                         type="xsd:string"/>
        </xsd:sequence>
    </xsd:complexType>
</xsd:schema>
```

4. This concludes the external representation of the process-driven application, but
   we still need the description of the interface to the Business Warehouse, where
   the collected orders will be processed. The XSD representation looks like this:

```
<xsd:schema xmlns=http://demo.vst.com
            xmlns:xsd=http://www.w3.org/2001/XMLSchema
            targetNamespace="http://demo.vst.com">
    <xsd:element name="PurchaseOrderListMsg_MT"
                 type="PurchaseOrderListMsg_DT"/>
    <xsd:complexType name="PurchaseOrderListMsg_DT">
        <xsd:sequence>
            <xsd:element name="poLineItems"
                         type="PurchaseOrderList_DT"/>
            <xsd:element name="totalAmount"
                         type="xsd:decimal"/>
        </xsd:sequence>
    </xsd:complexType>
    <xsd:complexType name="PurchaseOrderList_DT">
        <xsd:sequence>
            <xsd:element maxOccurs="unbounded"
                         name="poLineItem"
                         type="PurchaseOrder_DT"/>
        </xsd:sequence>
    </xsd:complexType>
    <xsd:complexType name="PurchaseOrder_DT">
        <xsd:sequence>
            <xsd:element    name="productID"    type="xsd:string"/>
            <xsd:element name="quantity" type="xsd:decimal"/>
            <xsd:element name="price" type="xsd:decimal"/>
        </xsd:sequence>
```

```
      </xsd:complexType>
    </xsd:schema>
```

First, let us look at the complex type PurchaseOrderListMsg_DT. This tells us that the interface consists of two parts: the collected items of type PurchaseOrderList_DT and a field called totalAmount, which provides the total value of the collected items. The type PurchaseOrderList_DT comprises a list (maxOccurs="unbounded") of individual items of type PurchaseOrder_DT, which consists of the elementary fields of an item, namely the product ID (productID), order quantity (quantity), and price (price).

An important point to note here is that only interfaces 2 and 3 are part of the external representation of the process-driven application. Interface 2 represents the services that the process-driven application expects to be implemented externally, and interface 3 represents the services that it provides itself and expects to be called externally. Accordingly, only interfaces 2 and 3 belong to the service contract. Interface 1 is a purely internal interface of the process-driven application and is the result of my placing the order request step outside the process. The input form itself still belongs to the composite, as mentioned earlier. Interface 4 is part of the implementation of interface 2, and is specific to this scenario and the current system landscape. It is not generally applicable and is therefore not relevant to the external representation of the process-driven application.

If interfaces 2 and 3 are also put in a repository, as I recommended earlier, it is easy for the developer to find out which business functions the process-driven application needs in order to function correctly. Also, new generation tools are available that enable you to generate proxies from the XSD interface definitions; these are empty code fragments that the developer simply has to fill with the necessary business logic.

The interfaces themselves can be created easily with standard XSD editors. SAP Process Orchestration uses the XSD editor that is part of the Eclipse WTP project (Web Tools Platform).

4.2.3.4 Persistence

One of the main ideas in the implementation of loose coupling between the process-driven application and the service contract implementation layer is the local caching of request data as part of the composite, so that the end user gets an immediate confirmation in his user interface that the request data has been saved successfully. This requires local persistency. In the Java world, the Java Persistence API (JPA) is the tried-and-tested solution. SAP Process Orchestration also provides developers with a JPA-based solution that enables them to model objects graphically. These object models can then be used to generate database tables automatically, as well as classic CRUD lifecycle methods (Create, Read, Update, Delete) and search methods; these are exposed as Web services and can be integrated as such in user interfaces and processes. The model for the internal reservation is shown in Fig. 4.23.

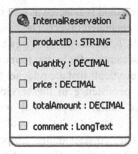

Fig. 4.23 Data model of a reservation

It consists of the selected product (`productID`), the order quantity (`quantity`), the price (`price`), and the total order amount (`totalAmount`), as well as a comment from the requester (`comment`). Figure 4.24 shows the automatically generated methods:

Existing Operations

Contains List with all available operations in this object.

Operation Name	Description	Visibility	Return Type
create	create	public	Output:InternalReservation
read	read	public	Output:InternalReservation
update	update	public	void
delete	key	public	void
findByMultipleParameters	findByMultipleParameters	public	Output:InternalReservation
findAll	findAll	public	Output:InternalReservation

Operation Parameters

Contains tree with all input and output parameters and faults for selected operation.

```
□ create
  □ Input Parameters
       productID:STRING
       quantity:DECIMAL
       price:DECIMAL
       totalAmount:DECIMAL
       comment:LongText
  □ Output Parameters
     □ Output:InternalReservation
          key:Id
          createdBy:UserId
          createdAt:DATETIME
          modifiedAt:DATETIME
          modifiedBy:UserId
          productID:STRING
          quantity:DECIMAL
          price:DECIMAL
          totalAmount:DECIMAL
          comment:LongText
  □ Faults
       CAFCreateException
```

Fig. 4.24 Automatically generated methods of the reservation

In the figure, the `create` method is selected as an example. You can see that the method call returns the whole generated object. The unique primary key (`key` field) and the administration fields (`createdBy`, `createdAt`, `modifiedBy`, and `modifiedAt`) are generated automatically by the framework, leaving the developer to concentrate on modeling those fields that are relevant from a business perspective.

We also access the local persistence in the service contract implementation layer. In the cross-reference table, the internal reservation numbers of the process-driven application are related to the externally generated order numbers of the back-end system. The corresponding object model with the fields `internalReservationID` and `orderID` is shown in Fig. 4.25.

Fig. 4.25 Data model of the cross-reference table

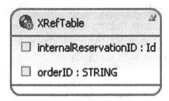

Unlike the `InternalReservation` object, this time the `create` method of the `XRefTable` is called directly from the process model. Only the technical implementation using Web services is the same.

4.2.3.5 User Interfaces

As we can see from the process models that we have created for the example, a total of five user interfaces are required to implement the scenario. The *Enter Purchase Request* and *Approve Purchase Request* (see Fig. 4.21) UIs are most interesting for us as they implement the interaction between the requester and the approver. The other three interfaces *Rework Purchase Request*, *Care For Error*, and *Confirm Notification* complete the process model but do not provide any new insights.

Generating user interfaces is surely one of the most complex and time-consuming tasks in application development. If you are developing process-driven applications, this is exacerbated even further by the fact that the interfaces have to collaborate with the process framework. For instance, the UI for approving the order request not only has to signal that the entry is complete in the form of an event; it also has to ensure that the data is passed to the process context. Process Composer from SAP BPM supports developers in this task by enabling them to generate UIs from the data of the process context. The tool uses the data definitions in the process context to automatically generate screens with input fields and tables. Of course, the developer has to check these automatically generated forms and may have to rework them, but this is a significant improvement as far as productivity is concerned.

As we want to implement a loosely coupled scenario, the call to save the data locally is particularly important for the *Enter Purchase Request* process step as it ensures that the user gets some form of immediate visual feedback that the data has been saved. SAP Process Orchestration has two technologies for modeling user interfaces: SAP NetWeaver Visual Composer and Web Dynpro. SAP NetWeaver Visual Composer

(SAP NetWeaver VC) is intended for less complex user interfaces. It enables you, with just a few clicks, to integrate services and it then interprets the input and output parameters to generate forms and tables automatically. All the developer has to do is make any cosmetic adjustments to the appearance of the generated user interfaces that he deems necessary, and add verification scripts and logic to control the screen flow. A graphical editor is provided for this purpose. SAP NetWeaver VC is also used for the graphical display of analytical evaluations. If you are dealing with diagrams and charts that are visually quite demanding, using Microsoft Silverlight on which SAP NetWeaver VC is based will give you much more versatility when designing your user interface. You cannot, however, program in Visual Composer, which means that developers have to make do with the standard functionality shipped with the product. If you have more demanding interfaces, I would therefore recommend Web Dynpro. This is a UI framework from SAP developed on a Java servlet basis; it has a comprehensive component library containing UI components such as calendars, navigation trees, and tables with integrated filter, sort, and personalization functions. It also provides services for business environments, such as input helps, internationalization, scrolling in mass data, and accessibility features. Developers are not bound to SAP proprietary solutions when designing their interfaces. As the foundation of SAP Process Orchestration is a standard-compliant JavaEE server, the UIs can also be programmed as servlets, JSP, or JSF interfaces. Recently SAP has added the UI Development Toolkit for HTML5 to the UI mix which allows you to develop highly sophisticated, modern UIs utilizing the latest HTML5 enhancements (see SAP 2014 for more details). Irrespective of the used technology, the SAP BPM API is used for the interaction with the process framework: to notify the process engine that a process step is complete, for example, or to transfer the entered form data.

Since we are using a simple example, SAP Visual Composer is quite sufficient for our requirements. Figure 4.26 shows the data flow for the *Enter Purchase Request* step in SAP Visual Composer.

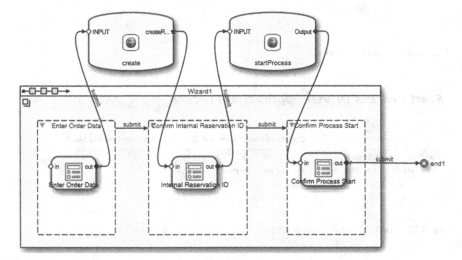

Fig. 4.26 User interface development with SAP Visual Composer

The model shows a wizard UI consisting of three forms: *Enter Order Data* (see Fig. 4.27), *Confirm Internal Reservation ID* (see Fig. 4.28), and *Confirm Process Start* (see Fig. 4.29).

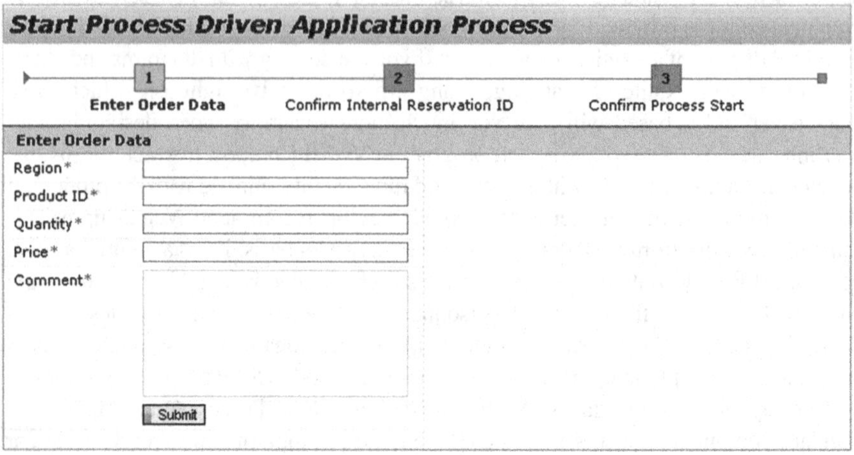

Fig. 4.27 Order form

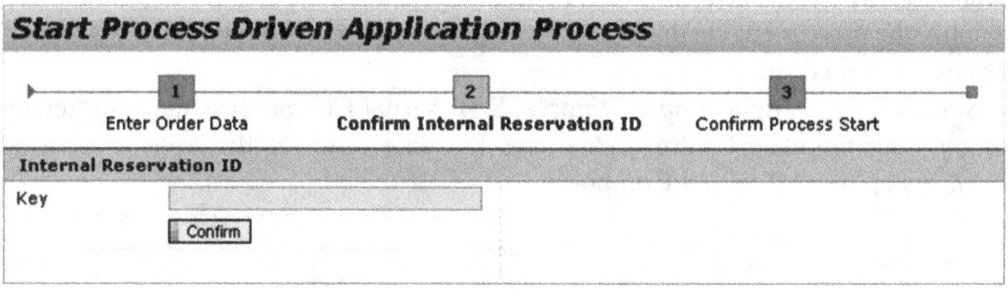

Fig. 4.28 Order confirmation

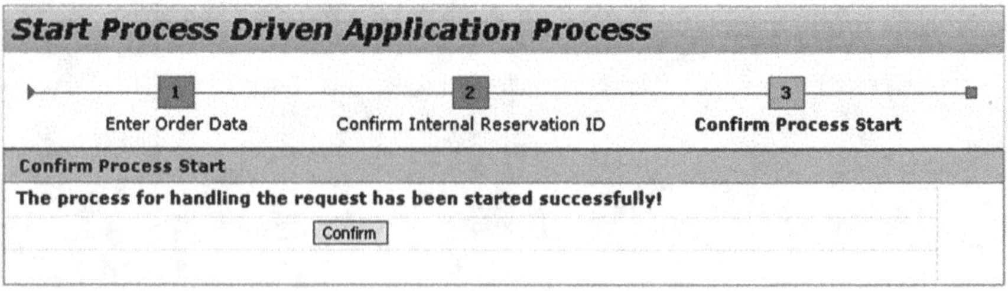

Fig. 4.29 Confirmation of process start

The user enters the order data in the *Enter Order Data* form. Once he has finished making his entries, he chooses *Submit* and the data is transferred by Web service to the `create` method of the `InternalReservation` object (which persists the data locally). A reservation number is generated, which is displayed to the user in the second step of the wizard UI. The user chooses *Confirm* to close the screen and the data is transferred to the start event of the process by an asynchronous Web service call. The *Confirm Process Start* screen of the wizard tells the user that the process has been started successfully (Fig. 4.29). Once the process starts, the entered data is transferred simultaneously to the process context.

I have used Web Dynpro technology to implement the user interface for approving the order. In contrast to the order form, it is not necessary to make any service calls from the approval UI; it simply displays the values entered by the requester. The approver can approve the request by selecting the *Approved* checkbox, or reject it by leaving the checkbox empty (Fig. 4.30).

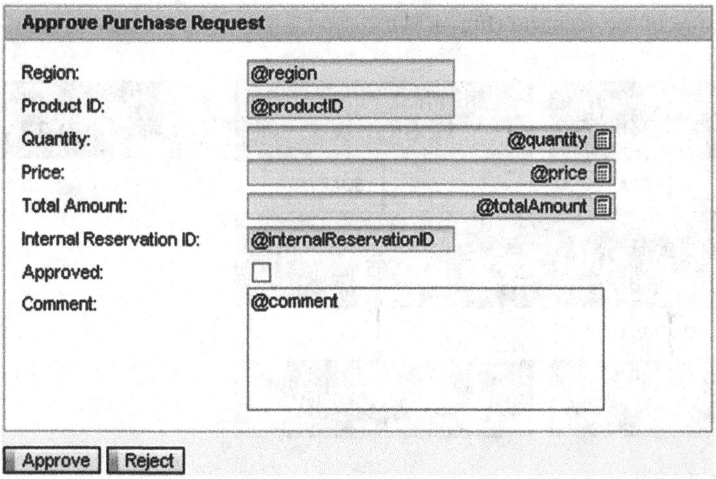

Approve Purchase Request

Region:	@region
Product ID:	@productID
Quantity:	@quantity
Price:	@price
Total Amount:	@totalAmount
Internal Reservation ID:	@internalReservationID
Approved:	☐
Comment:	@comment

[Approve] [Reject]

Fig. 4.30 User interface for approving the request

This interface was generated automatically from the process context. It takes care of the data transfer and the interaction with the process framework SAP BPM. The state of the *Approved* checkbox determines the behavior at the subsequent gateway, and the Comment field is used for communication between the process participants.

We have to deal with the issue of how to determine who will execute the individual tasks. Specifying particular users at development time would make the solution too inflexible, so SAP BPM uses a role concept instead. You can assign a process role to each lane in the pool, and then link this process role to existing groups or roles in the company's user management solution (for example, an LDAP directory, an SAP user management solution, or a JDBC database). The activities within this lane will then be executed by those users that belong to the assigned groups or roles in the user management system. Therefore, it is not until runtime that the process engine determines which user or users can actually perform the task. Even in the event of organizational changes, tasks will still go to the correct users because the users are automatically taken from the updated user management system.

4.2.3.6 Supplementary Implementation Details

So far, I have taken you through the main development steps for implementing the individual components of the process-driven application. You can assign the user interfaces to the user tasks, and the generated Web services to the service tasks of the process model. Next, I would like to explain the connection between the pools, which we have not yet looked at in detail. We use an enterprise service bus (ESB) to handle the communication between the *Process-Driven Application* and the *Service Contract Implementation Layer* pools, and between the *Service Contract Implementation Layer* and the *Business Warehouse* pools. Let's take a look at the logical architecture of the scenario (Fig. 4.31):

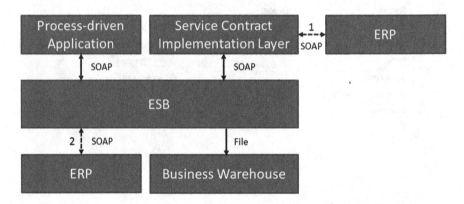

Fig. 4.31 Logical architecture

You can see in the figure that the two process pools are connected to the ESB by SOAP connections, and the Business Warehouse is connected to the ESB by a file interface. You do not have to structure the architecture like this, this is simply my choice. Of course, the *Process-Driven Application* and *Service Contract Implementation Layer* pools could communicate directly with one another, but our chosen arrangement gives us more flexibility if messages from any of the pools have to be sent to other participants as well. However, this is a matter of personal preference.

You will have noticed that there are two ERP systems in the figure; these illustrate two different implementation variants for connecting the ERP system. Since the service contract implementation layer is already a technical implementation of the business requirement from the process-driven application, it is not necessary to use the ESB again to connect to the ERP system. Therefore, I have chosen to use variant 1 for the implementation of our example scenario. Variant 2, where the ESB is used to communicate with the ERP backend, is more streamlined (all communication goes through the ESB, supporting central management of the communication within a company) and can also be recommended.

In SAP Process Orchestration, message handling in the ESB is modeled using the *Process Integration Designer*, a new perspective within the SAP NetWeaver Developer Studio that has been developed specifically for this purpose. You can use it to define how messages will be processed in the ESB, for example, how the message will be routed, which interfaces will be used in the target systems, and which mappings will take care of the transformations between the interfaces. In our scenario, I have chosen interfaces that need no mapping, so the implementation of the resulting integration flow is relatively simple. Figure 4.32 shows an example of the integration flow from the service contract implementation layer to the Business Warehouse system:

Fig. 4.32 Integration flow
from the service contract
implementation layer to the
data warehouse

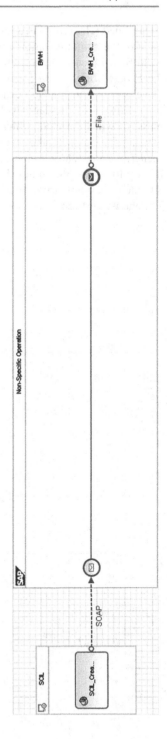

SAP uses BPMN notation for the integration flows as well. This makes them easily recognizable across the various participating roles and reduces communication difficulties. The viewer can see at a glance who is communicating with who and which processing steps a message passes through on its way through the integration server. The model contains the following details:

- Sender system
- Sender interface
- Receiver system(s)
- Receiver interface(s)
- Communication channels for technical connection of systems
- Message processing steps

On the left hand side you can see the sender system *SCIL* (SCIL stands for service contract implementation layer); on the right hand side you can see the receiver system *BWH* (BWH stands for Business Warehouse). Both have their own separate pool. In between the sender and the receiver there is a third pool that visualizes the processing steps within the SAP Process Orchestration integration server. In our simple example, no processing steps are required because the messages are transferred unchanged. Therefore, the start event is connected directly to the end event by a sequence flow. You can see that the sender and receiver pools both contain an activity with a new icon in the top left corner that is not defined in the BPMN specification (⬤). This is the icon for an interface. The model shows that this system uses the specified interface to send messages; therefore, a message flow connects the activity to the start event in the middle pool. Likewise, on the receiver side, an activity with an interface icon is connected to the end event of the message processing process, signifying that the system receives a message of the type that we assigned to the activity in the receiver pool. The message flows between the pools are labelled with *SOAP* and *File*, which indicate the technical connections that are used between the systems. They represent the communication channel, which defines how systems are connected to the ESB. The *SCIL* system sends its message by SOAP adapter, whereas the receiver system receives the message in the file system. Other configuration details can be added, depending on the communication channel; for example, you could specify the target file for the file adapter or the transport or message protocol for the SOAP adapter.

Since the above model describes the message transport from the service contract implementation layer to the Business Warehouse system, it has to be linked to the *Send Order List* step of our process model for the implementation layer in Fig. 4.22. The SOAP adapter provides a WSDL description of the interface, which we can use for the implementation of the *Send Order List* step.

We know now that the pools are connected by an integration flow, from which we can conclude that two other integration flows are required to realize the complete scenario, because an integration flow is required for each direction of communication between the *Process-Driven Application* and the *Service Contract Implementation Layer* pool. This is a simple matter though, because we can use the SOAP adapter. Since the whole scenario runs on one server (SAP Process Orchestration combines the BPM engine and the Integration Engine in one JVM (Java Virtual Machine)), communication is quick and efficient and does not require the HTTP protocol.

We have established that we need two more integration flows to complete our scenario: The first connects the *Create Purchase Order* step of the *Process-Driven Application* pool with the message-based events in the SCIL pool; the second connects the *Confirm PO Creation* step with the message-based intermediate event *Wait for Confirmation* in the opposite direction.

Message handling is rarely as simple as in our examples, but the Process Integration Designer is well able to deal with more complicated integration scenarios, and can take on responsibility for stateless integration processes. Figure 4.33 shows a more complex example:

Fig. 4.33 Complex integration flow

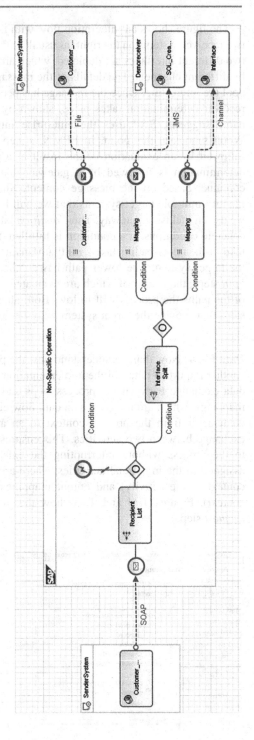

The figure shows an integration flow with the sender system on the left and the two receiver systems on the right, as usual. In the lower of the two receiver systems, two different interfaces are depicted, which are connected to the integration server by different channels. The details of the message processing process in the middle pool are interesting: Once the message has been received via the SOAP channel, a receiver determination takes place, shown by the *Recipient List* activity. As the name suggests, SAP uses the enterprise integration pattern from Hohpe and Woolf's book at this point. In BPMN, a step that prepares a decision is usually followed by an evaluation of the result at a gateway; accordingly, the receiver determination is followed by a gateway that determines how the process will continue, based on the message content. Since the receiver determination can identify multiple target systems that we will have to send messages to in parallel, we use an inclusive gateway. The *Condition* labels on the sequence flows represent concrete conditions: if a condition is fulfilled, this is the path that the process will take. If the upper path is taken, all that remains to do is map to the target format of the target system. The lower path has another interface determination (*Interface Split* step), the results of which are evaluated using conditions to determine which of the paths the process will follow. Both alternatives are concluded by mapping steps that provide the target system with the correct interfaces.

Data Flow Now that we understand how the pools are linked, let us take a look at another important detail of the implementation: the data flow within a process. The data exchange between the process steps and the process context is realized by mappings, which are modeled as a data flow either from an activity to the process context, or from the process context to an activity, but never as a direct data exchange between two activities. This ensures that additional steps can be added to the process without interrupting the existing data flow. The mappings are assigned to the individual activities. There are input mappings (from the process context to the activity) and output mappings (from the activity to the process context). Figures 4.34 and 4.35 show the mappings for the *Approve Purchase Request* step.

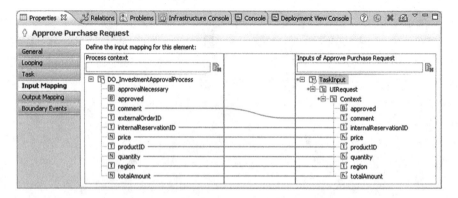

Fig. 4.34 Input mapping

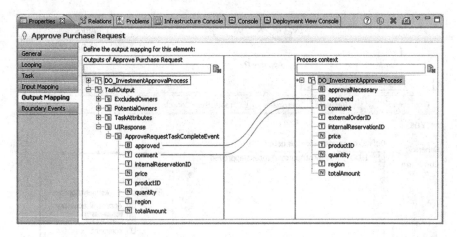

Fig. 4.35 Output mapping

In mappings, the data flow runs from left to right. In the output mapping, only those fields that can actually be changed in the respective user interface are mapped. As shown in the screenshot in Fig. 4.35, these are the Approval checkbox and the Comment field. The other fields of the context have all already been filled by the output mapping of the *Enter Purchase Request* step and do not need to be assigned again.

Conditions at Gateways If you use an exclusive gateway, suitable conditions must be placed on all sequence flows leaving the gateway. To ensure that the process is always executable, SAP BPM stipulates that one path is always executed by default, that is, the process follows this path if none of the other paths from the gateway have their conditions fulfilled at runtime. In the process model, the default path (also referred to as default flow in BPMN) is identified by a diagonal slash through the path in question (see also Fig. 4.36). In this example, the default flow is the path that is followed if the request is rejected. Whether or not the *Yes* condition is fulfilled is determined by evaluating the status of the process context field *approved*: If it has the Boolean value `true`, the process will take the *Yes* path at the gateway. In Process Composer, you can enter a condition as a script, and you are provided with all the fields of the context. For the example process, we only need to specify the field itself as a condition because it is already a Boolean value (Fig. 4.36), but the editor also allows you to formulate much more complex expressions, even those using predefined functions.

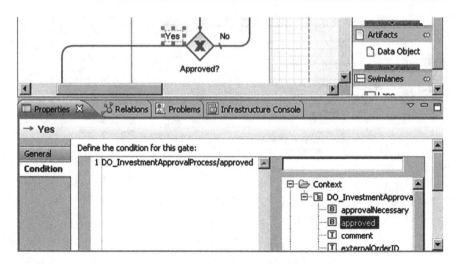

Fig. 4.36 Default flow and condition for the exclusive gateway

Correlations for Message-Based Intermediate Events The last issue we need to address is how the messages and processes that belong together will find one another. Let me explain. It is perfectly conceivable that several instances of the order process will have to be processed at the same time. However, the business and the technical process are loosely coupled together, which means that once the business process has sent the order, there is no longer any physical connection between the two processes. If the technical process wants to return a confirmation, it no longer knows which sender to address it to; all it knows is which interface to use for the response, but this information is not sufficient, as there may be several business process instances all waiting for confirmation. The process framework needs some way to determine which instance should be activated by the incoming message. A simple implementation would be to delegate this task to the waiting processes: When messages arrive from a particular interface, all waiting instances are activated, and these then apply certain criteria to determine if a message is intended for them. This could have a detrimental effect on performance for the whole system, however, because parallel threads would constantly be being started for the waiting process instances, only to find out that in most cases they are not the intended receiver anyway. Therefore, SAP BPM uses another approach: the definition of *correlation conditions* and their evaluation by the process framework. The correlation condition (which determines when an instance should be activated) is specified *in the process model* during modeling, but the actual activation of the process instance or instances that meet the condition is undertaken by the *process framework at runtime*. In our example scenario, the correlation condition evaluates a comparison of the internal reservation number that was generated earlier and transferred to the technical process, and a field of the same name in the confirmation interface. Figure 4.37 shows the correlation condition for the intermediate message event *Wait for Confirmation*.

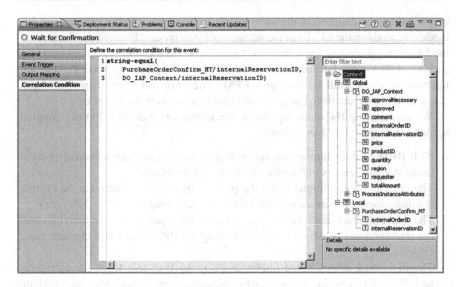

Fig. 4.37 Correlation condition for the message intermediate event

The condition is:

```
string-equal(
    PurchaseOrderConfirm_MT/internalReservationID,
    DO_IAP_Context/internalReservationID)
```

If the internal reservation number of the process context (referenced in the condition by the data object DO_IAP_Context) is identical (string-equal) to the internal reservation number that was transferred when the confirmation interface was called, then the corresponding process instance will be activated.

This pattern can also be applied to the message-based intermediate event *Wait for next msg.* of the technical process for collecting messages for the same product. You will remember that we can only send bundled messages to the Business Warehouse, with each bundle containing messages relating to a particular product. In this case, the correlation condition relates to the product number:

```
string-equal(
    PurchaseOrderMsg_MT/purchaseOrder/productID,
    DO_PurchaseOrderMsg_DT/purchaseOrder/productID)
```

This enables us to package the messages neatly by product number. There is another point we need to consider when implementing the technical process if messages are to be aggregated: the same interface must be used for the message-based start and intermediate event. With message aggregation, the sender cannot know whether it should send its message to a start or intermediate event; this has to be determined by the process framework. When the order process sends its message, the process framework first has to determine whether there is already a running process instance dealing with the product number associated with this message. It can do this using an active correlation condition. If it finds an existing instance, it simply passes the message to the intermediate message event of this process instance. Otherwise, a new process instance has to be started for this product. Based on this logic, it is clear why the start and intermediate events have to be assigned to the same interface. However, whether you can use this method depends on the BPMN implementation of your process framework. The method used here is simply one interpretation; the BPMN specification does not cover this aspect, nor does it stipulate the assignment of one and same interface to both the start and intermediate event. Find out from your BPMN engine provider how they recommend you should implement the aggregation of related messages in their engine.

We can sum up the main aspects of the implementation of a loosely coupled scenario with SAP BPM as follows:

- SAP BPM enables interaction between the business and the technical process using standardized asynchronous Web service interfaces.
- The correlation conditions allow the process framework to activate the correct waiting process instances without placing an unnecessary load on resources.
- The data flow itself comprises input and output mappings between activities and the process context, which is modeled using the BPMN standard element *Data Object*.
- The individual activities are implemented using Web interfaces for user tasks and Web services for service tasks. Message start events and intermediate message events are also provided with asynchronous Web service interfaces.
- A role concept is used to determine which employees will perform the tasks: groups/roles of a company's user management solution are assigned to a process role, which is assigned to a lane in the process model. All activities in this lane are then executed by the users determined in this way.

4.2.3.7 Overview in Composite Designer

Process-driven applications can comprise a number of very different components, as we have seen, and it is very important to the developer to be able to display a compact overview of the relationships between the individual components. The development environment of SAP Process Orchestration has a dedicated perspective for this in SAP NetWeaver Developer Studio: the Composite Designer. Figure 4.38 shows the overview of the business process. The connections to the components that can be reached directly from the selected process are clearly shown by arrows.

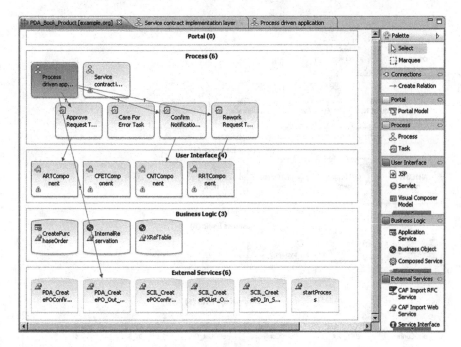

Fig. 4.38 Business process: overview in Composite Designer

One of the first things we notice is that the process-driven application is divided into layers: *Process, User Interface, Business Logic,* and *External Services*. This corresponds to the architecture of process-driven applications as discussed in this book.

The Composite Designer is not simply a tool for visualizing the dependencies between components; it can also be used as a starting point for creating new components. For example, you can create new business objects by dragging the *Business Object* icon from the palette to the *Business Logic* layer. The Composite Designer is a central cockpit for developing process-driven applications within SAP Process Orchestration. Figure 4.39 shows the same Composite Designer view for the technical process.

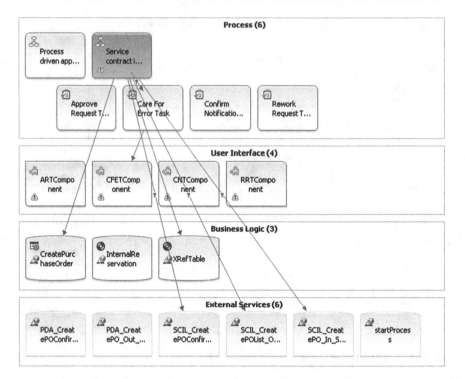

Fig. 4.39 Technical process: overview in Composite Designer

You can clearly see the local persistence call for the cross-reference table (XRefTable), as well as the call to the waiting business process using the SCIL_CreatePOConfirm_Out_Service interface. By clicking the components, you can easily identify the relationships within the composite application; this enables developers to quickly find their way around a process-driven application.

4.2.4 Runtime Behavior of the Example Scenario

You can deploy any of the components of the process-driven application on the JavaEE-based server by clicking them. After deployment, you can start the application immediately: instantiate the business process by calling the standalone user interface for entering the order data. There is no need to perform administrative steps such as linking the service interfaces used in the model with their concrete implementations as the development environment and the runtime are aligned in such a way that service calls and their implementations find each other automatically. The Visual Composer UI for entering the order data can be called directly by a URL; the screen shown in Fig. 4.40 is displayed:

Start Process Driven Application Process

|➡ — 1 — 2 — 3 — ◀|

| Enter Order Data | Confirm Internal Reservation ID | Confirm Process Start |

Enter Order Data

Region *	EMEA
Product ID *	HT-1000
Quantity *	10
Price *	10
Comment *	10 ok?

Submit

Fig. 4.40 Entering the order data at runtime

This is the wizard UI modeled with Visual Composer. The first step is to enter the order data. When the user chooses *Submit*, the Web service for persisting the data locally is called in the background. This generates the internal reservation number, which is displayed to the user in the second step of the wizard as confirmation that the data has been entered successfully (Fig. 4.41).

Start Process Driven Application Process

|➡ — 1 — 2 — 3 — ◀|

| Enter Order Data | Confirm Internal Reservation ID | Confirm Process Start |

Internal Reservation ID

| Key | 7dc491f8-61f2-11e1-af4f-0000003698c2 |

Confirm

Fig. 4.41 Confirmation of reservation at runtime

We could have connected to the start of the business process at this point, but I have intentionally put this action in a separate step of the wizard. When the user chooses *Confirm*, the asynchronous service that starts our processing process is called. This call does not pass through the ESB; it goes straight to the process framework. Figure 4.42 shows the UI confirming that the process has started successfully.

Fig. 4.42 Confirmation of process start at runtime

The requester completes his entry by choosing *Confirm*, which simply exits the user interface.

At the start of the process, the data is transferred via the Web service interface to the start event of the business process; from here it is written to the process context using an output mapping at the start event. Following the modeled process flow, the next step is to activate the approval step *Approve Purchase Request*. The process framework does this by sending a notification (for example, an e-mail) to those people who have been assigned to the *Approver* role (either at the start of the process or at runtime). Alternatively, the current tasks can be displayed in a central task list, usually on a company portal (see also Fig. 4.43). This list represents the current worklist of the logged-on user.

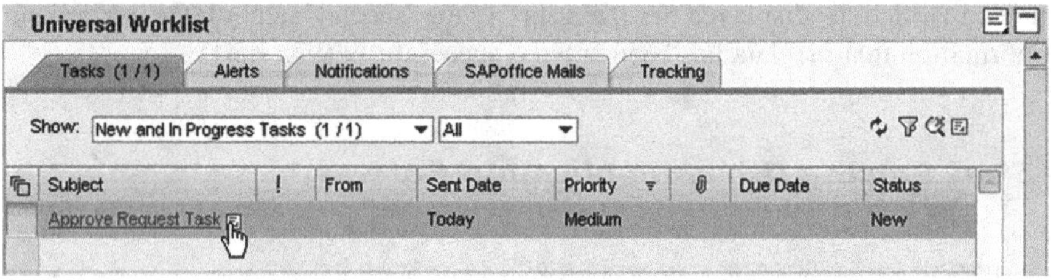

Universal Worklist							
Tasks (1 / 1)	Alerts	Notifications	SAPoffice Mails	Tracking			
Show: New and In Progress Tasks (1 /1) ▼ All ▼							
Subject	!	From	Sent Date	Priority ▼	⊘	Due Date	Status
Approve Request Task			Today	Medium			New

Fig. 4.43 Task worklist

The approver uses the link provided to navigate to the active task. An interface is displayed showing the data entered by the requester and provided by the process framework from the process context in accordance with the input mapping guidelines (Fig. 4.44).

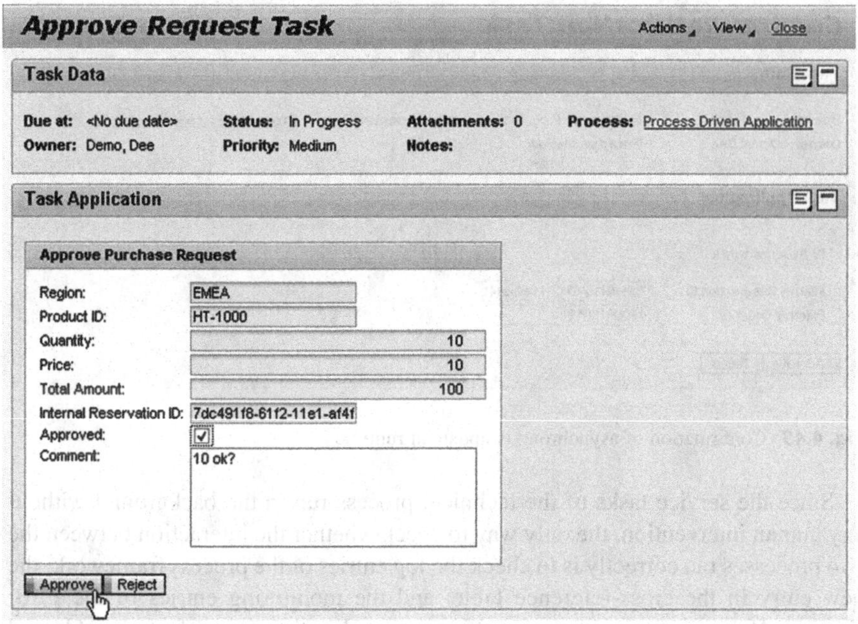

Fig. 4.44 Approval step at runtime

The approver confirms the order by selecting the *Approved* checkbox and completes the step by choosing *Approve*. This returns the changed data to the process context via output mapping.

The interaction between the process-driven application and the service contract implementation layer via the ESB now takes place in the background. The process-driven application starts the technical process by transferring the product ID, order quantity, and internal reservation number, and then waits at the intermediate message event. The technical process calls the back-end system to update the order data, and then stores the internal reservation number together with the external number generated in the backend in the cross-reference table. It then calls the Web service corresponding to the interface of the intermediate event where the process of the process-driven application is waiting. This process, once reactivated, adds the externally generated order number to the process context, from where it is displayed to the requester in a confirmation step (Fig. 4.45).

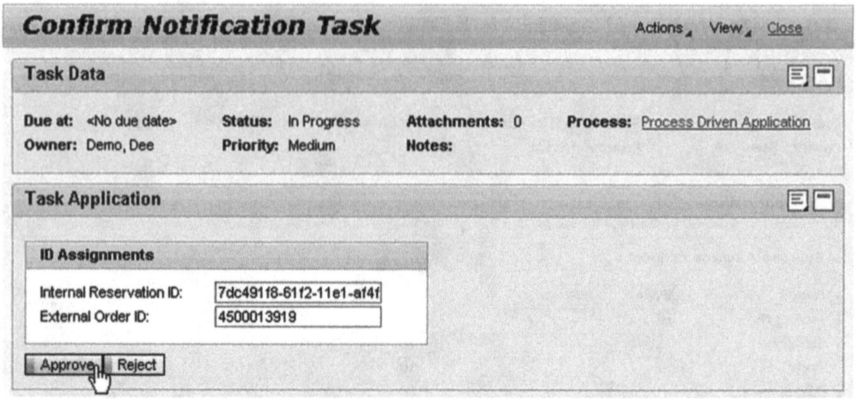

Fig. 4.45 Confirmation of asynchronous update at runtime

Since the service tasks of the technical process run in the background without any human intervention, the only way to check whether the interaction between the two processes ran correctly is to check the log entries of the process framework, the new entry in the cross-reference table, and the monitoring entries of the ESB. Figure 4.46 shows the new entry that is generated in the cross-reference table and Figs. 4.47 and 4.48 show the details of the process execution of the business process and the technical process, respectively.

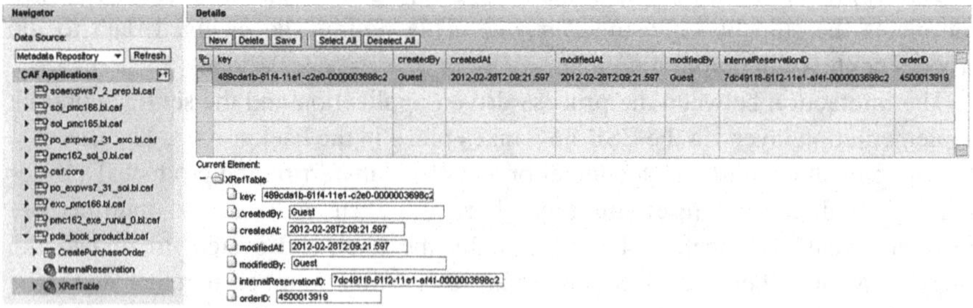

Fig. 4.46 Entry in cross-reference table after completion of process

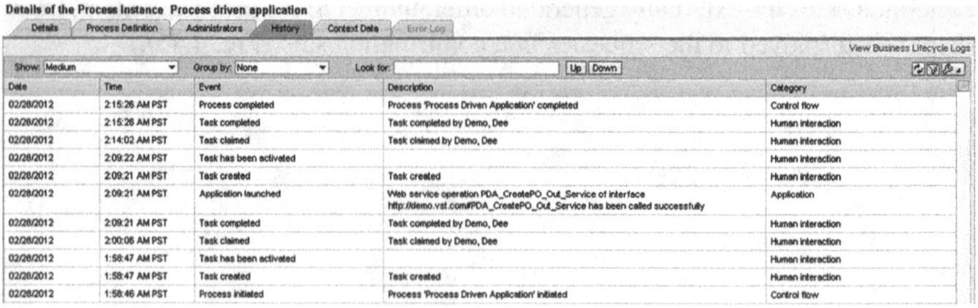

Fig. 4.47 Process execution of business process

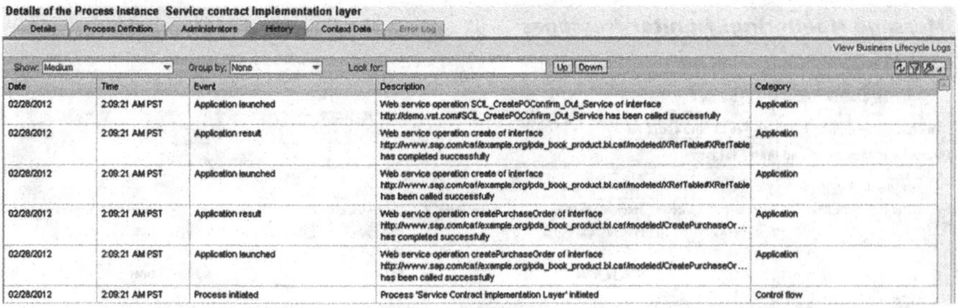

Details of the Process Instance Service contract implementation layer

Details	Process Definition	Administrators	History	Context Data	Error Log

View Business Lifecycle Logs

Show: Medium ▼   Group by: None ▼   Look for: [   ] [Up][Down]

Date	Time	Event	Description	Category
02/28/2012	2:09:21 AM PST	Application launched	Web service operation SCL_CreatePOConfirm_Out_Service of interface http://demo.vst.com/SCL_CreatePOConfirm_Out_Service has been called successfully	Application
02/28/2012	2:09:21 AM PST	Application result	Web service operation create of interface http://www.sap.com/cat/example.org/pda_book_product.bi.cat/modeled/XRefTable/XRefTable has completed successfully	Application
02/28/2012	2:09:21 AM PST	Application launched	Web service operation create of interface http://www.sap.com/cat/example.org/pda_book_product.bi.cat/modeled/XRefTable/XRefTable has been called successfully	Application
02/28/2012	2:09:21 AM PST	Application result	Web service operation createPurchaseOrder of interface http://www.sap.com/cat/example.org/pda_book_product.bi.cat/modeled/CreatePurchaseOr... has completed successfully	Application
02/28/2012	2:09:21 AM PST	Application launched	Web service operation createPurchaseOrder of interface http://www.sap.com/cat/example.org/pda_book_product.bi.cat/modeled/CreatePurchaseOr... has been called successfully	Application
02/28/2012	2:09:21 AM PST	Process initiated	Process 'Service Contract Implementation Layer' initiated	Control flow

Fig. 4.48 Process execution of technical process

The logging entries read from bottom to top. In the business process log, you can see the user task for confirming the input data first, followed at 2:09:21 AM by an asynchronous call to instantiate the technical process. Asynchronous calls have only one log entry, whereas synchronous calls have two (*called successfully* and *completed successfully*). The first logging entry of the technical process confirms its instantiation at 2:09:21 AM, concurring with the call from the business process. The first action of the technical process is the synchronous call (hence two entries) to the SAP back-end system to create the order. The next two entries show the synchronous write call to the cross-reference table (also at 2:09:21 AM). Since the data is written to the local database, this is practically instantaneous. The last entry for the technical process is the reactivation of the waiting process; this is asynchronous, so there is no visible change in the time stamp. The technical process then continues to wait for messages, so there are no more entries.

The business process continues immediately (2:09:21 AM) with the creation of the user task for the requester, and ends when the requester closes the confirmation screen.

By executing the process and examining the log entries, we can see the advantages of this architecture: back-end calls are decoupled from the process-driven application; local database calls are swift, allowing end users to work on their tasks without delays or interruptions. Furthermore, as you are not bound to any particular data type or proprietary Web service interfaces, you can easily replace the implementation for external access with an alternative solution, enabling you to adapt the process-driven application to other system landscapes. These advantages do come at a price: increased complexity; but this is easily managed by modern development environments.

You may have noticed that the whole round trip, from the business process to the technical process and back again, via the ESB, takes less than a second. We can confirm this by taking a closer look at the message transfer in the ESB. Figure 4.49 shows a summary of all messages processed within a specified time range.

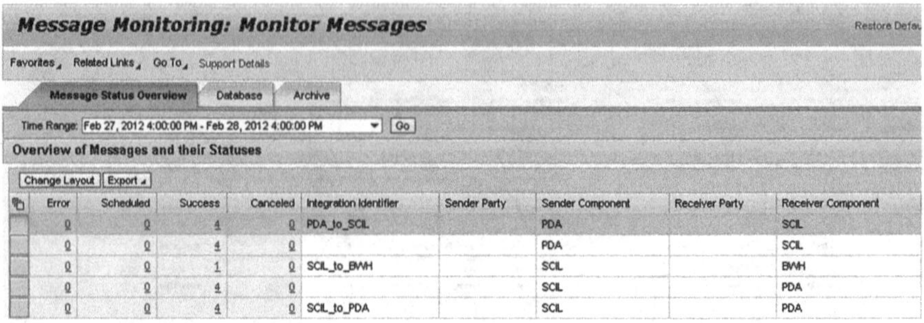

Fig. 4.49 Message monitoring in the ESB

The *Sender Component* and *Receiver Component* columns are particularly interesting. They show the message traffic between the process-driven application (*PDA*) and the technical process (*SCIL*). We can see that both components have sent the same number of messages to each other, but what we are really interested in is the last message in each direction. To find out more, we display the details of the last messages that were exchanged. These are shown in Fig. 4.50 (from *PDA* to *SCIL*) and in Fig. 4.51 (from *SCIL* to *PDA*).

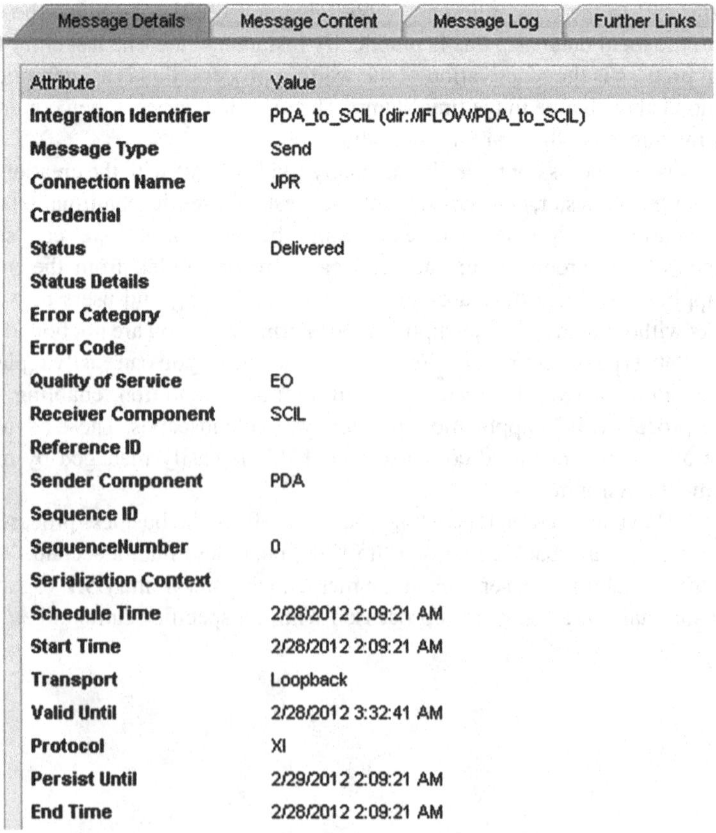

Message Details	Message Content	Message Log	Further Links

Attribute	Value
Integration Identifier	PDA_to_SCIL (dir://IFLOW/PDA_to_SCIL)
Message Type	Send
Connection Name	JPR
Credential	
Status	Delivered
Status Details	
Error Category	
Error Code	
Quality of Service	EO
Receiver Component	SCIL
Reference ID	
Sender Component	PDA
Sequence ID	
SequenceNumber	0
Serialization Context	
Schedule Time	2/28/2012 2:09:21 AM
Start Time	2/28/2012 2:09:21 AM
Transport	Loopback
Valid Until	2/28/2012 3:32:41 AM
Protocol	XI
Persist Until	2/29/2012 2:09:21 AM
End Time	2/28/2012 2:09:21 AM

Fig. 4.50 Message details (*PDA* to *SCIL*)

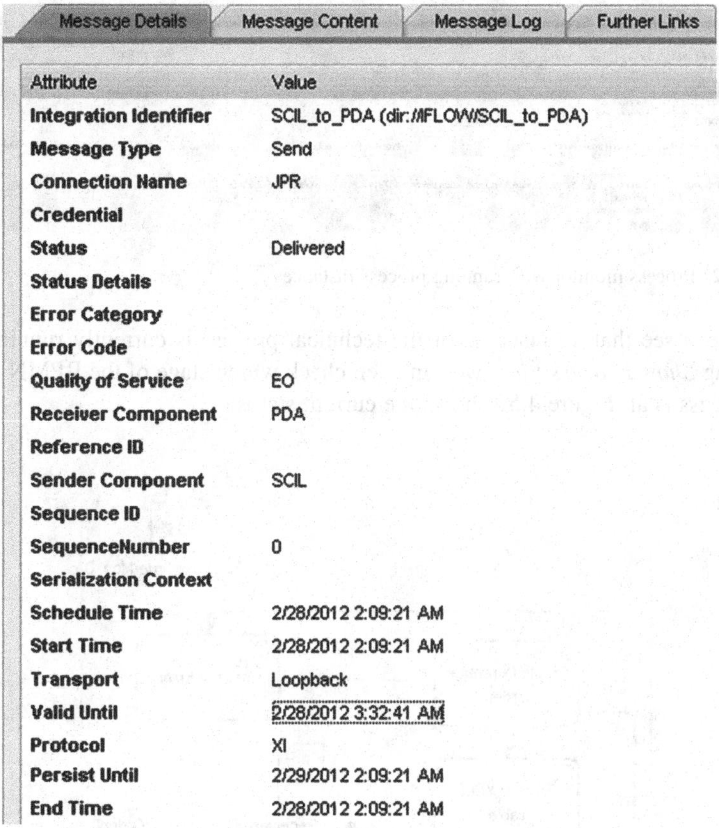

Message Details	Message Content	Message Log	Further Links

Attribute	Value
Integration Identifier	SCIL_to_PDA (dir://IFLOW/SCIL_to_PDA)
Message Type	Send
Connection Name	JPR
Credential	
Status	Delivered
Status Details	
Error Category	
Error Code	
Quality of Service	EO
Receiver Component	PDA
Reference ID	
Sender Component	SCIL
Sequence ID	
SequenceNumber	0
Serialization Context	
Schedule Time	2/28/2012 2:09:21 AM
Start Time	2/28/2012 2:09:21 AM
Transport	Loopback
Valid Until	2/28/2012 3:32:41 AM
Protocol	XI
Persist Until	2/29/2012 2:09:21 AM
End Time	2/28/2012 2:09:21 AM

Fig. 4.51 Message details (*SCIL* to *PDA*)

By comparing the entries for the start and end time, we can see that both messages were processed within the same second; the log entries in the BPM Engine and the Integration Engine match up exactly.

The last test is a functional check of the step sequence in the technical process that collects the messages and stores them as a package in the file system. First, we check whether a process instance of the technical process is currently running and, if so, which stage of the BPMN model it is at. SAP Process Orchestration provides dedicated monitoring tools for this: The *Process Monitor* enables you to analyze all process instances, irrespective of whether they are already completed, are still in progress, or have encountered errors. The example in Fig. 4.52 shows an overview of the processes that are currently running:

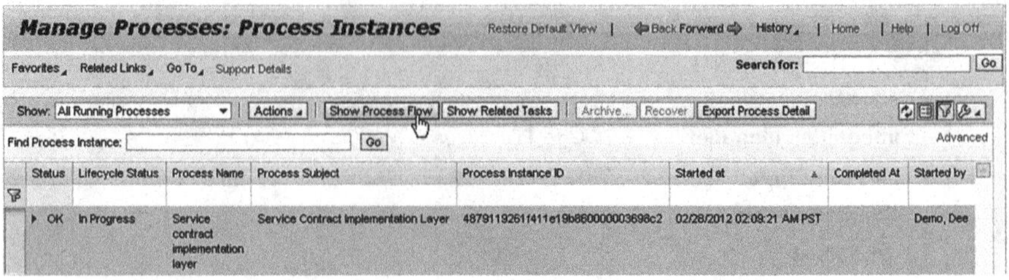

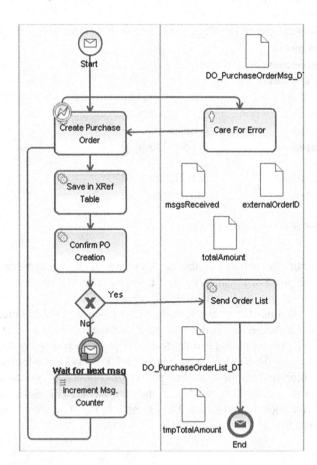

Fig. 4.52 Process monitor with running process instances

We can see that an instance of the technical process is currently running. By choosing *Show Process Flow* we can even check which stage of the BPMN model the process is at. Figure 4.53 shows the current status:

Fig. 4.53 Current process status of technical process

The marker tells us that the process is at the intermediate message event, waiting for other orders for the same product as in our first order to arrive. We are using a correlation condition at the intermediate event to bundle the messages by product number. It is very simple to verify whether this step is functioning correctly: Simply send another order with a different product number than the original order, for example, *HT-1001* instead of *HT-1000*. If we then check the process monitor, we see that there is indeed a new instance of the technical process, dedicated to aggregating orders for the product *HT-1001*. Figure 4.54 shows the new process instance in the process monitor.

Fig. 4.54 Process monitor with two *SCIL* process instances

We now want to bring the technical process that we have started to a successful conclusion. To do this, we have to send two more orders for the product *HT-1000* (one for 20 units, one for 30 units), and then check whether the process instance completes correctly and if it saves a new message with the three product orders in the file system via the ESB. Once the third message has been sent, we can check the target folder representing the Business Warehouse system. Figure 4.55 shows the file with the aggregated message that has arrived there and Fig. 4.56 shows its content.

Address	🖿 D:\public\PDA_Book\ReceivedFiles				▼
Folders		×	Name ▲	Size	Type	Date Modified
⊟🖿 PDA_Book			🗒 purchaseorder20120228-061559-348.xml	1 KB	XML Document	2/28/2012 6:16 AM
🖿 ESR_Export						
🖿 iFlow_Export						
🖿 ProductExport from NWDS						
🖿 **ReceivedFiles**						
🖿 VC-UI-Export						
🖿 WSDL-Files						
🖿 XSD-Files						

Fig. 4.55 Aggregated message in target folder

```
- <ns1:PurchaseOrderListMsg_MT xmlns:xsd="http://www.w3.org/2001/XMLSchema"
    xmlns:xsi="http://www.w3.org/2001/XMLSchema-instance" xmlns:ns1="http://demo.vst.com">
  - <poLineItems>
    - <poLineItem>
        <productID>HT-1000</productID>
        <quantity>10</quantity>
        <price>10</price>
      </poLineItem>
    - <poLineItem>
        <productID>HT-1000</productID>
        <quantity>20</quantity>
        <price>10</price>
      </poLineItem>
    - <poLineItem>
        <productID>HT-1000</productID>
        <quantity>30</quantity>
        <price>10</price>
      </poLineItem>
    </poLineItems>
    <totalAmount>600</totalAmount>
  </ns1:PurchaseOrderListMsg_MT>
```

Fig. 4.56 Content of aggregated message

Our test was successful. All that remains to do is check the process monitor, which gives us an insight into the statuses of the various process variables in the process context. This includes instances that have already finished, so we can verify the list of collected messages in the monitor as well. Figure 4.57 shows a screenshot of this.

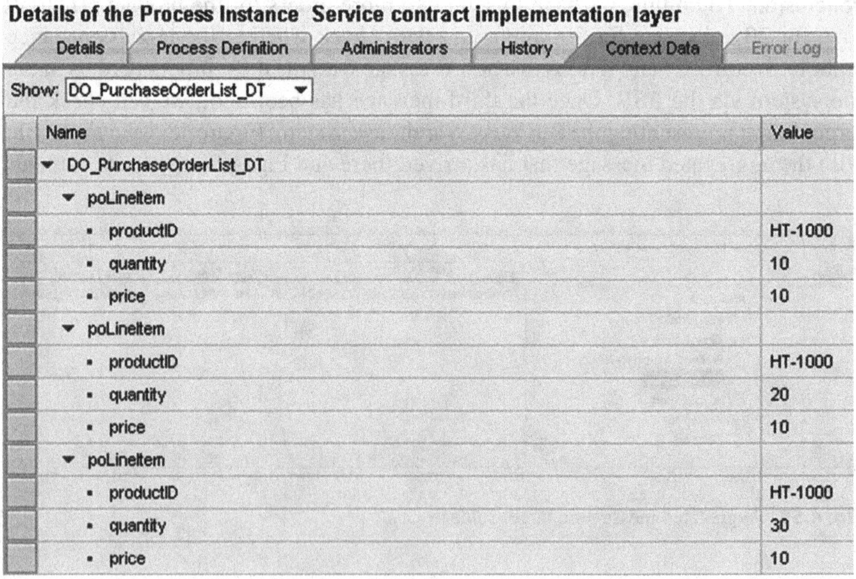

Details of the Process Instance Service contract implementation layer

Details	Process Definition	Administrators	History	Context Data	Error Log

Show: [DO_PurchaseOrderList_DT ▼]

Name	Value
▼ DO_PurchaseOrderList_DT	
▼ poLineItem	
• productID	HT-1000
• quantity	10
• price	10
▼ poLineItem	
• productID	HT-1000
• quantity	20
• price	10
▼ poLineItem	
• productID	HT-1000
• quantity	30
• price	10

Fig. 4.57 Analysis of the process context in the process monitor

This concludes our practical lesson on how to implement the basic architecture of process-driven applications using SAP Process Orchestration. I would stress once again at this point that this method can be applied to any other environment that can execute BPMN models. Personally, what I like about SAP Process Orchestration is that BPMN can be used seamlessly across all layers: in the business user-centric processes, in stateful integration-centric processes, and in stateless message processing processes—one single notation for all process-like flows. This allows BPMN to function exactly as set out in its objectives, that is, as a means of communication between the participating roles.

4.2.5   Role of Model-Driven Development

The example implementation emphasizes yet again how we can use loosely coupled BPMN processes to implement the proposed architecture. By also using a modern model-driven development environment, we can reduce development effort to a minimum (as you have seen, we did not have to develop one single line of program code to implement this proof of concept). However, I do not want to suggest that applications can be developed without any programming whatsoever. There are some gaps in the scenarios we have covered; in reality, we cannot expect to be able to model the service logic and the detailed form logic of the user interfaces without some programming input. What is certain though is that convoluted and difficult tasks such as designing user interfaces, persisting data, programming concurrency, and coupling different systems using service interfaces can all be simplified by model-driven approaches. Moreover, thanks to the options now available to us, we can efficiently implement exactly those architectures that we would previously have discounted because of the effort involved. By using the BPMN intermediate message event or receive task, it is a relatively uncomplicated procedure to implement loosely coupled architectures. All vendors that implement the BPMN specification have to include suitable solutions for these elements in their frameworks and provide an infrastructure for process cooperation. One of BPMN's particular strengths is the modeling and execution of process federations.

4.3   BPMN Implementations of Different Vendors

The intermediate message event has a central role in the implementation of loosely coupled scenarios. It is used in the business process to implement the wait function once the technical process has started, and is not released from this state until the required message arrives from the technical process. A first glance at the process model does not suggest any problems, but closer examination reveals the possibility that a deadlock situation or an endless loop could arise. Whether or not this situation does in fact arise depends on how the message-based intermediate event from the vendor of the BPMN implementation is implemented.

Theoretically, the back-end process could be completed before the intermediate event is activated, that is, before the token that travels through the process reaches the intermediate event. This poses the following problem: What happens to a message sent from the technical process if it arrives at an intermediate event that is not ready to receive it? This problem is exacerbated further if the message receipt is monitored by an event-based gateway with a parallel timer intermediate event, as modeled in Fig. 4.58.

Fig. 4.58 Time monitoring of message receipt using an event-based gateway

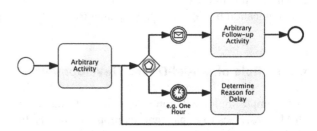

If the intermediate timer event fires before the message arrives, our token passes to the next activity *Determine Reason for Delay*. What happens to a message if it arrives when there is no token at the event-based gateway? In the BPMN 2.0 specification (OMG 2011), the chapter on execution semantics states the following:

P. 429: "An Activity is Ready for execution if the REQUIRED number of tokens is available to activate the Activity. The REQUIRED number of tokens (one or more) is indicated by the attribute StartQuantity."

P. 430: "Receive Task: Upon activation, the Receive Task begins waiting for the associated Message. When the Message arrives, the data in the Data Output of the Receive Task is assigned from the data in the Message, and Receive Task completes."

P. 440: "For Intermediate Events, the handling consists of waiting for the Event to occur. Waiting starts when the Intermediate Event is reached."

All the specification tells us is the point in time as of which messages can be received, namely, when the token reaches either the receive task or the catching intermediate message event. It does not tell us what should happen to messages that arrive at a time when neither a receive task nor an intermediate event is ready to receive them. Bruce Silver describes the behavior at the event-based gateway as follows:

P. 90: "The event that occurs first determines the path enabled out of the gateway. Any trigger signals arriving after that are ignored."

Based on these statements, we could conclude that any messages that arrive at a time when no receivers are ready will be discarded. In the situations outlined above, this would result in a deadlock or endless loop. In our example we find ourselves in an endless loop: The expected message is discarded and the token can never leave the process model by way of the intermediate message event. It circulates endlessly between the event-based gateway and the task for finding the reason for the delay.

SAP does not follow this approach in its implementation of the intermediate message event (for details, see Balko 2010a). All messages that meet the correlation condition are put in a queue at the intermediate message event, even if a token is not yet waiting at the intermediate event. Messages are taken out of the queue as soon as a token reaches the associated intermediate event. This method avoids the risks of deadlocks, endless loops, and lost messages.

If vendors do not follow this approach and thus run the risk of losing messages, help is at hand in the form of the BPMN model shown in Fig. 4.59.

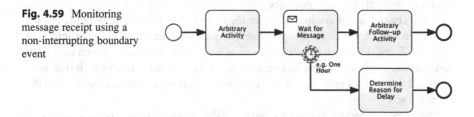

Fig. 4.59 Monitoring message receipt using a non-interrupting boundary event

In this process model, the wait for messages is not interrupted by the intermediate timer boundary event. This prevents messages being lost while the cause of the delay is being investigated. However, it does not solve the general problem of messages being lost if they arrive while the token is still at the activity before the receive task, for example. In the SAP implementation, messages cannot be lost here either, as long as the correlation condition for the receive task is met. As we saw in the example implementation, in SAP BPM the correlation condition is made up of fields from the process context. If this context is filled by the process start event, the intermediate message event is activated automatically and messages can already be added to the queue.

By using this simple example, I want to make you aware that even a seemingly clear-cut BPMN model can run into unforeseen errors at runtime, and for this reason it is essential to know how your vendor has implemented the various BPMN elements.

4.4   Version Management

Business processes in process-driven applications can run for an extended period of time, in some cases even for several years, although this is uncommon. However, runtimes of weeks or months are not unusual. We need to think about how these processes will behave if new versions are introduced (new versions of the processes themselves, or new versions of the content referenced in the processes, that is, service calls and user interfaces).

For referenced content, we can deal with this issue by using suitable names: We make the version number part of the component name. If a process references a user interface for entering an order, for example, the reference for the associated process step is given the name *OrderEntry_V1.1*. The process step and the UI component are explicitly linked by this name. If you want to use an updated version of the UI, you have to decide whether the new version is valid for process instances that are currently running. If so, and the changes to the UI are purely cosmetic (for example, colors have been changed to fit in with a new corporate identity, or the position of fields on a UI has been changed), you can provide the new version under the same name *OrderEntry_V1.1* in the version management system. The versions are differentiated within the version management system, but not at runtime. Once the new version has been deployed under the same name, all running process instances will call the new interface.

If the change is not compatible with the old version because new fields or tabs have been added, for example, you need to adapt the name of the user interface (to *OrderEntry_V1.2*), and update the references in the processes, which also get a new version number. If a new instance of this updated process is started, it runs with the new UI, while all processes that were already running continue to work with the old interface.

The same procedure applies to service calls. Here as well, you use names to control whether or not new versions of a service are used for process instances that are already active.

The general rule for process changes is that processes that are already running will continue to use the process model that they started with. If it is necessary to make changes to process instances that are already running, BPM systems that support such scenarios must have an architecture that can deal with this: They must allow ad hoc changes but employ prechecks to make sure that executability and robustness can be maintained for all subsequent steps, even after adaptation. You should also consider process schema evolutions, that is, migrations of running process instances to new process models. I would direct anyone looking for more information on this subject to the results of the ADEPT research project by the University of Ulm (Dadam et al. 2009a, b; ADEPT2 2014).

Advanced Concepts for Architecture Support in Process-Driven Applications

5

Let us summarize what we've discussed so far: In the last two chapters we have deepened our knowledge of process-driven applications and demonstrated a specific implementation based on a small scenario. In the remainder of the book, we will examine further useful concepts in the area of process-driven applications that increase the robustness of the architecture in question. I will discuss the following main topics:

- Locking behavior of the connected systems
- Idempotence requirements on the called services
- Events as prerequisites for sending response messages to the waiting process-driven application
- Error handling in communication with the back-end systems
- Wizard-like user interfaces compared with user interfaces being used in process flows

I will also show you some of the process patterns that have proven to be useful in the service contract implementation layer. These patterns demonstrate typically encountered problems and how they can be solved. The chapter concludes by describing how the flexibility of process-driven applications is improved by using rules in combination with analytical applications.

5.1   Locking Behavior of the Connected Systems

In accordance with the architecture described in this book, process-driven applications are loosely coupled with the back-end systems using stateless service calls. Therefore, we do not know in which intervals we access the back-end systems. This is particularly crucial in read-write cycles, since it is not possible to predict when the data is written to after a read operation (if at all). This means that we can discount any pessimistic locking methods if they lock the data after a read operation while being edited by the user. The back-end systems are not available

V. Stiehl, *Process-Driven Applications with BPMN*, DOI 10.1007/978-3-319-07218-0_5,   173
© Springer International Publishing Switzerland 2014

exclusively to the process-driven application and other applications compete for them. This means that pessimistic locking applied by a process-driven application inevitably causes disruptions in other applications that also need to access the data.

Reads performed by services, therefore, must be made using optimistic locking. The signature of the services can be used to identify whether a back-end system supports optimistic locking in its service calls. If the outbound or inbound data contains a time stamp of the last read or write (or at the least a sequence number modified incrementally each time the data is updated), optimistic locking is supported. If a write operation is then performed, the back-end system compares the resulting time stamp or sequence number with the current value in the database. If the values do not match, a write conflict is indicated by an exception. You can decide on the appropriate reaction to this exception.

If, however, the back-end system does not employ this type of processing, again the functionality must be provided by the service contract implementation layer. This could be done, for example, by copying the data to the implementation layer too when it is read. In the write operation, the data is read once more from the back end before the actual update by the implementation layer, locked in the back end at the same time, and compared with the copy. If this data matches the data in the copy, no further write operation has taken place in the meantime and the data can be written. If it does not match, a write conflict exists, indicated by an exception. In this case, the locked data must be unlocked.

The procedures described above do have a significant drawback: Read and write operations must work together, and hence be implemented as matching pairs. In *reads*, either the full object (if the back end does not support optimistic locking) or the time stamp/sequence number (if the back end does support optimistic locking) must be saved in a separate table in the service contract implementation layer. This table must then be accessed at *write time* to apply the conflict recognition function. Another difficulty is presented by the assignment of the data to the reader client: how do we know which UI or which process read the data? In other words, either the session ID of the client or the process ID of the process in question needs to be saved in the table together with the data. What happens, however, when the UI or the process is ended without being followed by a further write operation? Who is responsible for cleaning up the table (which itself is only of relevance during the lifetime of the UI or process)? If this were not the case, regular background jobs could, of course, check whether processes are still running and clean up tables if necessary. Furthermore, the entries for the logged active clients could be removed, if there is no response for a specified period of time. This requires, however, that the time of the last communication is also logged in the case of UIs. This would increase the amount of administration and the risk of errors significantly. Consider whether a simpler alternative is possible.

One simpler method is based on making the process-driven application pass the original unmodified data (from read time) as parameters when writing the new data. A read operation and a comparison of the data read from the back end with the original data passed from the composite must be performed before the actual write operation to the back-end system or systems, for conflict detection purposes. However, this method does not require any additional administration work in the service contract implementation layer, since all information for detecting conflicts is made available by passing parameters from the process-driven application to the write operation. This means that the read operation does not need to collect any administration data that could be required by later write operations.

This method also has a further advantage: the comparison is based only on the *change-relevant* fields of an object. Here, "change-relevant" means those fields that the process-driven application wants to modify.

The following short example illustrates the method I have just described. The delivery address of an order is changed from "New York" to "San Francisco" in the composite. In the write operation, both cities are returned (new/old) and a check is made to see whether "New York" is still specified in the original order in the back end, before the actual update is made. If this is the case, the update can be made; if not, a conflict exists. If another application modifies the street of the billing address in the order in parallel, the write operation for the city of the delivery address is not affected. This is because, in this case, only the city is considered to be the change-relevant field.

This would not be possible in methods where only the object "Order", as a unit, can be locked optimistically. In this case, the change made to the street in the billing address would result in a change being made to the time stamp or sequence number for the entire order. In the subsequent write operation of the delivery address change (which also references the order), a conflict is unavoidable. To summarize, the method described here is both simpler and less prone to conflicts than the implementation of additional administration tables in the interaction of read and write operations. The drawbacks are a more complex interface (since both the modified data and the original data need to be passed by the caller), an additional read operation, and the comparison of the object states in the process-driven application and back-end system. However, because the write operations are processed asynchronously (due to the loosely coupled architecture), the delays incurred should be minimal.

The optimistic locking method is recommended for long running transactions where there is relatively little demand for the data in question. Each conflict needs to be traced. Once detected, a conflict could be resolved by specialists who compare the data from the database with the new data record and merge it using appropriate guidelines. Merge operations of this type can be partly automated, requiring only a minimum of interaction with experts. An alternative is to split the business object in question into subobjects to reduce the likelihood of conflicts. A further option for reducing the chance of write conflicts is to use check or simulation services as found, for example, in SAP systems. These services must also be provided by the back-end systems and enable the write operations in question to be simulated without actually updating the data in the back end. Instead, only the prerequisites for a successful potential update are checked. Services of this nature are no longer a rarity in modern systems based on participation in loosely coupled scenarios in SOA environments. They are called from the UI of the process-driven application using the service contract implementation layer. They are not able to guarantee a complete absence of write conflicts, since they do not lock the data either, but because the simulation is called directly after the actual update (and time-consuming user interaction cannot be inserted) there is very little time between the two calls and the likelihood of a conflict is reduced significantly.

Both of the methods described here may seem complex and their implementation may involve overcoming a few hurdles, but think about the following: These methods only become essential if the process-driven application is genuinely in conflict with other applications. Often, business objects in back-end systems can be separated using number ranges or special IDs so effectively that there is no chance of conflicts arising. And in many conflict situations, it is not a problem if the data of the most recent write operation is applied. Consider, therefore, whether one of the simpler methods can solve your problem and only resort to one of the algorithms discussed here if there is no other option.

What should definitely be avoided is an explicit check-in/check-out mechanism at the application level. This is not a suitable solution because existing applications that also work with the data also need to implement it. This alternative therefore fails to meet the non-invasiveness requirement for process-driven applications and can be discarded.

5.2   Idempotence

The idempotence requirement for service calls is certainly one of the central properties in loosely coupled architectures and must itself be implemented by the back-end systems. In their book *Enterprise Integration Patterns* (Hohpe and Woolf 2004), Gregor Hohpe and Bobby Woolf describe the *Idempotent Receiver-Pattern*. The main purpose of idempotence is to detect when a single service call can occur more than once due to technical defects. This can cause problems of a specialist nature and appropriate measures must therefore be taken. One classic example is when an expensive consumer item is ordered: After you order your new Porsche, the vendor does not reply with a confirmation and you submit your order again. What you do not know, however, is whether your request was interrupted on the way *to* the vendor or whether the confirmation was lost on the way *back to you*. This makes it possible that the Porsche is delivered to you twice, in the event that the first order was processed successfully by the vendor and only the subsequent receipt went missing. While the sight of two Porsches is certainly pleasant, it's not something everyone can afford.

A relatively simple algorithm has been established to avoid this problem. Again, a new parameter is added to the service interface. This parameter contains a unique number, which typically can be generated by library functions of modern programming languages (for example, by the function `java.util.UUID.randomUUID()` in Java). The service call reuses a once-generated number only in retry cases and otherwise generates a new identifier for each call. The service implementation itself now updates a table of identification numbers. Before the data is updated, a search is made for the passed ID in this table to identify a duplicate. If the number is not yet in the table (because this is the first call), the data is updated in the back-end system, the response message is created, and sent back to the caller. Before the data is actually sent, however, the passed identification number is saved in the table together with the reply data. If the call is made again with the same data, the table entry now makes it possible to detect the duplicate. In this case, we do not update the data again in the back end and the message saved for the ID is sent to the caller instead.

The signature of the service, therefore, makes it possible to tell whether a back-end system provides this function. Here, the service contract implementation layer also needs to step in if idempotence is not supported. This implementation is not too difficult, however, as shown in the description of the algorithm.

5.3 Events

In the chapter about the basic architecture of process-driven applications, the notification of the waiting business process by the technical process using an event (expected by the business process) is a significant factor in the case of asynchronous write operations. Of course, the business process does not always have to wait and this might even be pointless if the further process flow does not depend on the result of the service call. Instead, the process can proceed as normal.

If, however, it is essential for the further business process flow that updates are made successfully in the back end, we need to provide a suitable eventing mechanism in the service contract implementation layer to release the business process from the wait state. In the BPMN model, we have illustrated this using the intermediate message event in the business process.

From the perspective of the service contract implementation layer, there are now three different cases for identifying a successful update in the back end and notifying the business process:

- The back-end system is addressed synchronously: In this case, success is detected using the return parameter of the synchronous call. The return data can be combined as a single event and sent to the composite (in accordance with the requirements of the business process).
- The back-end system is addressed asynchronously and the back end sends a corresponding time-delayed acknowledgement as an event: In this case, the back-end system itself can trigger events and the technical process only needs to wait for them. From the perspective of the technical process, this is a classic *Request-Reply Pattern* (Hohpe and Woolf 2004) described in more depth in the chapter about patterns (Sect. 5.6). After the event is received, the technical process transforms only its content into the format expected by the business process and then sends it.
- The back-end system is addressed asynchronously and does not itself send any receipts: To handle this case, the technical process must itself be active and poll the back-end system at regular intervals. It does this until it can detect success or non-success in the business object being written to, using a state flag. Figure 5.1 shows one way of implementing polling in BPMN.

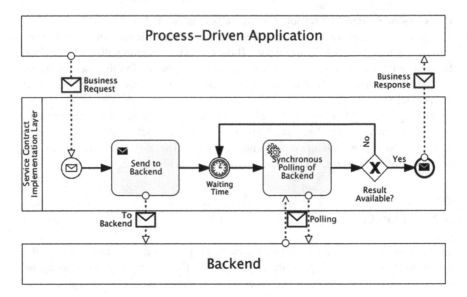

Fig. 5.1 Synchronous polling

This model shows the process-driven application in the top pool, the service contract implementation layer in the middle, and the back-end system at the bottom. The data exchange is initiated using an asynchronous message from the composite. The technical process now forwards the request to the back-end system, which we know will not show a reaction. Therefore, this technical process must query a status from the back-end system after a specific wait time. If the correct result (positive or negative) is received, a corresponding event is fired to the waiting business process. If back-end processing is not finished, however, and the expected result was not received, the back-end system is queried once more after a specific wait time.

As so often in BPMN, there are several possible implementations for this example too. One alternative to the model shown here is to map the loop using a subprocess with loop condition, as shown in Fig. 5.2.

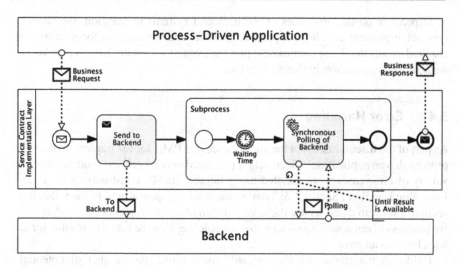

Fig. 5.2 Polling using a subprocess with loop condition

The subprocess shown in the figure is repeated as often as necessary until the loop completion condition is met. We do not know the number of loop passes in advance, therefore the symbol for the default loop is added to the subprocess in BPMN.

The back-end system was polled synchronously in both process models. I have visualized the implementation of an asynchronous polling in Fig. 5.3.

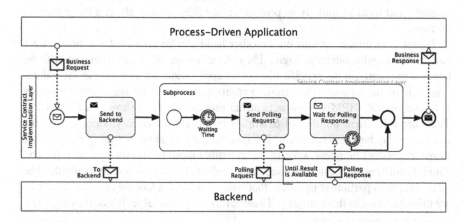

Fig. 5.3 Asynchronous polling

The time needed to wait for the response is also monitored in this model to avoid deadlock situations. In BPMN, this is implemented using the timer boundary event attached to the receive task.

Depending on the properties of the back-end systems in question, the service contract implementation layer is provided with several mechanisms for creating the required events to release the business process from its wait state. BPMN provides a suitable implementation in these cases too.

5.4   Error Handling

As part of the discussion about the significance of BPMN for the implementation of process-driven applications (Sect. 4.1), I presented several process models where a variety of error cases were handled using suitable BPMN constructs (Sect. 4.1.3: Exception Handling; Sect. 4.1.5: Transactions and Compensation). In the following section, I want to discuss how these very different error situations can be detected for process-driven applications and how suitable steps can be taken to resolve (or at least bypass) an error.

Unlike in traditional (tightly coupled) applications, the number of potential errors in loosely coupled scenarios can rise significantly. Just the number of components involved (software, hardware, connections, and so on) and the ways they can be combined give you an impression of the risks we are looking at. On a basic level, we can categorize errors as *technical* errors or *business* errors. Technical errors cannot be predicted and cannot be resolved by the end user of an application. These errors are usually fixed by specialists such as system administrators, experts for special hardware, or software developers. Included in this category are software errors (or bugs), database crashes, router errors, or connection problems. They tend to occur more rarely (ideally) and need to be detected and fixed as quickly as possible, since they usually affect a large number of users.

Business errors/exceptions on the other hand can be predicted and hence are a part of the regular business logic. They occur much more often and need to be handled explicitly in the specification of an application, for example in the validation logic on the UI and, if violated, in appropriate error messages. Another option is to use suitable BPMN constructs at the process level, as shown in Sect. 4.1.3. There are a limitless number of examples in this error category, since they come from everyday business scenarios. For instance, users can make typing errors, enter incorrect product numbers, specify incompatible input fields (for example, the end date is before the start date), or encounter products that are no longer available. The last example in particular indicates that write conflicts in loosely coupled scenarios are to be included in this category: These errors are predictable, hence they require a conflict resolution strategy.

The question now surely arises, how can both of these sources of errors be handled in process-driven applications, including the service contract implementation layer? Let us first consider the process-driven application itself. It is relatively simple to implement error handling here: Business errors can be shown to the end user directly on the UI. The user is also the best person to resolve the error, due to his or her business knowledge. The software supports end users using appropriate validation logic. Technical problems can also be detected immediately, since only synchronous calls should be produced by the UI. For the end user, however, they need to be presented as user-friendly, meaningful messages. Presenting the user with a Java stack trace, for example, makes little sense. Ideally, a service team should be informed automatically in the background in cases like these and respond to the problem as quickly as possible.

In asynchronous scenarios, error handling is divided between the process-driven application and the service contract implementation layer. In accordance with the service contract, the business process passes the data gathered during its process flow to the technical process, asynchronously. From this point in time, the technical process is responsible for any further error handling. Only the business error messages specified in the service contract are returned to the waiting process. This process is, by definition, prepared for the error and can address it using a suitable sequence flow in the BPMN model and handle it explicitly and correctly.

Technical errors, on the other hand, must be processed in full in the service contract implementation layer, since a process-driven application does not recognize any connected systems. The process-driven application and back-end systems are separated from each other by asynchronous communication, which means that the initiator of the communication cannot be consulted immediately anyway.

Instead, the technical process has several error handling strategies at its disposal. Temporary conflicts (such as locked objects) can, for example, be addressed using an automatic retry mechanism: After a specified delay, the failed call is simply tried again. The number of retries and the time delay can be configured to meet your requirements. For example, it is possible to specify whether the call is retried after a specific (constant) interval or whether the wait time increases automatically after each error using an algorithm. Furthermore, an escalation can be initiated if the defined number of retries is reached and an expert (business and/or technical, depending on the error) can be brought in. If automatic error resolution fails, therefore, the next stage is to attempt a manual correction. In this case, a business expert can make corrections to the data in place of the end user of the process-driven application and ensure that it can be processed further and correctly. It is often the case, however, that errors in the settings in the back-end systems are the cause of the error. Here too, the expert can provide support and in both cases a restart of the original message guarantees that the process is resumed.

If the message cannot be restarted, however, the data can be entered manually in the back-end system. Business experts are required here too, since they have knowledge of the business processes in the back end and can use this knowledge to perform the transactions in question. If necessary, the expert can consult the end user and discuss the best way of meeting his or her requirements without error.

Today, modern ERP systems support error handling in loosely coupled systems using technical frameworks specialized in the error handling of failed service calls. In SAP back-end systems, for example, forward-error handling (FEH) has become established as described briefly in the following (for details, see SAP 2010d). The aim of this framework is to avoid duplicate work in error handling and during the implementation of services. In a similar way to cross-cutting concerns in aspect-oriented programming, the actual error handling is delegated to the framework and hence removed from the implementation of functions in the service. Here, each service merely defines which errors and conflicts it throws. An individual resolution strategy can be assigned to each error or conflict in an administration console of the framework. This includes, for example, the retry intervals mentioned above, delay strategies, and escalation paths. A framework of this nature therefore also covers a workflow environment that integrates both business and technical experts. If a callback function is also implemented between the service implementation and the error handling framework, the service with the error can also be called back by the framework during error resolution. This enables the service to perform tasks such as closing files or database connections.

Further functions in an FEH framework include the grouping and categorization of errors, to enable them to be processed using uniform strategies. This makes configuration easier, since each error does not need to be assigned a separate handling method. Instead, errors of the same type are placed in the same group and assigned to a category. The category itself is assigned an error handling strategy. This approach is particularly beneficial when a large number of distinct causes of errors are encountered, since it reduces administration overhead significantly.

The errors encountered are listed in a monitoring console at runtime. The strategies already described can be applied depending on the cause of the errors. The framework guarantees that errors are handled quickly using escalation paths and appropriate notifications and also organizes communication with the services in question using the callback interface. The monitoring of error handling using a central framework makes it possible to trace the route of a message through the infrastructure at any time. The increasing compliance requirements in many of today's enterprises make the ability to trace how errors are handled a significant factor.

5.5   Wizard UIs vs. UIs in Process Steps

A recurring problem when implementing process-driven applications is the development of UIs. Within a process-driven application, we can use a UI either at the start of a process or during process execution as the implementation of a process step. Here, the technical requirements made on UIs for process-driven applications are significantly more demanding than for classic applications, where programming only takes place on a database dedicated to the application. A UI for a process-driven application, on the other hand, must always accommodate the heterogeneity of the system landscape when calling external services, plus associated problems such as transactionality, an increased likelihood of downtime in the systems, and increased response times. For this reason, I recommend in this book that you process the synchronous calls from the UIs only and that you pass the write operations asynchronously to the service contract implementation layer in a follow-on process step. Furthermore, tasks in process-driven applications are usually performed by different roles and they are consequently distributed to the process participants using task lists. From the task list, the end user navigates to the UI that is assigned to the process step in question. This method differs fundamentally from traditional, data-driven applications where end users call fixed transactions (and hence UIs) actively.

In the case of process-driven applications, we now need to tackle the question of how granular the UIs of a process step need to be. We know that the UI for a process-driven application has to be role-oriented and must cover the maximum number of functions possible at execution time. Conversely, this requirement makes fine-grained UIs associated with each other for the same role using *two process steps* superfluous. Modeling two BPMN user tasks in direct sequence for one and the same role is therefore redundant. On the contrary, a process modeled in this way demands to be routed through the task list to proceed to the next process step. This behavior is often annoying and to keep complex UIs usable, it is a good idea to implement wizards or use tabs. In a wizard, we split the UI into related screens that the end user has to process (the screen sequence is defined by the UI itself). In the example implementation from Sect. 4.2.4, a wizard of this type was used to enter an order and save it locally. This gives the UI a process-like quality, without actually having to access an over-heavy process. The procedure also enables the developer to develop complex logic, while keeping it usable. The end user, on the other hand, can make corrections at any time simply by navigating back along the wizard screens. At the end of the wizard, the local write to the database of the process-driven application takes place, before the back-end systems are updated in an automated follow-on process step.

One alternative to a wizard is to use tabs. A complex UI can be divided into multiple tab pages, with associated data bundled under each tab (as in the wizard UI). The difference between the wizard and the tab method is that each screen can be accessed at any time. In a wizard the end user must move backwards and forwards to get to a particular screen, but in the tab method, any page can be selected at any time in the tab method and the relevant data entered. This method is always recommended if the data on each screen is not associated with the data on the other screens. Wizards, on the other hand, are best used whenever the content of a follow-on screen is determined by the input on the preceding screen.

Regardless of which method is chosen, they both help to structure the complex, role-oriented UIs often encountered in process-driven applications and also prevent two consecutive user tasks from being used for one and the same role within a process.

As repeated throughout this book, only synchronous calls should be made from UIs, to ensure short response times and increase the acceptance of process-driven applications. Synchronous calls too, however, require service contract interfaces to be defined. The implementation of these interfaces though is designed with performance requirements in mind. This means you should choose the technology with the best performance for the involved systems. If the response times encountered in load tests are still not acceptable, however, caching needs to be considered as an optimization method. If this does not improve things either, the alternative is to make a local copy of the data in the database of the process-driven application. This is no rare situation, as shown by real implementations of process-driven applications in practice. Master data (such as customer data, vendor data, or product master data) is especially suited here, since it is rarely modified and, particularly in large enterprises, processes for distributing master data changes are well established. This makes it a relatively simple task to add a new receiver for changes.

The requirement that only synchronous calls are made from UIs can cause problems if the functions needed in the back-end systems can only be provided asynchronously. In these cases, a synchronous-asynchronous bridge has proved to be useful, as shown in the form of a BPMN pattern in Fig. 5.4.

Fig. 5.4 Synchronous-asynchronous bridge

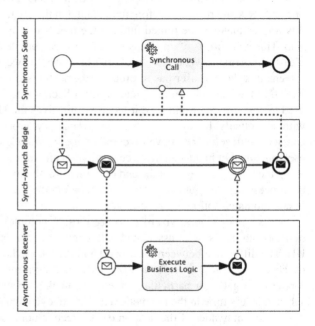

The synchronous sender requests a service that can only be provided asynchronously by the back end. Figure 5.4 shows nicely how the synchronous-asynchronous bridge preserves the technical connection to the synchronous caller, while the bridge itself calls the receiver asynchronously. It then waits (using the intermediate message event) for the response from the back-end system in the usual way. In SAP BPM, this behavior is produced, for example, by assigning the same synchronous interface to the message-based start and end events of the synchronous-asynchronous bridge. This signalizes to the framework that the process is being called synchronously and hence the connection to the caller must not be broken once the data is passed.

Once the response is received from the asynchronous receiver, the message-based end event immediately forwards the result to the waiting caller.

The reverse case is also a possibility, where the process-driven application demands asynchronous processing, but the back-end system only provides synchronous services. In this scenario, the asynchronous-synchronous bridge is also a good idea, and is itself shown as a BPMN pattern in Fig. 5.5.

Fig. 5.5 Asynchronous-synchronous bridge

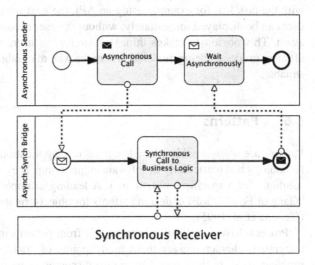

This time, the sender makes an asynchronous call and waits at the receive task. The asynchronous-synchronous bridge itself calls the business logic synchronously in the back-end system and packs the received response in a message, which itself releases the sender from its wait state.

It is clear that both bridges are intermediaries between the process-driven application on the one hand and the back-end systems on the other. This makes them part of the implementation repertoire of the service contract implementation layer. This is how the different communication demands (synchronous and asynchronous) made on the composite application are handled.

The final part of this section discusses another method for synchronizing the demands of loose coupling with UIs. Erl 2008 refers to the *UI Mediator Pattern*, which recommends using a service human interaction layer (SHIL). This layer simulates synchronism with the waiting end user by showing the status of the back-end query during execution of the asynchronous back-end calls. These screens are displayed depending on the response time behavior of the back-end systems. If the response is made immediately (for example, in under two seconds), the screen is displayed right away without an intermediate dialog. If more than two seconds pass without a response, however, the SHIL displays a dialog informing the user about the delay. If a second period of time then also passes (for example, a total of 12 s), a timeout occurs and a second dialog informs the user that the service is currently not available.

The basis of SHIL is a synchronous-asynchronous bridge with extended functions for controlling the dialog with the end user. In a more advanced variant, SHIL operates across process steps, in cases where two consecutive steps of one and the same role were modeled as two separate user tasks. Usually, the end user has to navigate to the second step using a task list. If, however, the SHIL is able to operate with the task list, for example using an API, the next interactive step for the same user can be displayed immediately, without the user needing to consult the task list again. This obviously makes things easier for the user, but can also lead to less efficient processes being modeled, where the wizard or tabs methods would be more suitable.

5.6　Patterns

Patterns are indispensable when designing new applications in modern information technology and particularly in software engineering. They represent tried and tested solutions for a specific problem area. A leading example here is the work of the "Gang of Four" (GoF) in design patterns for object-oriented software development (Gamma et al. 1995).

Process-driven applications can benefit from patterns in many ways, since their integrative character gives them many points of contact with a wide range of problem areas. In this book, I have also discussed some pattern-like solutions, for example in the discussions about the synchronous-asynchronous bridge in the preceding section, about the variety of UI technologies, or about the different process solutions using BPMN in Sect. 4.1. It is not my aim here to examine each individual pattern known from the literature and judge its relevance for the different layers in a process-driven application. Instead, I want to move the focus to the handling of patterns for the service contract implementation layer, since this layer plays a central role in the development of process-driven applications. The technical processes are handled by this layer, which is why the rest of this chapter discusses various process fragments for different problems in this layer. The modeling language used to implement the patterns is (of course) BPMN.

The description of the architecture of process-driven applications makes it clear that the service contract implementation layer (from the composite to the service contract) is given a focused job, to provide a specific business function. This is then implemented by reusing existing functions from legacy systems. Here, the implementation layer actively gathers information from the back-end systems or triggers activities or standard processes there. The implementation layer is therefore given an *active* part. Patterns like this are discussed in the section *Composition Patterns*.

Unlike the composition patterns, integration-centric patterns tend to be *passive*. They are instantiated by specific messages on the composite side and do not approach the back-end systems actively to gather information. Instead they wait passively for relevant messages, messages that are forced by defined business process flows. They then take the information needed by the process-driven application from these messages and send it to the composite.

As usual in patterns, I will sketch the problem addressed by the pattern in the following and then explain a possible solution (or solutions) using BPMN process fragments. These process fragments can be interpreted and executed by BPMN engines, which means that the following models are to be seen as executable program code. The finished process diagrams are therefore suitable to be used directly in your own implementations.

I would also like to note that I do not handle any workflow patterns in this section, as typically required by the user-centric processes of a process-driven application (business composition). They are discussed in depth, both theoretically as workflow patterns by Professor van der Aalst (van der Aalst et al. 2003) and in their implementations in BPMN diagrams or in UML 2.0 activity diagrams (in White 2004).

5.6.1 Composition Patterns

In this section, I discuss the various composition patterns used within the service contract implementation layer. They are characterized by an active role in the implementation layer, which means that, after the data is passed, the contract is met actively by calling service providers.

The first pattern addresses the most simple case of service fulfillment, when a request is forwarded to one system only and this system provides the service in full. This is known as a classic request-reply integration pattern (Hohpe and Woolf 2004) and is shown in Fig. 5.6.

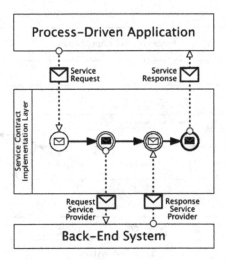

Fig. 5.6 Request-reply integration pattern

The process-driven application sends a message to the implementation layer, in accordance with the agreed contract. The implementation layer itself forwards the message (asynchronously) to the back-end system in question and then waits for its response. The message-based intermediate event is used here too. Once the response has been received, it is passed to the waiting composite. This layer is responsible for protocol and data format adjustments, alongside the actual sending of messages. In this way, the message received from the composite is transformed from the canonical data model of the process-driven application to the target format of the target application. This involves both structure mappings and data mappings. Structure mappings communicate between different data structures and map fields with the same semantics. The fields can be assigned directly in the differing data structures but they either have different names in the source and target structures or they are located on different hierarchical levels. Data mappings are always needed in cases where data transformations have to be made in accordance with specific conversion rules. The most simple type of transformation is the switch between different data types, such as from String to Float or from Date to String. A further example is the merging or splitting of fields, for example the first and last names can be separate in the received message for a customer structure, but the target format requires both name parts to be in the same field. Finally, it can also be the case that the field content needs to be changed completely. For example, a source system may only use consecutive numbers to represent a form of address (1=Ms, 2=Mr), whereas the target system requires plain text. These tasks and others also need to be implemented in the service contract implementation layer.

In the example above we only need one system as a service provider, but if multiple systems are involved the process flow changes as shown in Fig. 5.7.

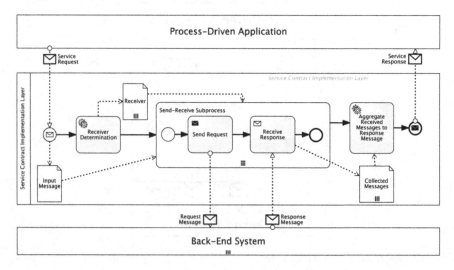

Fig. 5.7 Request-reply integration pattern with multiple systems in sequence

Multiple systems need to be triggered for a single inbound message to provide a service. The list of the receivers is determined at runtime and saved in a data object. Then, the systems are queried one after the other as made clear by the sequential multi-instance subprocess. The back-end systems in question are addressed using one and the same data format and also respond using a unified format. This is shown in the model in the messages *Request Message* and *Reply Message*. This model is useful whenever the addressed back ends are similar types, for example SAP systems with the same release level but in different regions. Once all messages are received, they are packed as a response message for the process-driven application and sent.

This scenario assumes that processing is done sequentially. It is indicated by the *sequential multi-instance marker* (≡) in the *send-receive subprocess*. If, however, processing in each back-end is fully standalone and independent from the other back ends, these back ends can be addressed in parallel as well. BPMN represents this using a parallel multi-instance marker,(III), as shown in Fig. 5.8.

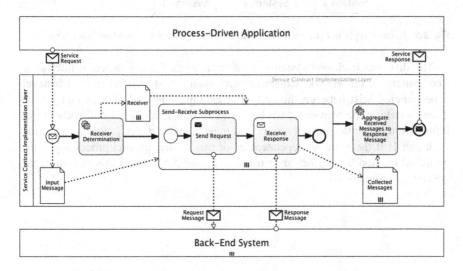

Fig. 5.8 Request-reply integration pattern with multiple systems in parallel

What can also be seen here is parallel execution in the back-end systems, also indicated by the multi-instance marker. As before, this pattern also assumes that the messages for the addressed systems are of the same type. This is not able to be implemented, however, in typical scenarios for process-driven applications, since highly heterogeneous landscapes and varying interfaces and protocols are encountered in the enterprises for historical reasons. The pattern shown in Fig. 5.9 is a good solution to this problem.

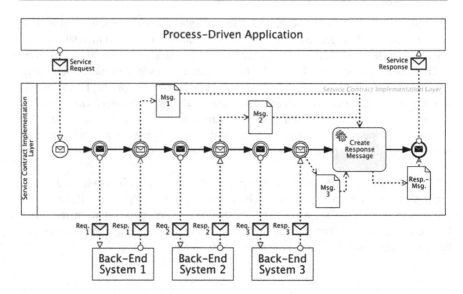

Fig. 5.9 Request-reply integration pattern with multiple systems with different interfaces

The different back-end systems are now addressed using different interfaces. The pattern itself shows sequential processing first, to be used whenever dependencies exist between the calls. For example, the call of back-end system 2 uses a field in the response from back-end system 1. Making a call without this information is pointless and hence the call must be made directly after the call from back-end 1. If there are no dependencies of this nature, parallel processing is the preferred method for performance reasons. Figure 5.10 shows this pattern in the BPMN representation.

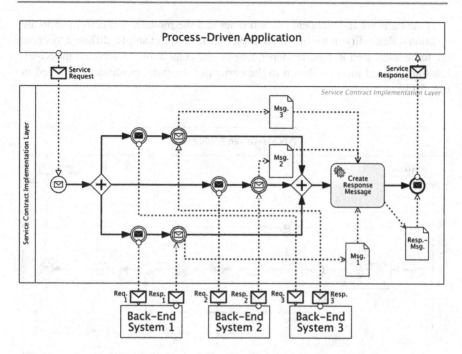

Fig. 5.10 Request-reply integration pattern with multiple systems in parallel with different interfaces

The parallel gateway starts the sequence flow at the same time in all three outbound paths and addresses the back-end systems using different interfaces (as expressed by the three different requests and replies in the model). The parallel gateway at the end of the three send-receive paths forces the sequence flow to continue by creating the reply message only after all replies from the back-end systems are received. This pattern is preferable to the sequence pattern for performance reasons (if usable in the scenario in question). In actual fact, it is the dependency criterion that specifies which method is used.

One further benefit of this pattern is its implicit solution of the problem that the reply messages are not always received in the order they were sent. In Hohpe and Woolf's *Enterprise Integration Patterns* it is the *Resequencer Pattern* (Hohpe and Woolf 2004, page 283) that solves this problem explicitly. The parallel gateway or, as will be seen in a further example, the inclusive gateway, solves the problem automatically. Since the gateways in question wait for different messages in parallel and the paths are synchronized in the gateway, it is guaranteed that all required messages are received in the sequence flow after the gateway, regardless of which order they arrive in. Unlike the resequencer (in which the received messages are then sent individually and in a different order), the pattern presented here creates and sends only one message, however the problem of the messages being received in different orders is the same in both patterns.

If the calls are independent of each other and the modeler wants to incorporate additional flexibility in his or her solution (because, for example, different systems are to be addressed in parallel depending on the content of the inbound message), rules are a good idea, as shown in the variant of the parallel scenario depicted in Fig. 5.11.

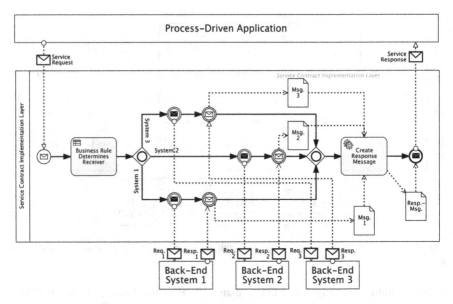

Fig. 5.11 Using rules to determine the receivers in the request-reply pattern

The task of the type *Business Rule* (⊞) uses the message content to determine the next steps in the flow by finding the systems involved for the subsequent inclusive gateway. This means that the gateway only passes tokens to the paths whose associated condition matches the condition of the business rule. The condition for a path does not need to be complicated, and in fact the rule could create a list of system names. Each system name corresponds to precisely one path that leaves the inclusive gateway. Hence the condition for each path is merely whether the system name representing the path exists in the list.

The paths activated in parallel are themselves merged using an inclusive gateway. In the semantics of the merged inclusive gateway, the BPMN specification stipulates that a token is not passed to the outbound path until all original paths have been closed. This is exactly the required behavior at this point.

The use of rules provides additional flexibility for executable processes. This approach also offers further benefits for process-driven applications, which is why we will look at it in more depth in a separate Sect. 5.7.

In the composition patterns used until now, the systems contacted asynchronously responded directly to the requests from the service contract implementation layer with a suitable reply message, also sent asynchronously. But what is the procedure when systems provide write or change operations in an interface, but do not themselves react directly and actively with messages? How can the process-driven application be released from its wait state in these cases? The solution here is based on cyclical queries of states of the modified business objects in the back-end systems in question. Each business system usually offers search and read operations on its managed objects and these operations are in fact usually synchronous. The implementation layer therefore reads and checks the content of this object using this read interface, to check whether the latest changes were processed. This check is made more simple using status fields that are usually a part of the object. If the required state is achieved, the process-driven application can be informed of the success of the operation. This wait to receive the required state is often associated with multiple read calls, which is why this pattern is a classic polling (see also Sect. 5.3 about the use of events to release a process-driven application from a wait state, where polling is also used appropriately).

The behavior can be explained when creating or changing an order: The back end is informed about the new order asynchronously, but itself does not create a separate confirmation message. The back end is therefore polled at regular intervals, such as when a new order is created using the *search interface* (because no order number that can be referenced exists yet due to the asynchronous processing) and when changes are made using the *read interface* with the order number as a pass-by parameter. In the case of the search interface, a suitable search parameter combination must guarantee the uniqueness of the new order as the search hit. In the case of purchase orders, this is often done by simply providing a unique purchaser reference number, passed with the purchase order. If the search itself does not return the required object immediately, the order data must be read again in this case. Finally, many potential criteria can be used to identify whether the original operation succeeded or failed. This state is of course highly dependent on the system in question, but one or more of the following criteria are applicable:

- When checking a status field, is the order now in the expected state?
- When checking the error status, did the last change cause an error? If yes, the associated error message must be analyzed.
- When checking the order history, does the order history contain the last change made to the order?
- When checking specific fields, does the order contain the changes?

When polling is implemented in BPMN, one of several variants can be selected. Figure 5.12 shows an initial variant where the system in question is queried synchronously and the read loop is modeled explicitly.

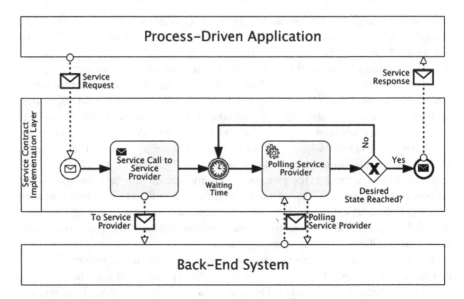

Fig. 5.12 Synchronous polling with explicit read loop

The process flow is triggered by the inbound message of the process-driven application. The service request is, as usual, passed to the business application asynchronously. The process is then passed to a wait state, which gives the back end time to update the request. Polling could of course take place immediately at this point. However, the extended runtimes in the back end increase the risk of a negative response significantly, since services have a low level of granularity by definition and have a specific business scope. This means it is not enough for a purchase order just to create an entry in a database table. It is more likely, for example, that a stock check is triggered, production started up, and vendors involved. The decision about the positioning of the timer in the BPMN model is, after all, dependent on the scenario in question and the actual functions provided by the called service.

Once the wait time has ended, a synchronous call is made to determine the object state. After this, the exclusive gateway detects whether the required target state has been reached. If this is the case, the process-driven application can be released from its wait situation. Otherwise, there is a wait at the timer intermediate event and the polling cycle starts again.

A more elegant way of monitoring for errors in polling that also provides more options, is modeling using subprocesses, as shown in Fig. 5.13.

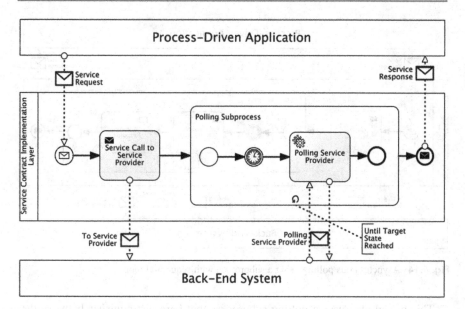

Fig. 5.13 Synchronous polling using a subprocess with sequential loop

This is characterized by the embedding of the polling activity in a standalone subprocess. This process is given a standard loop marker, since the number of loop passes is not known in advance and can only be identified once the target state is reached. Using the subprocess makes further improvements possible, since boundary events make it easier to monitor polling and to handle errors. We have already discussed appropriate error handling strategies at several points in this book, for example in Sect. 4.1.3 under the general topic of troubleshooting as part of BPMN. The solutions presented there can also be applied to monitoring in the context of polling and troubleshooting.

The two BPMN polling models we have looked at demand that the state is queried synchronously in the back-end system. If the back-end system only provides the services asynchronously, however, the model must be modified, as shown in Fig. 5.14.

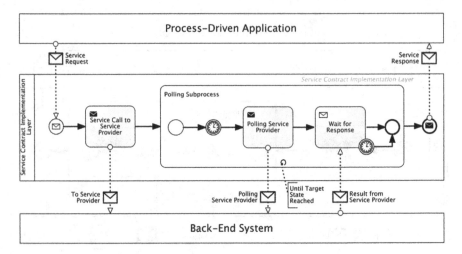

Fig. 5.14 Asynchronous polling using a subprocess with sequential loop

This model also uses a polling subprocess that here distinguishes between the separated calls for polling dispatch and polling receipt. Furthermore, the receive task W*ait for Response* is monitored using a timer boundary event to prevent it from waiting for the reply infinitely. Instead, a new polling cycle can start directly after the timer ends.

Within the architecture of process-driven applications, composite patterns are responsible for the important aspect of communicating between the final application and the business applications. They are characterized by their *active role* in the implementation of the service contract. Up until now, we have assumed that the reply can be sent back from the service provider in one *composite message*, but this is not always the case. The size of a message can, in certain situations, demand that it be split into fragments that are sent individually and combined again at the receiver side. The best way of proceeding in these cases is described in the following section about integration-centric patterns.

5.6.2   Integration-Centric Patterns

Unlike composition patterns, integration patterns are characterized by waiting *passively* for messages to be received, instead of actively requesting them using service calls (as shown in the preceding section). The focus here is on patterns in which the reply message does not comprise a single message but is instead provided in parts for technical or business reasons. A technical reason could be that the total size of the reply is too big to be communicated in full; a business reason could be due to the different ways that the individual parts of a service call are handled. For example, if the items in a purchase order are processed differently due to the products in question, individual messages are produced. The service caller, on the other hand, expects a complete message for the full purchase order, which can be processed further as such. In this case, the service contract implementation layer must modify its behavior when compared to the composition patterns. It must now wait passively for the individual parts of the message until a specific final criterion is met and the further processing can be triggered. This pattern is also known in the literature as an *aggregator* (Hohpe and Woolf 2004). Depending on the end criterion, there are various potential scenarios, which we will look at in the following. At the same time, the BPMN models depict only the collecting of the individual message fragments and therefore only the interaction between the back-end systems and the implementation layer. The process-driven application only appears in the models as a receiver of the full message. This is not a problem, however, since we are at the technical process level and our consistent separation of the layers allows us to test different implementations in the service contract implementation layer without affecting the process-driven application.

There is, however, one further interesting pattern for integration-centric processes, the *resequencer* (Hohpe and Woolf 2004). The resequencer also handles multiple messages, but unlike the aggregator it does not collect the messages with the aim of sending them to the target system as a single message and merely puts them in the correct order instead (the order in which the process-driven application expects them). In projects in the real world, the requirement to preserve the order of the messages is often encountered. The resequencer is the solution to this requirement and can meet it in various ways, for example it can work with only a single message type and the message parts are simply numbered sequentially or it must sort different messages defined using different interfaces. Another aspect to be considered by the resequencer is the question of whether all messages actually need to be received or whether the check on the order of the messages can be applied to a selected set of messages only. The final variant of interest is whether the resequencer is instantiated using a dedicated start message or whether it can (in principle) be started by any message in the sequence. We will examine all these questions in the section about the resequencer.

5.6.2.1 Aggregator Pattern

The aggregator pattern implements various end criteria for the aggregation, for example waiting for a specific number of messages, waiting for a dedicated end message, or waiting for a timer to finish. The example that follows defines completion using a total number of messages that need to be received. This total number is passed to the process in a specific field in the first message. The associated BPMN model is shown in Fig. 5.15.

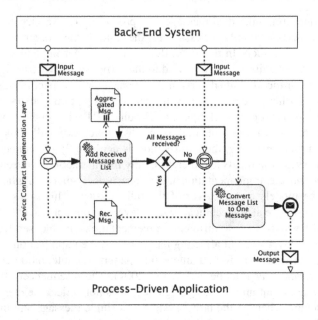

Fig. 5.15 Aggregator pattern with explicitly modeled wait loop

Once again, this model shows us the explicit modeling of the wait loop, ended when the last expected message is received. We can also see the explicit steps required to collect the messages in a separate data object and the transformation of the resulting message list to an outbound message. The inbound messages represent identical interfaces, as shown by their identical names (*Input Message*). This is important, since it expresses that the process only handles messages of the same type. The correlation condition for the intermediate message event is specified by the implemented scenario and could, in the case of order handling, be the unique order number to which the items belong.

One alternative to the explicit modeling of the wait loop is a subprocess with a sequential multi-instance marker, as shown in the model in Fig. 5.16.

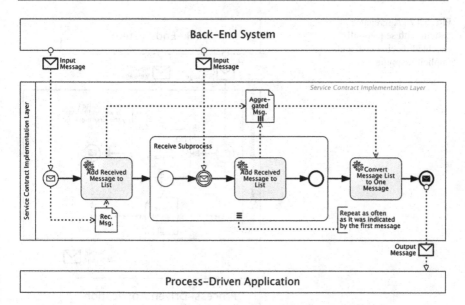

Fig. 5.16 Aggregator pattern with subprocess and sequential multi-instance marker

The number of loop passes is known at runtime, which is why the *Receive Subprocess* has a sequential multi-instance marker. The advantage of using a subprocess is the combination with boundary events for monitoring errors or time.

Both models include the collection of messages in a separate data object and the explicit creation of the result message using service tasks. This becomes unnecessary when the implementation of the BPMN specification supports the data mapping in the form discussed in the implementation chapter (with SAP Business Process Management). Here, the data content of a task was passed to the process context when a task was exited, with the process context itself consisting of all the data objects used in the model. Conversely, the content of the process context was passed to the step in question when a task was reached. If we consider this behavior of the process model, the implementation becomes even more compact, as shown in Fig. 5.17.

Fig. 5.17 Aggregator
pattern with sequentially
executed receive task and
implicit mapping

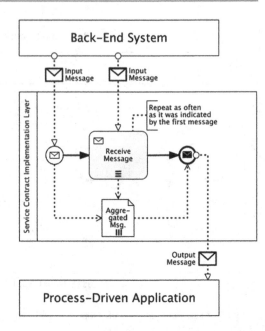

When exited, the message start event uses an implicit output mapping to add the first message to the collected list of messages. The use of the receive task instead of the intermediate message event is a further change here. Since the sequential multi-instance marker can also be added to this task, there is no need for explicit loop modeling for the time-consuming Receive Subprocess anymore. Furthermore, the received message is added to the data object *Aggregated Msg.* here too, using an (implicit) mapping. Finally, once the sending end event is reached, the message list is transformed to the data structure of the outbound message. The directed associations used here enable the data flow to be modeled in detail in this context.

All three models cancel the loop once the total number of expected messages specified in the first message is reached. This prerequisite is not, however, valid for all scenarios. In processes involving price bids, for example auctions, the time factor can be the limiting criterion. In this case, the arrival of the message is canceled when a timer runs out. Figure 5.18 depicts the process flow using a subprocess with a boundary timer event.

Fig. 5.18 Aggregator
pattern with time as end
criterion for the subprocess

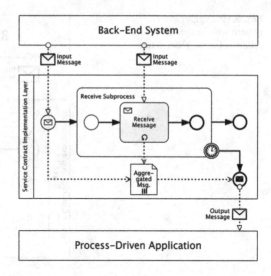

Unlike in Fig. 5.17, we have replaced the sequential multi-instance marker in the receive task with a standard loop marker, since the number of loop passes is not known when the process starts its execution. Furthermore, the receive task is now located in a subprocess, which itself is monitored by the timer boundary event. Once the time period specified for receiving the messages runs out, the receiver loop is interrupted and the information collected up to this point is sent to the process-driven application in a message. Of course, this pattern is not just restricted to attaching the timer event and can also be reused for other events such as messages, conditions, or signals.

When examining this model, the question arises of whether the work involved with the subprocess (which contains only the receive task) is worthwhile or whether the timer boundary event can be attached to the receive task as shown in Fig. 5.19.

Fig. 5.19 Aggregator
pattern with time as end
criterion for the receive task

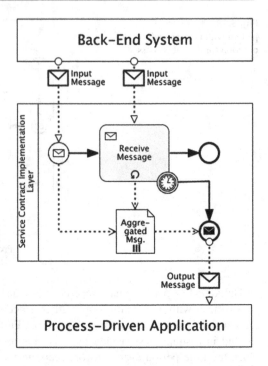

A comparison of the two models again emphasizes the significance of the validity scope of a boundary event. In the first case (Fig. 5.18), the validity scope can be found easily, since the entire subprocess and its encapsulated receiver loop are monitored. The subprocess is not exited during the loop pass, which means that the timer is not restarted each time a new message arrives. The model is semantically correct but how does it behave in the process from Fig. 5.19? Does the timer boundary event refer to the full loop or only to the arrival of a single message, which means that the timer is reset each time a message arrives? The BPMN 2.0 specification (OMG 2011, page 432) has the following to say:

"The loop activity is a type of activity that acts as a wrapper for an inner activity that can be executed multiple times in sequence.

Operational semantics: Attributes can be set to determine the behavior. The loop activity executes the inner activity as long as the `loopCondition` evaluates to `true`."

The loop activity does *contain* the receive task and hence the timer boundary event also refers to the loop and not to the individual task. This means that both models define the same behavior and I leave it up to you to pick a variant.

A further possible end criterion for the aggregator loop is to receive a dedicated end message. BPMN offers several interesting modeling options here and Fig. 5.20 shows one solution in the form of an explicit loop.

Fig. 5.20 Aggregator
pattern with dedicated end
message as end criterion
modeled as event-based
gateway

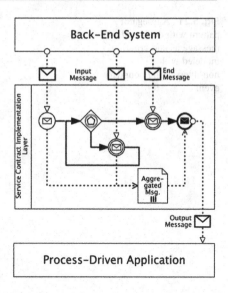

Once the process is started by the inbound message, it waits at the event-based
gateway for one of two different message types to arrive, depicted with different
names in the model. Further inbound messages are collected in the loop as usual,
whereas the end message stops the receiver loop when it arrives and also sends the
collected message to the process-driven application.

In this case too, the subprocess approach can be reused (instead of explicit
modeling) as in the context of a timer boundary intermediate event in Fig. 5.18.
In the figure, only the timer boundary event needs to be replaced by a message-
based boundary event. Hence the subprocess (which contains only the receive task
with standard loop marker) is interrupted by the arrival of the end message instead
of the timer running out. The remaining logic is not affected by this change.

A further interesting alternative is shown in Fig. 5.21.

Fig. 5.21 Aggregator
pattern with dedicated end
message as end criterion
modeled with
non-interrupting boundary
event

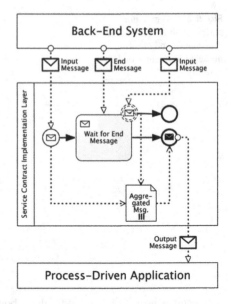

This model waits for the end message (!) at a receive task to arrive once the first inbound message has kicked off the process at the message start event. A non-interrupting message-based boundary event was attached to the receive task, however, which responds to arriving normal inbound messages. This makes it possible to process multiple messages that arrive at the same time in parallel, improving performance. The individual parallel paths end in a none end event, which means they do not end the full process. Instead, the process does not reach the message-based end event until the end message is received. The process flow is then complete.

To round off this discussion of patterns for aggregating messages, I would like to point to two special cases. In all cases we have seen so far, the aggregator process is initiated using exactly one well-defined start message. There are potential cases, however, in which activities are triggered in different systems and it is not possible to predict which system responds first. Another difficulty is that the systems respond using different interfaces. Hence the process must be prepared to receive different messages in an unknown order. A typical scenario for this problem is the merging of customer information from different systems, for example we may need to take classic customer master data and add account details, creditworthiness, purchasing history, recent orders, and so on. These data records can be requested from the back-end systems independently of each other, and only the order of the responses is unknown. A potential solution to this problem is shown in Fig. 5.22.

Fig. 5.22 Aggregator pattern with messages received in unknown order

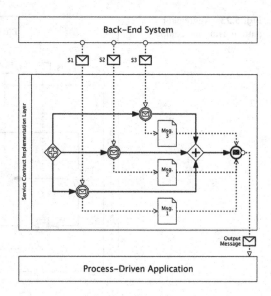

This model is characterized by its use of the parallel event-based gateway to instantiate the process right at the start of the sequence flow. This gateway is used to start the process as soon as one of the post-gateway events occurs. This means that one of the three messages represented by the different interfaces *S1*, *S2*, and *S3* are significant for the start of the process. After starting, the process waits for the remaining messages and the sequence flow continues by sending the collected result (using the message-based end event) only after they are received. All three messages are guaranteed to be received by using the parallel gateway in the merging of the parallel paths.

In conclusion, I would like to take a look at a slight modification of the scenario just described: In this example, we defined how the merge took place using the parallel gateway. Hence the process had to wait for all outstanding messages, but this is not necessary in all situations. In some circumstances, data is preserved redundantly in various back-end systems. These systems can be addressed independently and the same type of data can be requested from them. The balancing of the current load on the business systems determines the different response times of the systems. If, in this case, system A provides data that would also be provided by system B, it is pointless to wait for a response from system B. The required data is already there. On the other hand, it can be a good idea to contact multiple systems for the same data, since this makes the solutions more robust and improves overall availability. Furthermore, the response time for the process-driven application is reduced. In this case, however, the parallel gateway cannot be accessed to merge the parallel paths and the inclusive and exclusive gateways can't be used either as they don't provide the functionality needed here. In cases like this, BPMN provides the complex gateway instead, where any conditions can be defined for merges. Figure 5.23 depicts this approach.

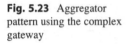

Fig. 5.23 Aggregator
pattern using the complex
gateway

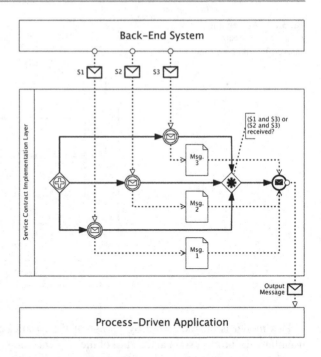

The model, however, can only be understood using the additional comment describing which conditions were actually assigned to the gateway. In the example above, therefore, this means that the process flow is resumed as soon as either the messages *S1* and *S3* or *S2* and *S3* are received. In this case, S1 and S2 must have the same type of data.

In the case of executable processes, the conditions must be formulated in the way shown in the implementation example from Chap. 4 for the paths of the gateway or the correlation condition for the intermediate message event. The use of the complex gateway provides the modeler with a new level of flexibility in cases like this.

5.6.2.2 Resequencer Pattern

The most important function of the resequencer pattern is the way it resequences associated messages in the order originally specified by the sender when they arrive. A classic example of this is when large messages are split into multiple smaller fragments on the sender side. These individual message blocks are passed to the network practically simultaneously and arrive in the resequencer at the receiver side in a different order, due to differences in runtimes, in particular in the communication between partners across WAN (wide area networks). Since the receiver cannot process the original large message as a complete message either, it is important that the fragments at least arrive in the correct order, and this is where the resequencer helps.

There are many potential constellations for the resequencer:

- Does the resequencer only handle messages of the same type or can the messages have different types?
- Do all messages need to be received or is there a distinction between mandatory and optional messages?
- Is there a dedicated start message that is guaranteed to arrive first or can any message in the sequence start the resequencer?

In this section, I concentrate only on the handling of messages with different types in the resequencer, where all messages need to be received. This does not mean I intend to neglect the other cases; they will be discussed in other sections. The handling of messages with the same type is described in Sect. 5.6.3.9 and the resequencing to a correct order in the case of mandatory and optional messages is described in Sect. 5.7.2.

Let us begin with the different ways in which the resequencer pattern can be implemented. We can further restrict the number of potential models, since the guaranteed arrival of a dedicated start message is a simplified special case of the more generic case where *any* of the messages can start the process. A first solution is shown in Fig. 5.24:

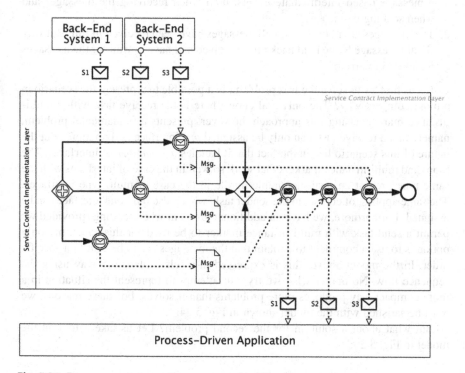

Fig. 5.24 Resequencer pattern with messages received in unknown order

As already shown in the aggregator pattern from Fig. 5.22, we use the instantiating parallel event-based gateway at the start of the process. This means that the start of the process is guaranteed as soon as one of the post-gateway events occurs. Hence, any of the messages *S1*, *S2*, or *S3* can trigger the instantiation. After starting, the process waits for the remaining messages and the sequence flow continues by sending the single messages in the correct order (using the throwing message-based intermediate events) only after they are received. All three messages are guaranteed to be received by using the parallel gateway in the merging of the parallel paths. If you look more carefully at the model, you will notice the explicit modeling of the sender systems using separate pools. The motivation here is relatively simple, namely since the messages have different types, they are most probably sent from different systems. If more than one of the message types involved is actually sent by a single system, we can of course reflect this using multiple message flows from the associated pool, as we did for *Back-End System 2* in the Fig. 5.24. Could we also represent the different sender systems using just one pool with a multi-instance marker? I do not see a problem here personally, but important information will be lost. The model no longer tells us here which system sent which message. More serious are the following two aspects:

1. A dedicated message with a dedicated associated event exists for each interface. In more complex sequences with n potential messages, we would have to model n message-based intermediate events, both when receiving the messages and when sending them.
2. The messages are not sent until all messages have been received in full. But why should message S1 be held back once received and have to wait for the messages S2 and S3 to arrive?

Let us first try to solve the first problem. Is it possible to represent the scenario in a more compact way? The only real choice here is the receive task with a multi-instance marker. Using this approach, however, presents a fundamental problem, namely that a receive task can only be assigned *one* interface and no more. But the nature of this scenario lies in the fact that it handles *any number* of interfaces. The loops and multi-instance markers that work so well in the case of interfaces with the same type present an insurmountable hurdle in the case of multi-type interfaces. The same applies, of course, to the sender task, where also only one interface can be assigned. Furthermore, we have an additional problem when sending (provided we permit a send task with multi-instance marker to be used for this case): my only option is to use a comment to explain that the messages are to be sent in a specific order. In the model above, this is expressed in a self-explanatory way using the sequence flow. No matter what we try, our attempt to represent the situation in a more compact way produces more problems than it solves. For these reasons, we must be satisfied with the model shown in Fig. 5.24.

But what about a solution for the second problem? Let us take a look at the model in Fig. 5.25:

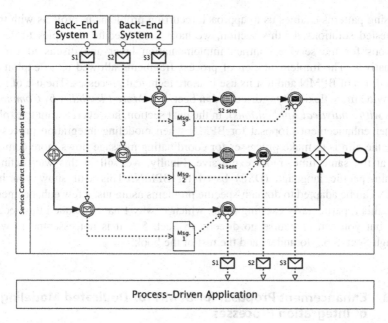

Fig. 5.25 Resequencer pattern with messages received in unknown order and sent immediately (if possible)

Surprisingly, the model for sending messages immediately is (if permitted by the relationships with other messages) similarly simple to the model from Fig. 5.24, in which nothing is dispatched until all messages are received in full. The only thing we need to do is to move the sender steps to the parallel processing branches and implement a catching conditional event to keep the order of the sequence. In detail, the process is again started using an instantiating parallel event-based gateway. The message that arrives first (no matter which one) instantiates the process immediately. After the message *S1* is received, the forwarding of it represented by a throwing message event is triggered immediately in the path of this message. This is because this message must arrive at the receiver first and there are no other relationships with other messages to be respected. The situation in the case of the messages *S2* and *S3* is different. *S2* must wait for the dispatch of *S1* and *S3* must wait for the dispatch of *S2*. This can be modeled in a very compact way in BPMN using the catching conditional event. Accordingly, a corresponding conditional event is located before each throwing message event for *S2* and *S3*. The conditional event makes the relationships to the other messages transparent to the reader of the model in an effective way. Finally, the parallel gateway before the end event synchronizes the paths and ends the process correctly. Hence, we have achieved our aim of implementing the resequencer pattern, namely using suitable BPMN models to dispatch the messages in a specified order while respecting different interfaces and guaranteeing that all messages in the sequence are received.

Using patterns enables us to approach recurring problems in projects with tried and tested solutions. In this section, we have used specific examples to design solutions for the service contract implementation layer and discussed various alternatives. The implementation of process fragments allowed us to exploit the capabilities of BPMN and test its use in more technical processes. The use of rules to provide more flexibility is discussed in Sect. 5.7 (*More Flexibility by Combining Rules with Analytical Applications*). In the next section, however, I want to explain another enhancement proposal for BPMN when modeling integration processes. Here, the aim is to make processes for coordinating message flows more compact and, at the same time, more expressive. Finally, we will in this way define a domain-specific language (DSL) based on BPMN. This will show you how BPMN can be adapted to domain-specific problems using just a few enhancements. I find this a particularly exciting topic, which is why I have included this section here, but you can of course go directly to Sect. 5.7. It is not essential to work through Sect. 5.6.3 to understand the rest of the book.

5.6.3 Enhancement Proposal for BPMN for Dedicated Modeling of Integration Processes

In both of the preceding Sects. 5.6.1 and 5.6.2, we have shown a range of patterns for the service contract implementation layer and how they are implemented using BPMN. It is clear that BPMN is well suited for implementing integration processes due to its many technically oriented components. The question arises of whether it is appropriate to make the enterprise integration pattern, as discussed in Hohpe and Woolf (2004), a component of BPMN. In their book, Hohpe and Woolf provide their own notation, based on simple symbols, with each symbol representing a specific enterprise integration pattern. The symbol in Fig. 5.26, for example, represents the aggregator pattern.

Fig. 5.26 Symbol for the aggregator integration pattern (from Hohpe and Woolf 2004, page 268)

A sequence of these symbols therefore expresses a processing chain (often called a *pipeline* or *route* in the literature or by the vendors of integration products) for a message within an integration solution.

The notation suggested by Hohpe and Woolf (also called *pattern symbols* or *pattern icons* in this section) has established itself in use by integration developers. Pattern symbols are now even supported by the Microsoft product Visio (see EIP 2011), which means that pattern icons can be used to formulate solutions for integration problems highly effectively. Despite this, however, this notation is also missing some important details with respect to semantics at runtime. For example, if the symbol for the aggregator integration pattern from Fig. 5.26 is used, the reader can see that messages are aggregated at this point, but exactly *how* this aggregation takes place, *where* the messages come from, and *the result* produced by the aggregator remains unknown. Furthermore, this notation does not indicate when the aggregation ends, namely whether a predefined fixed number of messages is expected, whether the aggregation ends after a fixed time period, or whether an external event has this task. We must therefore consider whether a combination of BPMN and the pattern symbols is a more expressive solution, providing the reader of the model with far more information than is possible when using only the pattern icons. Finally, a chain of pattern symbols represents a category of process that can benefit widely from the advantages of BPMN already discussed, especially with regard to how event processing can be expressed. The following section discusses this aspect in more detail.

5.6.3.1 Pattern Symbols as BPMN Language Extensions for Meaningful Representation of Integration Processes

It is natural to wonder whether a BPMN extension is really necessary or whether the existing task types already meet the requirements. I could, of course model integration processes using only service tasks, perhaps with an added comment to indicate which pattern is currently being processed by the task in question, but this is not my aim here. After all, we do not want to forget the readers of these models who rely solely on the BPMN sequence and/or message flows to understand what the author wants to say. This is not possible when using only service tasks, since here the semantics are not obvious. In the case of our aggregator patter, for example, it is not possible to detect when the aggregation ends only by using the service task. For this reason, we need more than just one new task type.

To understand my motivation for the language extension, a comparison with the existing BPMN task types may be useful: Even in its current form, BPMN contains task types that are not absolutely necessary: for example, the business rule task can be seen as a type of service. Here, too, I could exploit the service task to indicate a rule call. However, the business rule task also has its validity, for example a modeler could formulate in a much more detailed way in his process model that the services of a rules engine are used when the business rule task is reached. It is this type of precision at the business process level that I want to achieve for integration processes and the extension is, to my mind, more than justified.

In their book, Hohpe and Woolf discuss no fewer than 65 integration patterns, not all of which, however, are relevant for integration processes. Hohpe and Woolf split their patterns into six categories:

- Messages channels (which channels are used by applications and systems to communicate with integration solutions?)
- Message construction (what does the construction of messages look like?)
- Message routing (what does the message processing within an integration solution look like and how is the destination of a message determined?)

- Message transformation (how can the various data formats in the systems and applications in question communicate with each other?)
- Message endpoints (how are applications and systems not originally designed for integration scenarios made compatible?)
- Systems management (how is it guaranteed that the implemented integration scenarios operate correctly and are monitored?)

As we know by now, BPMN is strongly aligned with the sequence control of process flows. Furthermore, it focuses on both the associated data flow within the processes as well as on the message flow with external partners in the form of collaboration diagrams. Taking this into account, we can take a close look at the patterns in the categories *message routing* and *message transformation* as extensions for BPMN. In the following, I also want to examine how the pattern symbols can be integrated in BPMN. As we will see, I will suggest a general extension to the task types in which the upper left corner of the task is labeled with the pattern symbol of the associated integration pattern for better visibility. We must still consider, however, whether adding a new task to the process flow is enough or whether further details (such as relationships to other elements in the form of associations) make the pattern and hence the full process easier to understand. And in the most complex patterns, such as the aggregator pattern, we need to decide whether their implementation needs to be made more detailed using a subprocess. Finally, we take to take the executability of the new tasks into account, namely which metadata needs to be added to the new task before it can be executed in a process engine. To answer this question, I will make use of the open source project Apache Camel (see Camel 2011) as a reference implementation for the enterprise integration patterns (EIP) discussed by Hohpe and Woolf and compare which parameters it implements for a specific EIP. The sources used here are Claus Ibsen and Jonathan Anstey's book *Camel in Action* (Ibsen and Anstey 2011) and the online documentation of the company FuseSource, which provides a graphical Camel editor based on the EIP symbols (FuseSource 2011a). The following discusses the individual patterns but in no specific order and without any claims to being complete. The explanations below also do not claim to specify every last formal detail of the pattern in question, but to sketch out the main ideas on which the patterns are based instead. I will leave it to other authors to analyze the language extension in a form in which it could be submitted to the OMG as a BPMN extension. To summarize, I hope to achieve the following benefits of this combination of BPMN and the notation proposed by Hohpe and Woolf:

- Respecting user tasks when executing technical processes: As seen, specialists must be consulted even when executing processes that are more technically oriented. By viewing the new tasks as extensions to existing task types, we can emphasize the involvement of people using the user task.
- Exception handling using boundary events or event subprocesses: One particularly powerful property of BPMN can now be used for integration-centric processes and hence for the patterns, namely controlled event handling during process execution. This category includes the use of event-based gateways and the time-based monitoring of the individual steps or sequences of steps.

– Using activity markers such as a standard loop, parallel or sequential multi-instance marker (for new tasks too), and hence a more compact representation of more demanding loop processing and parallel processing situations.
– Structuring of complex process flows using subprocesses nested in a hierarchy.
– Explicit modeling of the data flow (even between the new activities) to increase transparency across the data processing within the process.
– Explicit modeling of the transaction behavior of integration-centric processes using the standard BPMN transaction handler elements.

These points cover a few of the drawbacks discovered in previous implementations of modeling tools for creating integration processes, when using only the notation proposed by Hohpe and Woolf. A combination with BPMN solves these drawbacks in an elegant way and is explained in detail in the following sections.

5.6.3.2 Aggregator Pattern

We start with one of the most complex patterns, the aggregator pattern. We discussed this pattern intensively as one of the integration-centric patterns in Sect. 5.6.2. To recap, the pattern groups multiple associated messages in a single new message. In the discussion in Sect. 5.6.2, we found that the many potential parameters demanded many different BPMN models to implement its behavior. This means we need to respect three basic properties in the implementation:

3. Correlation: Which inbound messages belong together?
4. Completion condition: When does the process stop waiting for further messages to arrive?
5. Aggregation algorithm: How are the various messages processed as the new single message?

It is a good idea, therefore, not to represent this pattern as a single new task, but to design a full subprocess instead, labeled only with the symbol from Fig. 5.26 in the top left corner when closed. When opened, however, all details of the implementation are respected and the various implementation options (as discussed in Sect. 5.6.2) are depicted in the graphic. Figure 5.27 shows the aggregator pattern in the compact subprocess view and Fig. 5.28 shows the subprocess details.

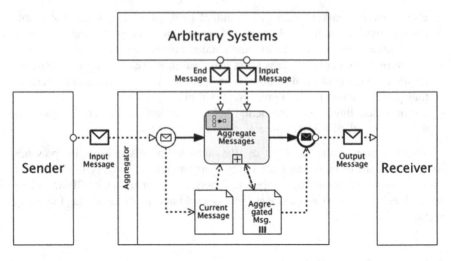

Fig. 5.27 Aggregator pattern in compact view

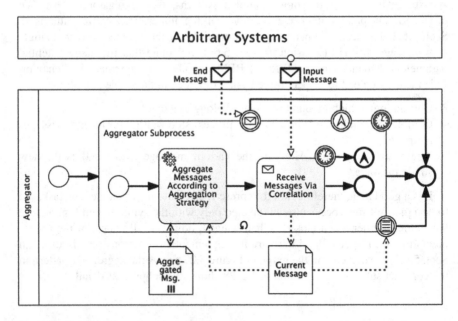

Fig. 5.28 Details of the aggregator subprocess

Figure 5.27 starts by showing the arrival of the first message that actually instantiates processing. The inbound message is saved in a data object *Current Message* that can, at the same time, be used to communicate with the subprocess (the data object has the same name in both models). Figure 5.28 starts by adding the new message to the list of aggregated messages in accordance with the aggregation strategy. Next, a receive task waits for further messages and adds them (once received) to the aggregated list in accordance with the correlation condition and the aggregation strategy. The configuration properties of the aggregator pattern mentioned at the start (correlation, completion condition, plus aggregation algorithm) can now be incorporated in the process model from Fig. 5.28 as follows:

- The correlation is defined as a property of the receive task from Fig. 5.28. This can, for example, be formulated using a script, as was shown in the implementation of the basic architecture of a process-driven application in Sect. 4.2.3.6.
- The aggregation algorithm that determines how inbound messages are grouped is assigned to the task *Aggregate Messages According to Aggregation Strategy* in Fig. 5.28 and refers to a component that incorporates the new data in the existing aggregated message. This could again be a script, but Java Beans is also an alternative.

We now need to implement the completion condition. Ibsen and Anstey (2011) name four basic completion criteria that need to be respected in the model as well:

1. Completion when reaching a specified total number of messages (completion size): We save this condition as a property of the Aggregator Subprocess from Fig. 5.28. This makes it an end criterion of the loop, but we then need to modify the marker of the Aggregator Subprocess. This is because, as always in these cases where the number of loops is known, we show this visually in the model using the multi-instance marker (≣).
2. Completion if no messages arrive for a specified period of time (completion timeout): This condition is represented in Fig. 5.28 using the interrupting timer boundary event attached to the receive task.
3. Completion at a specified time (completion interval): The model from Fig. 5.28 uses the interrupting timer boundary event attached to the Aggregator Subprocess. Once the target time for the full process is reached, the loop of the subprocess is interrupted and the message handling completed in full.
4. Completion in accordance with a condition predicated by the message content (completion predicate): I modeled this content-related monitoring in Fig. 5.28 using the interrupting conditional boundary event attached to the Aggregator Subprocess. A condition of this type can again be formulated in a script or (since it references the content of the message) using an XPath expression. Regardless of how the condition is expressed, it is part of the conditional event. The relationship to the data used in the condition is represented visually using an association between the data object(s) in question and the conditional boundary event. You can see how this is implemented in the model in the association between the *Current Message* data object and the conditional boundary event.

Alongside the four completion conditions above, we have, however, also met a further criterion, namely a completion when a dedicated end message is received. This is why I covered this dedicated message *End Message* explicitly both in the model for a compact view of the aggregator pattern (Fig. 5.27) and in the detailed model (Fig. 5.28). As we can see in the detailed process, its use as the interrupting message boundary event has the required effect of interrupting the Aggregator Subprocess and hence stopping further messages from being received.

The completion conditions can also be combined in any way, as dictated in the pattern in Hohpe and Woolf. Of course this makes the model difficult to read at first glance, but this is mainly due to the need to respect all possible completion conditions in a single model. In practical use of the pattern, we will almost certainly need only one completion criterion and the model will become much simpler.

If the aggregator pattern is used in a processing chain that includes further enterprise integration patterns and the aggregator pattern is not the first task used when a message is received, the implementation from Fig. 5.28 cannot assume that the data object *Current Message* is already filled. The sequence flow from Fig. 5.28 must, therefore, start by receiving messages before the aggregation strategy can be applied again. The model from Fig. 5.29 handles this situation.

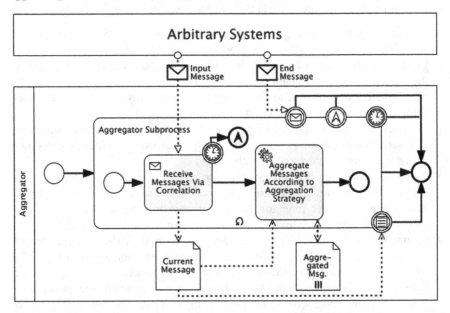

Fig. 5.29 Details of the aggregator implementation when using the aggregator within a processing chain

5.6.3.3 Content Enricher Pattern

The aim of the content enricher pattern is to enrich inbound data with information so that the message can be processed by the target system. On the other hand, the sender is often not able to provide all data required in the target system. In this case, the content enricher uses a synchronous call to determine the required data. The associated new BPMN task is shown in Fig. 5.30.

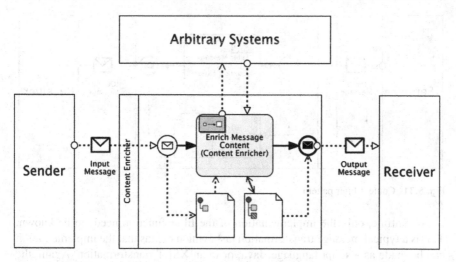

Fig. 5.30 Content enricher pattern

The content enricher is passed the original message as an input parameter, determines the missing information from a further system synchronously, and uses this information to enrich the original message. In this way, the function of the pattern is similar to the asynchronous-synchronous bridge. The enrichment of the data is also indicated by new symbols in the top left corners of the data objects, also taken from the symbol language of the integration patterns. The original data object has just one square, but is given a new square after the content enricher pass.

Before the new content enricher task can run, the following two pieces of information must be specified (FuseSource 2011b):

- The address of the source from which the additional information is requested. In the BPMN model above, this information could, for example, be assigned to the back-end system pool called *Arbitrary Systems*, which communicates with the content enricher.
- Aggregation strategy: Like the aggregator pattern, the execution engine must be told how to incorporate the requested data in the original message. The function itself can be provided using a Java bean or a script. The reference to the responsible bean or script, however, is one of the properties of the content enricher itself.

With this configuration, the content enricher can fulfill its task at runtime.

5.6.3.4 Content Filter Pattern

The content filter pattern performs exactly the opposite function to the content enricher: Specific parts of a message must be removed or the structure of the message simplified and the pattern can be mapped to BPMN in a similarly simple way. The new task is used as shown in Fig. 5.31.

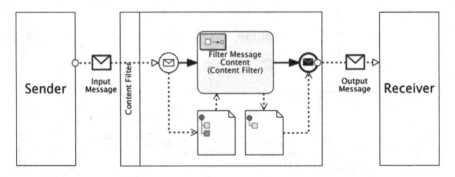

Fig. 5.31 Content filter pattern

At runtime, only the implementation of the filter function needs to be known. This is a typical message transformation task, which means that the implementation can be made as a script language, Java, or in an XSLT transformation. Again, the reference to the implementation is part of the properties of the content filter task. At runtime, the message being edited is passed to the content filter using the inbound data object. It now uses the filter function to simplify the message and the result is passed to the outbound data object and finally sent to the receiver using the message-based end event.

5.6.3.5 Message Translator Pattern

The content enricher and the content filter patterns are both message transformation patterns, responsible mainly for communicating between different data formats. This pattern category is made more general when the message translator pattern is included. This pattern can be used whenever transformations between different formats need to take place and it is shown in Fig. 5.32.

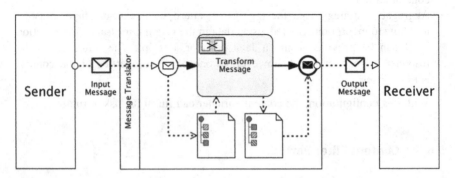

Fig. 5.32 Message translator pattern

The wide range of potential message transformations mean that it is not a good idea to use a separate symbol for every detail. The message translator uses a reference to the implementation of the transformation logic to specify whether message header data or the payload itself is affected, whether a transformation is taking place between objects and XML (marshal, unmarshal), or whether messages are normalized or packed in different structures. The implementation can again be made in script languages, Java, and XSLT transformations and the processing at runtime is the same as in the content filter pattern.

5.6.3.6 Content-Based Router Pattern

One of the tasks of a content-based router is to transfer a message to exactly one receiver, as determined by the content of the received message. This function can be implemented using a combination of a new BPMN task with the type content-based router interacting with an exclusive gateway, where each gate in the gateway has to define an expression specifying whether the message is to be forwarded to the associated receiver. The function is depicted in Fig. 5.33, which also shows how the standard flow always need to run if none of the conditions is met.

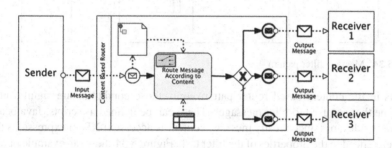

Fig. 5.33 Content-based router pattern

There are various ways of formulating those conditions that need to be free of conflicts (due to the demand that only one system has to receive the message): The reference to the implementation is saved in the properties of the task *Route Message According to Content*, whether in script languages, Java beans/Java programs, XPath expressions, or business rules. This can be depicted by a graphical association, as shown in Fig. 5.33 when using a business rule.

A similar pattern, the dynamic router pattern, can be shown in a similar way. The only difference is that the information about the conditions is saved in a database filled by the target systems in question at system start. To do this, the target systems send a type of notification of availability to the dynamic router. This notification does not just provide information about the availability of the receiver, but also provides the conditions under which the receiver is able to accept specific messages. These conditions are defined by the router in the database table and evaluated at runtime. As far as the representation as a BPMN task is concerned, only the association changes, since the new data store symbol (Daten-speicher) is used in BPMN 2.0 instead of the business rule (as shown in Fig. 5.33). Apart from this, the way the dynamic router works at runtime is identical to the content-based router, with the inbound message being analyzed in accordance with the routing logic and forwarded to *precisely one* assigned receiver in accordance with the truth value of the various conditions. If none of the conditions is met, the standard flow is followed and the message handled accordingly.

5.6.3.7 Message Filter Pattern

Unlike the content filter pattern, which is used to filter individual parts of a message, the message filter pattern removes unwanted messages from processing completely. The way the filter is used is shown in Fig. 5.34.

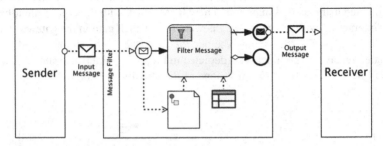

Fig. 5.34 Message filter pattern

As in the content-based router pattern, only those conditions are significant at runtime that are used to filter messages. These can be defined as scripts, Java beans, business rules, or (since mostly message content is accessed) XPath expressions that are referenced in the properties of the filter task. Figure 5.34 shows an example of how a rule set is used. If the filter criterion applies to the current message, the conditional sequence flow is followed and the untyped end event is reached with the result that the message is not forwarded. If it does not apply, the standard sequence flow is followed and the message end event is used to send the message to the receiver.

5.6.3.8 Recipient List Pattern

Unlike the content-based router pattern, the recipient list pattern passes a message to a *list* of receivers as specified by its content. This is implemented using a combination of the new BPMN task of type *Recipient List* and conditional sequence flows. Here, an expression must be defined for each conditional sequence flow, which determines whether the message is forwarded to the respective receiver assigned to the conditional sequence flow. Figure 5.35 shows how this works. Here, the standard flow is again used to guarantee further processing in case none of the conditions is met.

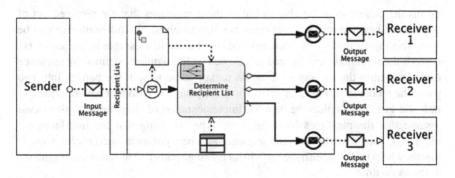

Fig. 5.35 Recipient list pattern using conditional sequence flows

The condition can again be formulated in various different equally suitable ways, using script languages, Java beans/Java programs, XPath expressions, or business rules. The reference to the implementation is saved in the properties of the task *Determine Recipient List*. Figure 5.35 shows an example of how a business rule is used. The routing logic is calculated at runtime and, depending on the condition, forwarded to the assigned receiver or receivers. The standard flow is followed whenever a receiver cannot be determined in advance.

As an alternative, the recipient list pattern can also be implemented using an inclusive gateway. This option is shown in Fig. 5.36.

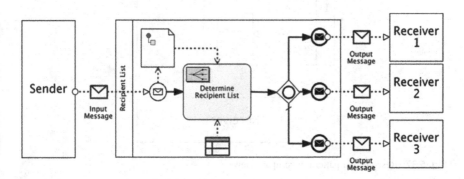

Fig. 5.36 Recipient list pattern using the inclusive gateway

5.6.3.9 Resequencer Pattern

The resequencer pattern is one of the patterns known as stateful (as already discussed in the aggregator patterns). A sequence of messages is supposed to reach the receiver in a well-defined order, but there is no guarantee that the messages arrive in an ordered way (see also Sect. 5.6.2.2, in which the resequencer pattern is considered in a different perspective). The resequencer pattern, therefore, is responsible for putting the individual messages in the correct order. This also means the pattern must be able to buffer those messages that are received out of sequence. Once the missing messages are also received, the full sequence can be sent. This means that the resequencer does not buffer all messages in the sequence, it sends them immediately instead (if allowed by the sequence defined by sequence numbers within the messages). It again makes sense to split the pattern into two parts, the model from Fig. 5.37 shows how the pattern is used as a new resequencer task and Fig. 5.38 depicts the detailed implementation of the pattern. Both models assume that the messages have the same type (meaning that the interfaces are identical). This is what makes the sequence numbers just mentioned useful, namely that they help to distinguish the individual message parts and to sort these fragments at the same time.

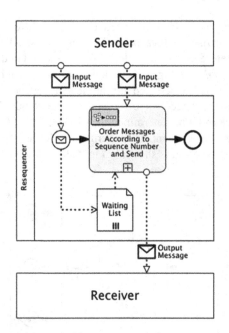

Fig. 5.37 Resequencer pattern in compact view

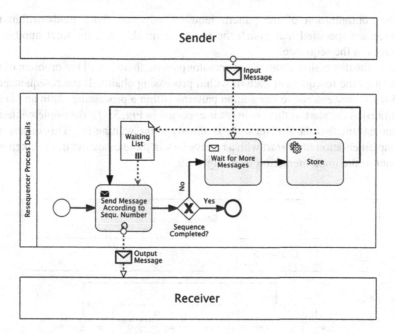

Fig. 5.38 Details of the resequencer subprocess

The way the resequencer pattern works at runtime can be explained as follows, beginning with the inbound message from the sender from Fig. 5.37 that starts the processing. The message is copied to a data object called *Waiting List*, which collects all messages that were not yet sent to the receiver. Furthermore, the list makes the connection to the subprocess implementation from Fig. 5.38 that accesses the same data object. The sender task from Fig. 5.38 now forwards as many messages as there are messages *with consecutive sequence numbers*. Sent messages are removed from the list immediately. It is also possible here that no messages are sent, because the sequence was interrupted due to missing messages. Once the send operation is completed (either because the list is empty or due to a gap in the sequence numbers), the exclusive gateway is checked to see whether the resequencer can be ended. This is the case whenever the waiting list is empty and all expected messages were received. In message sequences, the number of expected messages is usually provided as part of the message header. This means that every message contains the total number of parts in the sequence. The resequencer can, for example, take the information about the current sequence number and the total number of message fragments in the full message from two header fields called currentSequenceNumber and totalNumberOfMsgs. If the sequence is not yet complete, further messages are expected by the receive task *Wait for More Messages*. If this task is exited, this means that a new message is received that itself is included in the waiting list by the service task *Store* and the cycle can begin again from the start.

The configuration of the pattern requires only that those fields within the message are specified that match the sequence number and the total number of messages in the sequence.

As in the discussion about the aggregator pattern, there is still the problem of the position of the resequencer pattern within processing chains. If the resequencer is used with other enterprise integration patterns within a processing chain and is not positioned at the start of this chain (as is expected in Fig. 5.37), the implementation cannot assume that the first message is already in the waiting list. This means that the implementation must start with a receive task in these cases and this is taken into account in the implementation from Fig. 5.39.

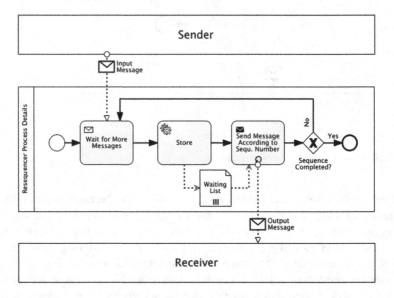

Fig. 5.39 Resequencer implementation with receive task as the first step

This modification does not change the basic logic; it merely guarantees that the resequencer starts when the message is received and only then does the sender loop proceed.

5.6.3.10 Splitter Pattern

In real scenarios, individual messages can often be very complex. Order data, for example, usually consists of an order header and multiple order items. Both the order header and the items themselves comprise a large number of further segments. If you want to process a message of this type, it is often a good idea to split the message into its parts and then edit them individually, possibly in parallel (for performance reasons). This is the precise task of the splitter pattern, as shown in Fig. 5.40.

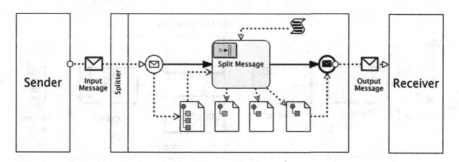

Fig. 5.40 Splitter pattern

Inbound messages are made available to the splitter using one data object. The splitter then splits the complex structure it receives into different fragments, each of which can now be processed individually in the remainder of the process. In the example in Fig. 5.40, only one message fragment is passed to the receiver.

The only information the splitter needs to split the received structure correctly is the way the message has to be split. This is specific to the actual construction of the message and can be done in many different ways. For example, each line in a text message can represent precisely one data record and the splitter detects the end of an entry using the line end marker. Alternatively, the individual parts are marked by special characters (@, ;), which must be made known to the splitter. In XML-based messages, a specific tag can be used as a separator of individual fragments. All this information must be indicated to the splitter when it is configured. In particularly complex cases, custom Java beans could be one way of splitting messages. Whatever method is chosen, it is implemented in the model using an association, for example an association with a script as shown in Fig. 5.40. Those properties that represent the splitter method must then be assigned to this association (for example, a reference to a Java bean or a special character or tag). Once configured like this, the splitter is ready to be used.

5.6.3.11 Composed Message Processor Pattern

The patterns we have discussed are particularly powerful in combination with each other. An example suggested by Hohpe and Woolf is the composed message processor pattern, comprising the splitter pattern, content-based router pattern, and aggregator pattern in a sequence. Figure 5.41 demonstrates the sequence of these patterns using the original symbol notation proposed by Hohpe and Woolf.

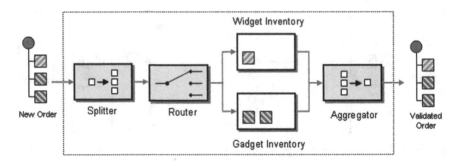

Fig. 5.41 Composed message processor pattern (from Hohpe and Woolf 2004, page 296)

As shown in Fig. 5.41 an inbound message passes a splitter that splits the message into its individual parts. It then uses the router to send each part (not shown in the model in Fig. 5.41 in detail) to two potential receivers. The aggregator collects their responses and aggregates them as a new outbound message. One typical scenario that uses this pattern is the validation of the individual items in an order, for example whether an item is in stock and hence able to be delivered. Figure 5.41 distinguishes two types of products that have to be compared with different stocks. The data (now including the validation) is then forwarded as one aggregated message.

Figure 5.42 shows this model now implemented with the extended BPMN.

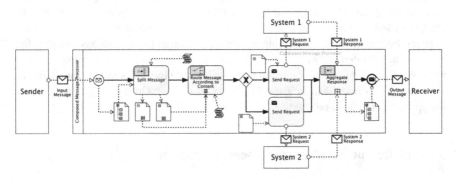

Fig. 5.42 Composed message processor pattern using the extended BPMN

When compared with the model from Fig. 5.41, the BPMN model from Fig. 5.42 is now much more precise. For example, you can now see how the inbound message is split into two different message parts and each part can itself appear more than once (expressed by the multi-instance marker in the associated data objects). The individual fragments are passed to the content-based router task *Route Message According to Content*, which has a sequential multi-instance marker. This makes it clear that execution is repeated for each message fragment. Here, a new token is produced for each message segment and passed to the exclusive gateway. The gateway is merely responsible for evaluating the result of the content-based router and forwarding the data fragment in question to the associated send task. The model makes

- the send operations,
- the individual message parts sent by the send task in question,
- and the systems involved

as easy to see as the response messages and their aggregation in the aggregator task *Aggregate Response*. The aggregator ends when it has received as many messages as queries were sent to the systems involved (which means that the end criterion is a specific total number of messages). If the patterns, interfaces, communication end points, gateways, and so on are configured as described in the discussion of the individual patterns, this model can then be executed right away.

One drawback of the model in Fig. 5.42 is the explicit modeling of the send operations to the systems involved. Each time we need to communicate with a new system, the model must be modified. This should come as a reminder that we have already solved a similar case in a more elegant way. Looking back at the model from Fig. 29, we see that we used an ESB to bypass the direct communication with the end systems in the stateful process part. This made the solution as a whole more flexible and easier to maintain and we should make use of these benefits for the composed message processor here.

5.6.3.12 Scatter-Gather Pattern

The scatter-gather pattern is a further example of a composite processing sequence. It combines the parallel sending of a single message to multiple systems (a broadcast) with an aggregator that collects the responses from the systems and aggregates them as an outbound message. Unlike in the composed message processor, one and the same message is sent to all receivers and also not all responses are necessarily received since a time limit applies. The associated original model is based on the pattern notation shown in Fig. 5.43.

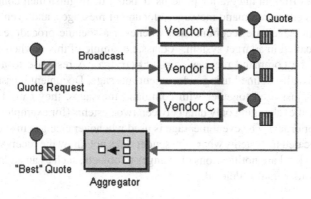

Fig. 5.43 Scatter-Gather pattern (from Hohpe and Woolf 2004, page 298)

Figure 5.43 uses the gathering of offers as an example of the scatter-gather pattern. The offer request is sent to three traders at the same time, in a broadcast. The aggregator then bundles the replies and sends them back to the original requester as a message with the best offer.

The implementation of this sequence flow with the extended BPMN does not require a separate pattern for the broadcast part of scatter-gather, since this function has identical semantics covered by the parallel gateway (see Fig. 5.44). The responses are gathered again by the aggregator subprocess, which, in this case, exits after a timeout. This aspect is not taken directly from the model in Fig. 5.44. Our discussion of the aggregator at the start of this section, however, reminds us that the completion condition is modeled within the subprocess *Aggregate Messages* and I have not modeled this subprocess again explicitly for this example.

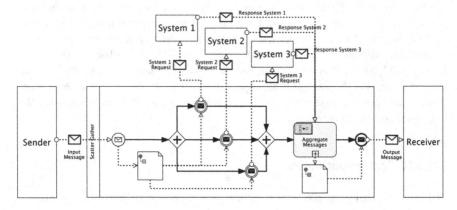

Fig. 5.44 Scatter-Gather pattern using the extended BPMN

5.6.3.13 Extensions for Messages

In their book, Hohpe and Woolf introduce new symbols for different message types, alongside the different integration patterns, to better distinguish their content. These new symbols cover command messages, document messages, and event messages. Command messages are recommended whenever a specific procedure or method needs to be called in a target system. A classic example of this is when creating an order using the command message createOrder. A response to a command message is usually defined using a document message. Document messages, however, are not just used together with command messages, they can also be used productively if exchanging only data between two systems (for example, the data of a customer or order). The event message is used whenever changes in states need to be communicated to systems where the sender does not know the receivers. Typical events of this kind are notifications of changes to objects, such as an address change or when an order item is deleted.

BPMN also recognizes the message symbol (as an envelope ✉), but does not distinguish further by message type. The different types suggested by Hohpe and Woolf are highly practical and provide important additional information. It is certainly worth considering whether to implement them in the BPMN, in particular when implementing integration scenarios with many different message types. It is therefore an obvious step to associate the symbols for the different message types with the message symbol in BPMN, producing the new symbols shown in Fig. 5.45.

Fig. 5.45 Indicating different message types

5.6.3.14 Using the Extended BPMN in Specific Scenarios

We now have a whole new range of BPMN elements for more expressive modeling of integration scenarios and I would now like to round off this discussion by illustrating their use in two scenarios. The first example is taken from a tutorial on the open source solution Apache Camel. Apache Camel is an integration framework whose most fundamental components are based on the enterprise integration patterns suggested by Hohpe and Woolf. Jonathan Anstey, one of the co-authors of the book *Camel in Action*, chose the message handling sequence shown in Fig. 5.46 in his Internet introduction to Camel (Anstey 2009).

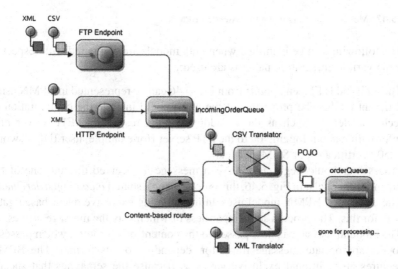

Fig. 5.46 Message handling using the pattern symbols (Anstey 2009)

The flow of the scenario is as follows (from Anstey 2009):

The fictional company that implemented this process is a vendor of spare parts for motorbikes and the customers of this company are primarily manufacturers of motorbikes. Over time, the methods used to order replacement parts from this company have changed. Originally, an order was saved on an FTP server as a CSV file (comma-separated values). As part of the SOA approach, the XML format was added and the company today offers both the CSV format and the XML format for purchase orders. As well as the classic file transfer, the XML format can also be sent using HTTP. The company recommends that any new customers only use HTTP to transfer XML files, but contractual requirements mean that it must continue to offer the old protocols and the old CSV data format. In the company's internal system, the purchase order data is processed further in the format of simple Java objects, known as POJOs (Plain Old Java Objects). This is why the incoming purchase orders must be transformed to POJOs, both for XML content and for CSV content. Figure 5.47 shows the equivalent process here, but now implemented with the extended BPMN.

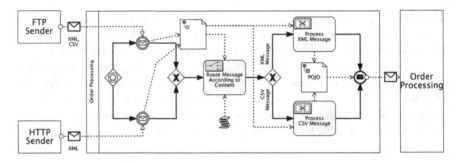

Fig. 5.47 Message handling using the extended BPMN

The following can be identified when both models are compared with respect to how the various integration patterns are used:

1. The FTP and HTTP end points from Fig. 5.46 can be represented in BPMN using different pools. The properties of the pools could include the configuration of technical details, such as the IP address of the responsible FTP server plus information about logging on to the FTP server (for example, user ID/password, X.509 certificates, or SAML tickets).
2. Processing should begin as soon as a message is received through one of the potential channels. In Fig. 5.46, this is done using a shared *incomingOrderQueue*. The associated BPMN model uses an instantiating exclusive event-based gateway for this. The process starts regardless of which way the message arrives.
3. The inbound message is now passed to the content-based router, which passes it to the appropriate message translator, depending on its format. The BPMN requires an additional exclusive gateway, because the semantics that specify that only one path is followed can only be realized using this gateway. In Fig. 5.46, the connections from the content-based router point directly to the appropriate translator pattern. This is not possible in BPMN, since it would express the same behavior as a parallel gateway, namely that both paths are given a token. This is not wanted in the scenario above.

4. The message translator patterns translate the inbound formats into a POJO and this POJO is saved to a queue in Fig. 5.46, which is where processing continues. In Fig. 5.47, this aspect is represented by adding an additional pool. Details of the queue would again be saved as properties of the pool.

Once again, this example indicates how classic integration scenarios can be implemented in a very expressive way using the extended BPMN, while preserving the compact nature of the original pattern notation.

The second example of implementing integration scenarios with the extended BPMN is a general process originally used for test purposes at SAP. Its many and varied message processing steps make it of great interest and its BPMN model is shown on the next page in Fig. 5.48.

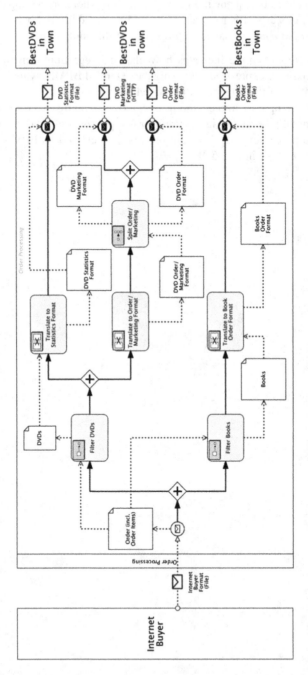

Fig. 5.48 Complex purchase order processing using the extended BPMN

The process shown in Fig. 5.48 addresses the following business problem: An Internet shop provider for books and DVDs receives purchase orders that it passes to two vendors specialized in books (the vendor *BestBooks in Town* in Fig. 5.48) or DVDs (the vendor *BestDVDs in Town* in Fig. 5.48). The vendor *BestBooks in Town* only wants to receive book purchase orders in its target format on a file server it provides itself. The vendor *BestDVDs in Town*, however, is more demanding and requires marketing information about which products are ordered alongside the regular purchase order data. It also needs aggregated data for its statistics, namely information about the total value of purchases on each day. The difficult part is that the statistics data must be saved in a different system than the order and marketing data. The order and marketing data is sent to one and the same ERP system, but different communication protocols are used, HTTP for the marketing data and file transfer for the order data.

To solve this problem, purchase orders incoming by file transfer are first copied to an internal data object *Order*. This object is the basis for how the integration process works. The different processes for the DVDs and the books are distinguished in the parallel gateway. A content filter pattern (not to be confused with the message filter pattern) filters the orders accordingly by branch, extracting the books from the original message for the book branch and the DVDs for the DVD branch. The filter results are passed to a standalone data object in which the branch in question can operate independently.

After the extraction, the format in the book branch must merely be transformed to the target format of the book vendor. Processing of the DVDs, on the other hand, continues using another parallel gateway, whose transformation steps effectively produce the expected target formats of the vendor. Here, the upper branch of the parallel gateway accepts the data for the statistics file. Once the target format for the statistics is created, the associated file can be sent using file transfer. In the lower branch the data is first transformed to a data object that includes both order data and marketing data. This data must be sent separately, which means a splitter needs to be used. The send operations of the order data and the marketing data, however, can be parallel. The implicit parallel join behavior of end events means that the process does not end until every token has disappeared from the process. This means that a further merging parallel gateway is not required.

The configuration required here is clear and the various message formats are hidden between the pools behind the message symbols. The pools themselves include the technical information about the end points (such as file server information or the HTTP address). The configuration of the individual patterns has already been handled in depth in this chapter and we can conclude that the integration scenario from Fig. 5.48 meets the requirements made at the start.

5.6.3.15 Comments on the Extended BPMN

As shown in the examples, it is a relatively simple task to implement integration scenarios using the domain-specific BPMN proposed here. Combining BPMN with the symbols from the integration patterns from the Hohpe and Woolf book produces a compact graphical notation for system integrations that enhances the options compared with the pure pattern notation, making data flows, for example, equally visible as well as the involved systems. On the other hand, system integrators are also reflected in the new notation, since they know the typical pattern symbols being used in the new BPMN tasks and subprocesses, enabling them to recognize what is actually happening technically in each task in the resulting process model. Furthermore, the new notation benefits from all the advantages of BPMN, namely that interrupting and non-interrupting boundary events can be attached to the new tasks. This makes it possible to respond to error situations in a highly dedicated way. Similarly, the markers can be applied to the new tasks, with standard loops, parallel or sequential multi-instance, or compensation all interacting expressively with the patterns in ways that the pure pattern notation cannot match adequately. Finally, whole pattern sequences can be grouped, reused, and controlled via boundary events in subprocesses. The new extensions proposed here do not necessarily have to be processed in a BPMN engine. In principle, code for ESBs can be generated from the new integration models, if they support the integration patterns. One obvious candidate is the Camel integration framework, on which these integration-centric process models could be executed. In short, a range of completely new possibilities are available to system integrators who need to solve typical integration problems in companies with heterogeneous system landscapes and/or intensive B2B relationships with customers, partners, and vendors.

5.7   More Flexibility by Combining Rules with Analytical Applications

Rules and their executability by rules engines are a vital component of today's solutions. They are used wherever quick adjustments need to be made to changing business conditions, the exact field in which process-driven applications are applied. This makes the use of rules in the area of composite applications in particular an obvious choice. Here, the constantly changing business logic can be formulated as business rules and adjusted again at runtime depending on business developments. It is not, therefore, necessary to embark on any complex implementation projects to match the strategy of the enterprise with the executed processes. Many examples exist that show how rules can be used in a meaningful way:

- Validation rules are used in form checks. A further example is checks to see whether a customer's claims are justified.
- Calculation rules for tax, prices, interest, commission, discounts, bonuses, and so on.
- Decision rules for deciding whether someone qualifies for a loan or whether a traveller needs further checks at customs.
- Recommendation rules for suggesting the further treatment of a patient or suggesting further purchases in online shops. Most of you will recognize texts

such as "Customers who bought this item also bought . . ." on Internet provider sites.

- Personalization rules, applied, for example, when visiting specific websites.
- Internationalization rules, such as customs legislation or different interpretations of insurance policies.
- Exception rules such as seasonal campaigns, advertising campaigns, or special arrangements.
- Optimization and configuration rules such as product configuration.

Finally, these rules are a way of keeping enterprise policies and strategy consistent and clear for all while also guaranteeing that they can be implemented. I do not, however, want to go into detail about the properties of rules in this chapter. Instead, I would like to look at how rules are applicable in process-driven applications and in particular how they interact with processes. If you want to learn more about the world of rules, I recommend Ronald Ross's book (Ross 2009) and the Business Rules Manifesto of the Business Rules Group (BRG 2003).

Together, rules and processes form an optimized symbiosis. Ronald Ross (Ross 2009) emphasizes the independent nature of rules and, hence, the strict separation of rules and processes. Instead, business rules are meant to lead the process and ensure that the processes themselves remain relatively stable. What can change frequently, on the other hand, are the basic rules.

What type of architecture benefits from this type of approach? When studying the literature I found several interesting approaches, and I will take one article as an example. In Graml et al. 2008, the authors focus on the use of business rules to support agile business processes. A business process is agile if both the control flow and the data flow can be modified at runtime. The article in question discusses potential solutions to this problem. Since process-driven applications are confronted with similar problems, the following section examines the proposed solutions for relevance to composite applications and adapts the solutions for composites (where possible). The authors also use BPMN to model the business problem, but transform these models to BPEL again for execution. The use of BPMN 2.0 permits new alternatives here.

Once we have discussed the use of business rules in processes to increase flexibility, a separate section then takes a look at their particular use in technical processes. This expands the spectrum for rules from the composite layer to the service contract implementation layer. Where possible (and worthwhile), I will also look at rules in more detail.

To conclude, we will use the combination of business rules and analytical applications to further automate processes. Here, the focus is on the methods for coupling rules and analytical applications to further reduce the number of interactive steps in processes.

5.7.1   Using Business Rules to Increase Flexibility

This section is based on the solutions for using business rules to increase flexibility of business processes as they are explained by Graml et al. (2008) in their article. Processes with fixed models have a severe problem: there are only limited options available for adapting running processes to changing conditions. Many of the problems are related directly to the Web service model in SOA environments, since the replacement of services (for example with services with new logic) is restricted to identical port types. Another difficulty is the fixed definition of the process flow as defined at design time.

Graml, Bracht, and Spies distinguish two strategies when solving these limitations. The first is known as *flexibility by selection* and attempts to predict potential process changes and respect them in the model at design time using different control flow combinations. The variant that matches the context in question best is then selected at runtime. The obvious drawback in this approach is the inability to predict every potential process variant.

The second alternative, known as *flexibility by adaption* is based on the idea of changing the port type, control flow, and data flow of both the process model and the running process instance directly at runtime. The authors' solution is a combination of both alternatives, using patterns to predict potential adaptions and using business rules to control the use of the patterns (among other aspects).

In the case of the rules themselves, three categories are defined: derivation rules, condition rules, and process rules.

- Derivation rules represent knowledge and specify how new information can be derived from existing information. A classic example is price determination for specific customers.

  Ronald Ross calls these rules structural rules or definition rules, which either classify or calculate when executed.
- Condition rules represent expressions that must be met at every point in time. A typical property of these rules is that they can be violated, for example when a specific customer is not allowed to exceed a predefined value when making orders.

  Ronald Ross calls these rules behavior rules or operative rules, applied whenever people are involved.
- Process rules represent the logic within a process that decides whether certain activities or subprocesses can be executed depending on the current process context. For example, international companies need to implement different processes for different regions, to conform to legislation. The process context can therefore be used to decide which process fragment applies at execution.

To explain how these different rule categories are used, I will take the purchase order process already used in this book. Figure 5.49 shows it without the details of the service contract implementation layer.

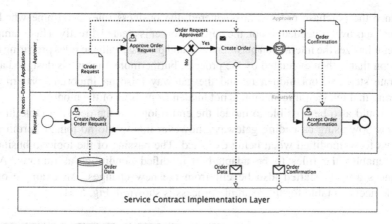

Fig. 5.49 Simplified purchase order process without rules

An important aim of each process implementation is to virtually completely automate the processes so that no human involvement is required. Every human interaction in the process flow is a potential source of error, can produce delays, and increase process costs. This is done by avoiding dialog steps as far as possible and only involving people in exceptional situations. The process from Fig. 5.49, therefore, can best be enhanced by a derivation rule directly before the call of the approval step. This requires only that the approver's knowledge about decision determination for this specific operation is mapped to rules. This formalizes expert knowledge for the enterprise and makes it reusable. In the example, the approval could be dependent on the purchase order region and the size of the order and the approver only needs to be contacted once a certain size of order is exceeded. In this case, a simple decision table is all that is needed for the implementation. Figure 5.50 shows the new process flow after the business rule task (newly introduced in BPMN 2.0) is added.

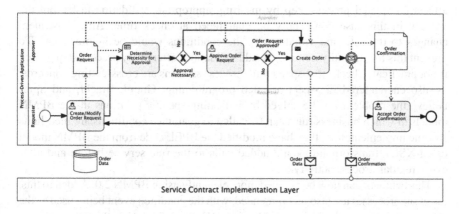

Fig. 5.50 Simplified purchase order process with rules

Once the purchase order data is entered, the business rules determine whether manual approval is needed. If not, the purchase order is created directly. This example also emphasizes the interaction between rules and process, with the rules preparing the decision that is then evaluated by the process. Furthermore, the rule is designed as a separate step and not hidden behind the gateway (also an important pattern for ensuring that relevant information is not hidden from users of the model).

It would also be possible to model the entire logic of the decision table in the process flow using cascading gateways, however this would no longer permit the process to be modified when being executed. The passing of the logic to business rules enables the rules to be adapted to modified conditions at runtime. Any instances already started also benefit from the new changes. An example of a simple decision table for the example process is shown in Fig. 5.51.

Fig. 5.51 Decision table for
the simplified purchase order

Country	Total Amount	Approval necessary?
EMEA	< 100.000	FALSE
	>= 100.000	TRUE
APJ	< 70.000	FALSE
	>= 70.000	TRUE
AMER	< 150.000	FALSE
	>= 150.000	TRUE

The region where the purchase order was made specifies which of several different order value limits trigger an approval. Depending on the health of the business, experts can modify these limits quickly and flexibly moving responsibility for the development of the business back to the expertise in the business departments.

Meeting certain conditions during the execution of a process, however, is rather more difficult, due to the static modeling of the process flow. As specified in the introductory definition of a condition rule, these are expressions that must be met *at every point in time*. Furthermore, these conditions apply to a certain range of validity, such as a specific sequence. It is, of course, possible to meet the conditions after a completed process step by inserting appropriate validation tasks, but the validity in this case could only be guaranteed at check time. Any subsequent changes to the data and violations to the conditions would be ignored here. To prevent this too, the only option is to add validations after *every* process step, which is not practical. Checks that span entire process sections are cross-cutting concerns, as also encountered in aspect-oriented programming. Graml, Bracht, and Spies believe the problem can be solved by indicating specific positions in the BPMN models in which business rules can be called to guarantee conditions are met. In its specific implementation, they have modified the BPEL code from the BPMN model using XSLT transformations and added calls to the rule service before and after every regular process activity.

This behavior can now be mapped more elegantly using BPMN 2.0. Added to this, event subprocesses are also recommended, with the condition event being used as the start event for precisely this event subprocess. Figure 5.52 depicts this approach.

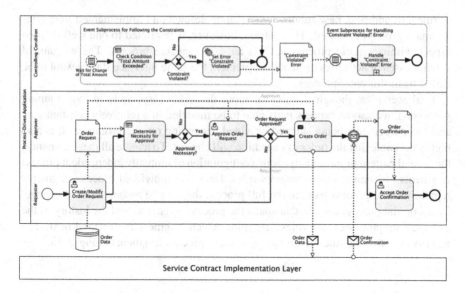

Fig. 5.52 Meeting conditions using event subprocesses

The main process is monitored by a non-interrupting event subprocess, which is activated whenever the monitored variable (or variables) changes (for example, the total value of the purchase order). If this is the case, the rule for meeting the condition is called. In the model above, this could be a limit to a specific total value, for example the rule could define an upper limit for the purchase order on the basis of customer and creditworthiness data. If the condition *Total not exceeded* is met, the subprocess ends silently and the main process can resume its process flow. If, however, the rule detects that a condition was violated, a data object (*"Constraint Violated" Error* in our case) is updated, with this change itself expected by a second event subprocess. This time, though, the subprocess starts with an interrupting conditional start event. This forces the main process to exit and triggers an error handler. Scenarios of this type that interact with rules are now supported by default due to the addition of event subprocesses in BPMN 2.0. This also makes it no longer necessary to modify the BPMN models using XSLT transformations.

Let us now take a look at the handling of process rules that have the task of controlling process fragments. The main idea is based on modeling certain process parts in advance that are not associated with each other statically, but that are linked dynamically at runtime using process rules. The implementation of this idea is precisely what Graml, Bracht, and Spies mean in the combination of *flexibility by selection* and *flexibility by adaption*. They present two patterns for this in their paper.

In the first pattern, an activity or a subprocess of a static process is held as an exchangeable activity or subprocess. The actual activity or subprocess that provides the function in question is not determined until runtime using a process rule. As an example, the authors give the delivery of a product as an exchangeable subprocess, defined differently according to the country of destination. The business rule has the task here of selecting the appropriate subprocess. The selection criteria for the activated subprocess can also be adapted at runtime because they are externalized as rules. In addition, new subprocesses can be defined and implemented long after the main process is started. This pattern, however, is restricted to one well-defined aspect within a static process held as an exchangeable process. The exchanged subprocesses or activities must also implement the same interface if they want to be called from the static process.

Real scenarios, though, require far more flexibility (especially in long running processes), with some process parts able to be modeled in a relatively constant way and other fragments being skipped or added depending on circumstances. It is also highly probable that the order of execution will change. To handle all these demands, the second pattern proposes a dynamic configuration of mutually independent process fragments at runtime using business rules. Here, the individual process fragments represent those process parts in the full process that can be assumed not to change. Based on the process context that spans the process fragments and the history of the executed subprocesses, the rules determine which fragment is executed next. The authors illustrate the rule-driven composition of process fragments in Fig. 5.53.

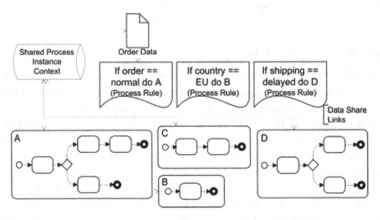

Fig. 5.53 Composition of process fragments (from Graml et al. 2008)

Finally, the idea of loose coupling can be applied here too. To implement this pattern, Graml, Bracht, and Spies use a central dispatcher process that calls the rules for determining the next subprocess in a loop. Immediately afterwards, the process fragment in question is executed. This assumes, however, that all subprocesses are matched to the shared process context. This method cannot be applied to reuse useful subprocesses developed in other projects (and mostly likely based on different data). This problem can also be solved relatively easily, though, when each process fragment provides its function as a service and the data in question is received using an interface. The central dispatcher process then no longer calls the process fragments directly, since it cannot know which specific interface implements each process fragment. Instead, it passes the information about the next process fragment that needs to be called, together with the data of the process context, as a message to an ESB. The ESB can now use its mapping function to map the data of the dispatcher process to the data of the next process fragment, which makes it now possible to involve subprocesses originally developed for a different scenario. The called subprocesses themselves pass their results back to the ESB as a message, so that it can again map to the interface of the dispatcher process. The full scenario is held together using a shared process ID generated when the dispatcher process is started. The dispatcher process is instantiated for every business case, which in the case of a purchase order process in the full scenario means one dispatcher process for each purchase order processing. The rules themselves become a kind of state machine, which uses the knowledge about the already executed subprocesses and the state of the process context to decide how to proceed. Figure 5.54 illustrates the procedure.

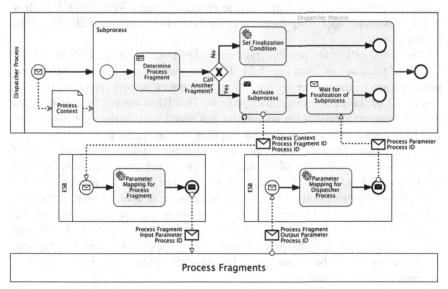

Fig. 5.54 Rule-based linking of process fragments using an ESB

The dispatcher process is started using an initial message. A loop subprocess is responsible for determining the process fragment, calling the process fragment, and waiting for it to exit. This loop is closed as soon as the end state has been detected by the rule-based step for determining the next process fragment. In the model, the setting of the end condition is indicated at the *No* gate of the exclusive gateway. The rules are used right at the start of the subprocess by the business rule task (newly introduced in BPMN 2.0). A simplified decision table for finding the process fragments that are called and defining the appropriate next state is shown in Fig. 5.55.

State	Region	Process Fragment	Next State
Start	EMEA	Order_Approval_EMEA	1
Start	US	Order_Approval_US	1
Start	APJ	Order_Approval_APJ	1
1	EMEA	Customs_EMEA	2
1	US	Customs_US	2
1	APJ	Customs_APJ	2
2	EMEA, US, APJ	-	End

Fig. 5.55 Decision table for finding process fragments

The decision table has two halves, with the columns *State* and *Region* reflecting the input parameters of the business rule and the columns *Process Fragment* and *Next State* reflecting the output parameters. In this interface between the process and the rules, it is important that the decision rule has access to the entire process context even if only a fraction of the data of the context is used for the decision initially. This means that new columns or new rules can be added at any time in the future if necessary. In the example table, the decision is made as to which process fragment is activated (column *Process Fragment*) depending on the region from which the process was called, and how to proceed (column *Next State*). It is clear that processes for approving orders and for customs procedures will differ from region to region.

The actual call of the process fragments takes place using the ESB in the *Yes* branch of the gateway from Fig. 5.54. The parameters passed to the ESB are the process context, the unique ID for calling the correct process fragment, plus the unique ID of the calling dispatcher process. This ID is needed later to dispatch the response message that the subprocess has ended back to the right dispatcher. The ESB itself is only responsible for mapping the data to the input parameters of the called process fragment. Every process fragment must respect the process ID of the calling process as a part of the interface, both in the input parameters and the output parameters. This is the only way to associate return values correctly via correlation. The process ID of the dispatcher process is after all used to bind the entire process chain and hence enables full end-to-end monitoring, important for tracing errors. The process fragment must, therefore, provide the ESB with the unique process ID after the process ends. After mapping the process fragment output parameters to the parameters of the dispatcher process, the ESB reactivates the correct dispatcher instance.

The question now arises of whether the rules could be handled directly in the ESB, removing the need for an explicit dispatcher process. This would produce a more decentralized "federal" solution to the problem, without a central controller process. This can certainly be implemented, but this solution must also respect the state in some form. The actual task of an ESB is to receive and forward messages while respecting typical tasks such as routing and mapping. This means that the handling of states must also be incorporated explicitly, for example by calling persistence using JPA. If not persisted explicitly, the alternative is to pass all process data from fragment to fragment, an unlikely situation since it limits the reusability of the process fragments. If a full process is viewed as the sum of the called process fragments, a full process for an investment operates on different data than a full process for a project, but both processes will surely want to reuse the process fragment *Invoicing*. The interface of the *Invoicing* fragment, however, cannot be dependent on the two usages (and with that on two completely different data types). This would not be manageable when the full context is passed and is therefore not a potential solution.

We need a type of state handling process and a central coordinating dispatcher process is a sensible solution with respect to tracing the process flow, monitoring, and troubleshooting. Handling the rules directly in the ESB does not seem to be an appropriate solution for the case in question.

But we have not nearly exhausted the possibilities of using business rules in process-driven applications. We will discuss some further applications in brief in the following.

The first case again examines the idea of the state machine, but this time varying the order of the process steps. If the individual steps in the process are known but their order can vary (or some steps are skipped), the use of decision tables is again indicated. The basic idea can be illustrated by the example process steps *Order-Eat-Pay* for different types of restaurants. In a classic restaurant, the diner first orders, then eats, and pays at the end. In a branch of a cafeteria, on the other hand, the diner pays directly after ordering and then eats. In a buffet system, the diner usually pays a set price first, selects a meal, and then eats without ordering at all. Implementing a process for all three restaurants requires the flexibility of rules. The two figures below show a decision table for this scenario and the associated process flow (Figs. 5.56 and 5.57).

Fig. 5.56 Variation of process steps using rules

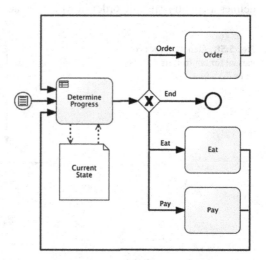

Fig. 5.57 Decision table for varying process steps

State	Restaurant	Process Step	Next State
Start	Classical	Order	1
Start	Cafeteria	Order	1
Start	Buffet	Pay	1
1	Classical	Eat	2
1	Cafeteria	Pay	2
1	Buffet	Eat	End
2	Classical	Pay	End
2	Cafeteria	Eat	End
End	*	End	

Once the start condition is met (in this example, entering the restaurant), the appropriate process step and the new state are determined simultaneously by the rules. The step is then executed before the next loop pass starts to determine the next step again. This pattern can be applied to a wide variety of similar scenarios.

Its drawback is the selection of process steps fixed in advance. Furthermore, it is now no longer possible to tell from the BPMN model in which order the steps are executed, an important advantage of BPMN. If this is your aim, you must create separate explicitly modeled sequence flows for each restaurant type. It is debatable whether, with this amount of freedom, BPMN can be recommended for executing the individual steps or whether these types of processes are not suited to BPMN and we should use other software products instead (as is usual when handling case records). We will study this topic again in detail in Sect. 5.8 and discuss various solutions.

It is also not possible to add completely new steps using the method above. This would again require a loosely coupled variant using an ESB. It is worth considering, however, whether all this implementation work is worthwhile for individual steps and in most cases the described flexibility in order is enough. Any order can be configured at any point at runtime. A more generic variant of this idea is shown in the model from Fig. 5.58 with the associated decision table in Fig. 5.59. This defines a country-specific order in which the activities are executed.

Fig. 5.58 Generic process variant for controlling process steps

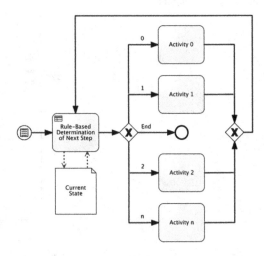

Fig. 5.59 Decision table for generic control of process steps

Country	Current State	Next State
DE	Start	0
	0	1
	1	2
	2	n
	n	End
US	Start	0
	0	2
	2	n
	n	End
Fr	Start	0
	0	2
	1	n
	2	1
	n	End

Each country has a different execution sequence, $0 \to 2 \to n$ for the USA and $0 \to 1 \to 2 \to n$ for Germany (ignoring the start and end states). Steps can be skipped, as seen in the USA, and the example for France shows how the steps can be called in a different sequence, namely $0 \to 2 \to 1 \to n$. Rules can be used to add or delete countries as easily as modifying the order of the steps. These are the arguments that speak in favour of using business rules, taking into account the restrictions caused by fixed activities mentioned above. Furthermore, the model above has the distinct drawback that the control flow is obscured completely since it is hidden in the rules. A solution of this type should therefore be considered carefully and implemented in very specific cases.

Rules can also be applied in the execution of processes in personnel departments. Here, the decisive questions are: who can perform certain steps, who is not permitted, or who can access the processes as an administrator. This exposes a weakness of BPMN, namely that it employs swimlanes to model roles. This prevents certain aspects from being expressed (or only expressed by adding comments). Furthermore, it does not provide associations with organigrams. It is not the role of BPMN to close these gaps and it is the strategy of the OMG to accommodate these aspects using other standards instead before merging them with BPMN. Figure 5.60 shows a process fragment from Allweyer (2010a) as an example for these clear weaknesses in BPMN.

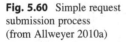

Fig. 5.60 Simple request
submission process
(from Allweyer 2010a)

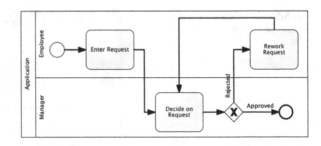

The step *Enter Request* in this submission process can be executed by *any* employee, which is not the case for the task *Rework Request*, even though it is located in the same swimlane. This activity is obviously only meant for those employees who submitted the request in the first process step. The *Manager* swimlane also has problems, since not every manager is supposed to be able to perform the task *Decide on Request*, only the manager of the submitter. These types of constellations must be accommodated and implemented again and again and rules are a sensible alternative here in interactions with user management systems. The actual assignment of users is made therefore *at runtime* while respecting the current context and is not associated statically with the swimlanes. The swimlanes themselves provide orientation as to which person group is responsible for which activities. This specific information is defined, however, by the rules, which makes the correct behavior at runtime possible here too. This is necessary whenever critical processes are delayed by absences (such as vacation or sick leave) and quick changes need to be made. Employees are not usually entered directly (too static) and groups and roles are usually referenced by classic user management systems such as LDAP-based systems, databases, or SAP systems. The relations between people are also saved in these systems. If special relations (such as a manager) are implemented, as in the scenario above, the user management system must provide an appropriate API, for example to make the assigned manager identifiable throughout the whole organizational hierarchy. These calls can either be made directly from the rules engine and the business rules provide specific names or the rules send appropriate instructions to the calling process and it identifies the person group using calls to user management. This assumes that the process and the business rules are closely meshed, with the process knowing how to implement a rule like *Find Manager* in calls to user management and hence produce the correct behavior.

The request submission example above touches on another problem, namely how to model a suitable double verification principle. The model shown in Fig. 5.60 illustrates the classic solution of a request being approved by a manager, with the requester and manager in two separate swimlanes. But what happens when the changes in the company structure demand adjustments to the principle? In certain constellations, such as when the cost of a request increases, the manager of the direct manager needs to be involved as well. In other cases, the direct manager is skipped intentionally, for example when a manager elsewhere in the hierarchy has the required signoff authority. Adapting the process to the context every time does not make sense and the flexibility must be produced from a combination of business rules and process instead. Again, it is the rules that provide stability in the actual business processes. A potential solution to this problem is shown in Fig. 5.61.

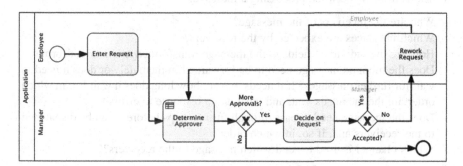

Fig. 5.61 Implementation of multiple approvals using rules

The approval is now handled in a rule-based loop. In the model, we assume that the user management API is called from the rule, the responsible employee identified, and then assigned to the swimlane. This ensures that the task *Decide on Request* is passed to the correct person. This approach can handle any number of combinations, regardless of how many levels are involved and without needing to adapt the process.

In the process patterns discussed here already, we have always included a time element by monitoring the duration of individual steps or step sequences grouped in subprocesses using timer boundary events and activating an appropriate exception sequence in the event of timeouts. Different time limits can also be defined for user tasks, making it possible to specify the time at which a task is started and by when it must be completed. If timeouts occur, a timer event activates the exception handling sequence.

The release point of tasks can also be governed using an activation timer, making it possible, for example, for interested parties to register for a survey while delaying the actual start of the survey until a later point in time. Once this time is reached, the associated step is released and the survey sent to the registered parties. The time instruction here guarantees a uniform start for the survey campaign.

A final example of the use of time instructions with rules is when defining an expiration date, namely the expiration of a task if not completed by a previously defined time (since its data is then no longer relevant for the remainder of the process). When applied to the survey just mentioned, the responses of participants sent after a particular date are ignored in the analysis.

In all these examples, the logic used to identify the times is passed to rules and hence can be adapted at runtime. Further applications for rules are as conditions for exceptions (which exception to raise under which conditions) and as completion conditions for loops (which constellation ends the loop). The following section now discusses further scenarios designed especially for technical processes.

5.7.2 Using Business Rules in Technical Processes

Rules are particularly recommended in the service contract implementation layer, where we implement technical integration processes. There are usually many decisions to be made when processing a message:

– Who are the receivers of the message?
– Which interfaces are expected by the receivers?
– How are the individual fields in the message transformed to the target formats?
– Does the inbound message need to be forwarded immediately or does it need to wait for further messages? If it needs to wait, how long does it wait for, in which order are the messages sent, and what is the response to errors?
– Does the message need to pass through further steps before it can be dispatched to the receivers and, if so, in which order?
– Which channel is used to send which message to the receivers?

This (incomplete) list shows you the wide range of applications for rules when used as implementation methods for the decisions above. The questions in the list represent classic integration problems, whose solutions are also illustrated in the book *Enterprise Integration Patterns*. They do not need to be repeated here and instead I will emphasize the specific use of rules in selected examples from the spectrum above. The areas in question are *Receiver Determination, Interface Determination, Mapping*, plus *Channel Determinations* and *Message Handling Logic*.

When a message is received in the service contract implementation layer, its sender, the inbound interface, and the channel that directed the message are all known. The *Channel* here is the method (or route) used to transport the message, be it by e-mail, JMS queue, Web service call, or file transfer. This is the first instance where we can think about using rules. Based on the information now known, one or more receivers can be determined. Alongside this, the message content, including metadata like the length or format of the message, can also be used for decision purposes. Both decision tables and traditional if-then rules can be implemented here. Some typical examples are illustrated here:

– If the message is received using the interface OrderOut and by e-mail from the sender system *ABC*, the receiver is *XYZ*.
– If the message is received using the interface InvoiceOut and the field totalAmount exceeds a value of 1,000,000 Euros, the receivers are *LMN* and *UVW*.

If we are able to determine the receiver(s) in this way, the next rule can be used to determine the target interface format, namely the response to the question of in which format the receiver is to receive the message. Here, we can also exploit the information that helped us to determine the receiver. It is also a good idea to split the rules between receiver determination and interface determination, since this makes the entire system more flexible and concentrates each set of rules on a particular aspect (separation of concerns). The administration of the rules becomes easier when each set of rules contains fewer entries, but at the same time there is a loss of overall clarity when the administrator has to edit the sets separately. The improvements in flexibility generally support this separation however. Examples of determining the target interface are as follows:

- If the inbound interface has the format OrderOut and is sent to the receiver *XYZ*, the target format is OrderInXYZ.
- If the inbound interface has the format InvoiceOut, is sent to the receiver *UVW*, and the field urgency contains the value critical, the target format is InvoiceInCriticalUVW.

We now know both the receiver(s) and target format(s) of the message. We now need to update the message from the input format to the output format, a suitable job for mapping rules that can define how input and output fields are mapped to each other. The focus here is on value mappings, which transform values that cannot be mapped 1-to-1. The fields of the interfaces represent the same semantic information, but they are shown with different values. For example, the inbound interface can have the value *1* for *male* and the value *2* for *female*. The outbound interface, on the other hand, cannot handle the values *1* and *2* and only understands the non-numeric texts just shown. This produces rules in the following form

- If the input field gender contains the value *1*, the output field gender is given the value male.

Another option for simple transformations of this type is transformation tables, since they are much simpler to edit in these cases than if-then rules. If we need more complex logical expressions, however, or even need to calculate a target value, classic if-then rules are the best choice. A typical example here is the determination of a price related to a large number of parameters, such as the customer, the amount ordered, the product ordered, the status of the customer. If the inbound interface provides all this data but without the price needed by the outbound interface, a complex logic must often be applied before the price can be determined. It is best, therefore, to transfer this logic to reusable rules.

After these steps, the message is now in its target format with fields filled correctly and ready to be sent. The rules that come next determine the method used to transport the message to the receiver. This step is known as *Channel Determination* and defines whether the message is sent by, for example, JMS queue, Web service, file transfer, or e-mail. Rules enable this to be specified in as detailed a manner as needed, for example differences in field content can cause different channels to be assigned to one and the same outbound interface and the same receiver. The associated rules are as follows:

- If the receiver *UVW* is sent the message `InvoiceInCriticalUVW` and the field `customerStatus` contains the value `gold`, the outbound channel *E-Mail* is used.
- If the receiver *UVW* is sent the message `InvoiceInCriticalUVW` and the field `customerStatus` contains the value `silver`, the outbound channel *JMS* is used.

The handling of the message is now finally complete. All information required to send the message is available and it can be sent as follows:

- In the correct format
- With the correct value
- Using the determined channel
- To the correct receiver

No less than four different sets of rules were needed to achieve this result.

Another example of the use of business rules within technical integration processes is the implementation of a specific message-handling logic. This is a requirement whenever message sequences with complex interrelationships occur. In these cases, the integration layer crossed by all messages has the task of monitoring and securing the correct flow of messages. Let us make this clearer using the example of a complete ordering process, which involves the following messages:

- Create/confirm/change/cancel a purchase order
- Create/change/cancel a sales order
- Create/change a delivery
- Create/change a goods movement
- Create/change an invoice
- Create an incoming payment

If the integration layer is now responsible for all these messages being in the correct order, the rules must define clearly how to proceed in cases where the messages are not received in the expected sequence. This can happen whenever outages in networks and computing systems cause disruptions. We can illustrate this using the simple case study of a car manufacturer who urgently needs materials for production. The manufacturer creates a purchase order electronically, but a fault in the network means that the message does not reach the vendor. The fault is discovered but cannot be repaired quickly and the manufacturer decides to call the vendor. The vendor enters the data directly in the ordering system, which then sends a purchase order confirmation message automatically. This means the integration layer receives a confirmation even though the activity should really start with the purchase order itself. Rules can now be applied to decide how to proceed, namely whether to hold the confirmation back until the matching purchase order is received (it is still held by the manufacturer and will be sent again when the connection is repaired) or whether to forward the confirmation and ignore the purchase order later?

An additional difficulty in this logic is that some messages are mandatory and some are optional. Some special messages need to be sent exactly once and other message types can be sent multiple times. All these properties must be respected when creating the business rules. The result of this, once again, is a state machine combined from BPMN processes and business rules that can decide how to proceed in any possible situation. A small example based on the decision table shown in Fig. 5.62 illustrates a potential solution.

Fig. 5.62 Excerpt from the decision tables for complex message control sequences

State	N0	N1	N2	N3
0000	F, 0001	H, 0010	H, 0100	H, 1000
0001	Invalid	F, 0011	F, 0101	H, 1001
0010	F, 0011	H, 0010	H, 0110	H, 1010
0011	Invalid	F, 0011	F, 0111	H, 1011
0100	F, 0101	C, 0110	H, 0100	H, 1100

In this example, we want to process four messages (N0 through N3). The state machine is initially in state 0000. The representation of the state has an important part to play here with each place representing which message was already received (encoded in binary and reading from the right). A 0 stands for "not yet received" and a 1 for "received". This means that the initial state 0000 indicates that no message has been handled yet. In addition, the following assumptions are made:

– The start message N0 occurs precisely once.
– The message N1 is an optional message.
– The messages N0, N2, and N3 are mandatory messages

The action executed by the process for the current message is now specified in the action fields of the table. They contain the information about what to do with the current message, encoded using the letters F (forward), H (hold back), and C (cancel) and also the next state of the machine.

The first row of the table represents the state transitions from the initial state. Once the start message N0 is received, it can be forwarded immediately and the first bit of the state representation is set to produce the next state 0001. When N1 is received, however, it cannot be forwarded yet and is held back since it has to wait for the start message N0. This means that only the next state 0010 is set, which stands for the received message N1. The same applies when the messages N2 and N3 are received.

The second row of the table is concerned with the transitions whenever message N0 is received (the state 0001). By definition, the message N0 cannot be received again, which explains the entry *Invalid* in the associated action field. The situation is different, however, when N1 is received. It can be processed immediately and the machine can switch to the state 0011. The next field, which represents the received message N2, is also interesting. Although N1 has not yet been received, N2 is processed further immediately (in accordance with the table entry) and the machine passes to the state 0101. This is because N1 is an optional message and does not have to be received. This means that it is possible to handle N2 immediately. The situation is, however, different yet again in the final table column where N3 cannot be processed immediately when received since the mandatory message N2 is missing. This makes it correct that the message N3 is held back by the entry (H, 1001) and only passes to the state 1001. In this way, the table above is really quite simple to decode.

A further interesting field can be seen in the final row of the table for the state 0100, which represents the case where only the message N2 has been received so far. If the optional message N1 is now received, we can feel free to cancel it and just set a new next state.

The only question now remaining is what to do with the messages that have been held back. These messages must be examined again (and all buffered messages), whenever a new message is received and handled by the process using a forward entry. This can mean that the prerequisites for other messages have changed and that they now also need to be forwarded. If these messages are also sorted in ascending order in the queue, it becomes more likely that they need to be processed in sequence or that those messages towards the back are ignored if the first message in the queue cannot be processed further. Figure 5.63 shows a suitable process model.

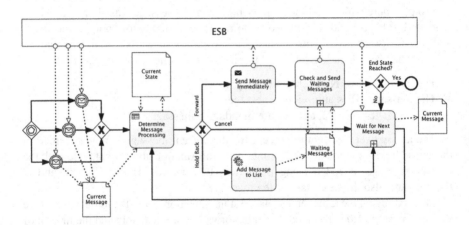

Fig. 5.63 Control of complex message sequences as a BPMN model

Since we do not know which of the potential messages is received first, we must start the process using an instantiating exclusive event-based gateway. For simplicity, the example above assumes only three possible candidates. Once they have been received, the rules determine their further processing based on the current state of communications. Here, the data object *Current State* is used as both an input and output parameter of the rule. The gateway that follows the business rule task handles the actions *Forward*, *Hold Back*, and *Cancel* determined by the rules. In the case of *Hold Back*, the message currently being processed is added to a waiting list. Next, the subprocess *Wait for Next Message* is applied, although the wait for different message types is encapsulated in a subprocess for clarity.

In the case of *Cancel*, the message can be ignored and the wait state can apply immediately. In the case of *Forward*, however, we can forward the current message to the receiver immediately. The action just executed gives us the option of sending other waiting messages, which means that the subprocess *Check and Send Waiting Messages* checks this aspect and responds to the constellation in question accordingly. This also exploits the rules used at the outset. The subprocess ends at the precise moment when checks on the waiting list can no longer identify any candidates to be sent. Once the subprocess has ended, the subsequent gateway determines that the end state has been reached. The wait state applies to this branch too only if the end state is not reached, otherwise the entire process can be ended.

Once the subprocess *Wait for Next Message* is executed, the rule task is visited again to determine the further processing based on the new information and to start the lifecycle one more time.

There are, of course, limits to this method, not least that in the case of n messages, we would have to consider 2^n state changes. In reality, however, we can exclude a large number of transitions, making the actual scope much smaller. And we have seen here how it is possible to implement message-handling logic using rules.

In a final example, I would like to illustrate how rules can be used to validate messages, since even when messages with correct syntax are forwarded to the integration-centric process they can still be semantically incorrect. In the case of field combinations in particular, rules can filter messages with errors automatically and forward them to an expert to be checked and corrected. A classic example of this kind of problem is surely errors in currency conversions, where it is always easy to divide instead of multiply with a conversion factor. Usually, a message like this gets stuck in the middleware (since the local validation logic in the receiver application refuses it) or it reaches the target system and damages it accordingly (which often requires a lot of repair work). If the message is held in the middleware, it is often difficult to correct its content, since security restrictions in middleware products mean values cannot simply be modified. It is relatively easy to solve this problem by filtering messages using validation rules and implementing an explicit correction. Even if unexpected field constellations cause messages to encounter errors, a solution can be found by modifying or expanding the rules and restarting the message at runtime. After the correction, the message is again passed to the business rules for validation (where it can be filtered and corrected again). Each time an error occurs, the rules are developed and perfected further, and perform tasks automatically that were previously characterized by errors and follow-up work. In a final stage, rules can also perform automatic corrections in simple cases, if they follow repetitive patterns. This is how we can increase the level of automation and hence efficiency in the enterprise.

Figure 5.64 shows a suitable process model here too.

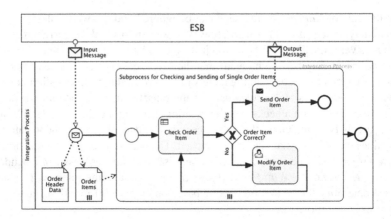

Fig. 5.64 Rule-based field checks in integration-centric processes

In this example, the inbound message contains an order consisting of an order header and multiple order items. These two parts of the message are first split into two dedicated data objects. Next, a parallel subprocess checks each order item on the basis of rules. Depending on the result of this test, we either initiate a correction to the item in a user task or dispatch it immediately. In the correction case, it is best to validate the item again (using the rules) to prevent errors in the input from reoccurring.

These examples demonstrate how we can address and solve standard integration problems elegantly using rules. In today's ESB implementations, on the other hand, each vendor offers proprietary tools for solving these problems. Within a single product, various tools are used to make a range of decisions, even though they could be addressed uniformly using a rules engine with an associated gain in flexibility. The benefits of using business rules are so obvious, however, that you can expect to see them implemented more and more often in integration products.

5.7.3   Increasing Automation by Combining Business Rules and Analytical Applications

We can increase the level of automation in business processes within process-driven applications by incorporating analytical data. Within a process model, there are two typical scenarios to consider when exploiting analytical applications to optimize processes:

– Within a service task to prepare rule-based decisions
– Within user tasks in the form of graphical diagrams for interactive decision making

Figure 5.65 shows our purchase order process again, this time with an additional service task added for finding specially aggregated data from a Business Warehouse (BW) system (the additional collaboration with the data warehouse is not shown explicitly in the model).

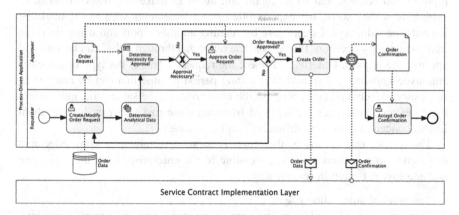

Fig. 5.65 Simplified purchase order process with analytical data

As soon as the data is entered by the requester, we read aggregated information from a BW system. This system provides, for example, predefined data analyses as Web services (known as analytics as a service). In our specific example, this could be a summary of the past purchasing behavior of the shopper, together with figures about the reliability of payments. This information is incorporated into decision making based on rules. The benefit of this approach is found in the combination of transactional and analytical data for improved decision making. The data aggregated in the BW system from various other systems enables analyses to be made that are far more reliable and accurate and with that support higher quality decision making. The provision of this service by the BW system (as Web services) and its interaction with business rules also makes further automation possible and improves flexibility in business processes. A combination of analytical data and rules is now a fully automated alternative to the time consuming evaluation of manual analytical diagrams and tables. Of course, not all decisions can be fully automated, which means the interactive analysis of data by expert employees continues to be a vital part of processes. The difference, however, is that the expert is now consulted in far fewer cases, since the majority of decisions are processed automatically.

The interactive analysis of data by experts could, when related to the process model above, be depicted in the form of graphical diagrams in the *Approve Order Request* step, with information from a BW system added to the decision interface of the employee during the process flow. This means that the employee is provided with the context-specific data relevant to decision making without needing to access the BW system itself and research it. Hence this scenario reflects the second application of analytical data in processes mentioned at the outset.

It is now interesting to consider how we can further optimize our processes once we have implemented a solution of this kind. The weak points remain the interactive user tasks and it is useful to examine the work methods of employees in their manual decision making. It is generally the case that an employee accesses the same reports, transactions, and so on again and again to make decisions. If asked to explain how they work, the experts often make statements such as "If field abc exceeds the value xyz, I make sure by running another report and using its value uvw to make my decision. If uvw is in the range aaa through bbb, I can be sure and approve the request. Otherwise, I reject the request". This is the type of priceless employee knowledge acquired over a long period of time that can be mapped to rules successively and conserved for the enterprise. At the same time, automation increases and employees are released from mundane routine work, leaving them free to concentrate on more difficult exceptional cases.

The aim of this approach, therefore, is to successively map knowledge and experience to rules and make it accessible to the enterprise. Both the enterprise and employees benefit in several ways:

- The level of automation rises.
- Employees are released from time consuming mundane routine work, increasing motivation by letting them work more intensively on more challenging and more interesting tasks (which itself improves quality).
- A reduction in risk for the enterprise when employees are absent or leave the company.
- The extracted decision-making knowledge is applied to other cases as "best practices".

In summary, the combination of the three elements processes, rules, and the incorporation of analytical data has enormous potential for optimization and automation. Dedicated tools and frameworks from many different vendors now support enterprises so well that they can respond more quickly, more specifically, and more precisely to ever changing market conditions. This enables them to either consolidate their position as market leader or even extend it.

5.8   Process-Driven Applications and Unpredictable Process Flows

By now, we have discussed a wide range of different process models in this book, but what they all had in common was a fixed sequence of steps. We have always stressed the importance of high levels of flexibility, but the existence of some static elements cannot be denied. This aspect is also criticized in the related literature, as summarized by Max Pucher in his blog (Pucher 2010):

> I have just been very vocal (and provocative) in the last ten years denouncing the all-out claims of the BPM-faithful that they can model a business and run it on rigid flowcharts.

His blog goes on to discuss research in the area of adaptive processes and how his patented method of User-Trained Agents (UTA) was created over the years. The idea is based mainly on agents that monitor and log user actions at every point in time. The experience gathered by this monitoring is then used to provide the user with suggestions about how to proceed. If the suggestion is used, the collected knowledge becomes more trustworthy. If not used, the level of trust falls and the agent attempts to detect better patterns in the collected data to improve the chance of success for the next proposal. In principle, this method is an automation of the determination of decision rules from the last section. But Pucher is not trying to fully eliminate human interaction and instead wants to help the user continue the process without it being frozen in advance. His work includes ideas from process mining (see also van der Aalst's process mining website (van der Aalst 2010) and his book (van der Aalst 2011) for further research on this topic), which uses the process event logs as the basis for changing proposals. But how can we support completely unpredictable processes, such as the treatment of patients in a hospital, legal procedures, tailoring offers to specific customers, or appraising an insurance claim using IT? The following examines the role of BPMN in these kinds of scenarios and how we can use a combination of structured, unstructured, and standard processes to address the problem.

The BPMN 2.0 standard specifies an activity called the ad-hoc subprocess for mapping non-fixed sequences of tasks. Figure 5.66 shows a subprocess of this type with multiple tasks.

Fig. 5.66 Ad-Hoc subprocess

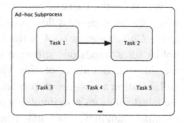

The semantics of the handling of this subprocess specify that first all tasks are activated *without* an inbound sequence flow (the tasks 1, 3, 4, and 5 in the example above). The end user selects one of the activated tasks to be executed. If the attribute ordering assigned to the ad-hoc subprocess is set to the value *Parallel Processing*, more than one activated task can be performed at once, which of course is not possible in sequential processing. Once a task is completed, the completion condition (represented by the attribute completionCondition) for the subprocess is evaluated and if the condition is not yet met, the set of activated tasks is recalculated and passed for execution (if required). If, on the other hand, the condition is met, the ad-hoc subprocess is ended without any new tasks being activated. In parallel processing, however, tasks can still be in editing even though the completion condition is now met. This makes the handling of the running tasks dependent on the value of a further attribute of the subprocess. If, for instance, the value of the attribute cancelRemainingInstances is set to the Boolean value true, all active tasks are interrupted and the sequence flow resumes directly with the task that follows the subprocess. In the case of false, however, the completion of all tasks being edited is expected.

This means that we can use an ad-hoc subprocess to dissolve the static nature of fixed execution sequences. This case also demands that all tasks are known at design time, but what happens when a completely new task is needed at runtime that was not originally predicted? This is illustrated particularly clearly in the case of hospital treatment. A doctor uses a diagnosis and the progress of the condition to trigger various examinations and treatments. This behavior cannot be mapped just by using an ad-hoc subprocess and we also need a case record in which all information such as analyses, reports, images, and graphs is collected and can be edited collaboratively by those involved in the process. But how can the case record interact with structured processes to span the full process? A period in hospital does, after all, also involve structured processes that should be supported by IT. A specific example is illustrated in Fig. 5.67, which shows the interaction of structured, unstructured, and standard processes.

The process starts with the admission of a patient, where the usual patient data is recorded in the step *Registration and Assignment to Physician* and a doctor on call is selected as the doctor responsible during this patient's stay in hospital. After examining the patient, the doctor must decide whether further examinations are necessary. If this is not the case, the patient can leave the clinic right away. Otherwise, the doctor selects specialists who can provide further details for a diagnosis on the basis of current information and starts the collaboration. This is where the fixed process flow is exited, despite there being an ad-hoc activity action in the *Collaboration* pool in the BPMN diagram. This is, however, only a place-holder for a standalone software solution concentrating on collaboration between the doctors. Solutions of this kind are also known as groupware and support collaboration across geography and across time. As well as people and information, the latest solutions also involve working methods in the form of dedicated tools, for example rankings, pro and contra tables, quick surveys, SWOT (strengths, weaknesses, opportunities, threats) analyses, cost-benefit analyses, and many more. For each piece of information, the collaborators can start discussions and add comments. The final aim is to guarantee that all decision-making steps can be traced and understood. This information must be preserved for the future and an archiving function is essential. Examples of products with these properties are SAP StreamWork and SAP Jam. You can find more details under SAP 2011 and SAPJAM 2014 respectively.

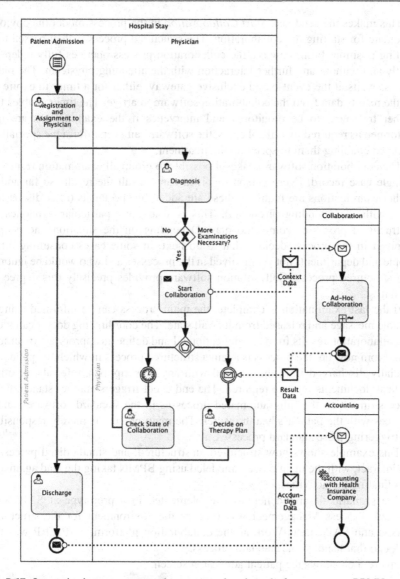

Fig. 5.67 Interaction between structured, unstructured, and standard processes as a BPMN model

In our specific example, the interaction between business process and collaboration software is supported by the following:

- Creating a new collaboration using the business process
- Selecting the doctors involved in this collaboration
- Handing over the existing patient data

This makes the send task *Start Collaboration* in the process model the obvious candidate for starting the collaboration. The structured process is then passed to a waiting position. From now on, the collaboration process operates fully independently and without any further interaction with the attending physician. The main process waits at the event-based exclusive gateway, either for a timer to expire or for the results data from the collaboration software to arrive. The timer enables the further treatment to be monitored and intervenes if the examinations are not performed as required. In critical cases, the software can even inform the specialists involved enabling them to speed up the treatment.

The collaboration software makes it possible to group all examination results in a single case record. Every person involved can consult the results so far and if further examinations are required, these are added by specialists (after discussing them with the attending physician). This is where the particular dynamics of unstructured processes come into play. Depending on the situation, the people involved in the process decide what to do next, in some cases consulting other people and departments not yet involved in the processes and who would be ignored in a structured process. Collaboration software provides precisely this degree of flexibility.

If the last examination is complete, the main process can be informed using a suitable message and released from its wait state. The coordinating doctor can view the collaboration results from an application UI and define an appropriate treatment plan. From now on, the process is again a structured process in which the patient is officially discharged from the hospital with any prescriptions, referrals, or other medical documents that are required. The end event triggers another standardized process, in which the fully automated processes in the standard software handle invoices with the patient's health insurer. The main process is merely responsible for triggering these standard processes.

This example shows how structured, unstructured, and standardized processes can interact, with the main process modeled using BPMN taking the lead again and coordinating the activities.

The scenario described here was implemented in a prototype at SAP. SAP Business Process Management was used as the environment for the structured process and SAP StreamWork as the collaboration platform. SAP ERP was the back end that handled the standard process.

Figure 5.68 shows the patient admission screen.

Fig. 5.68 Patient
admission form

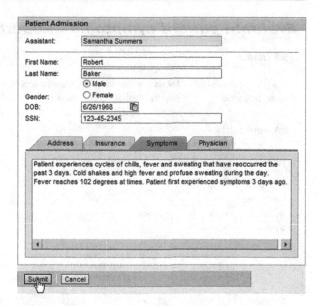

The image shows a typical data input screen organized into different tabs for entering patient information such as address, symptoms, insurance data, and the attending physician when first admitted (the *Physician* tab). Once all the information is entered, the doctor in question receives a notification that it is available when the patient is seen.

The initial examination produces the first results of relevance to the future collaboration with the specialist doctors. This means it must be possible to upload scanned documents or images (such as cardiograms or sonograms). Figure 5.69 shows the UI of the attending physician, which here is still a part of the structured process.

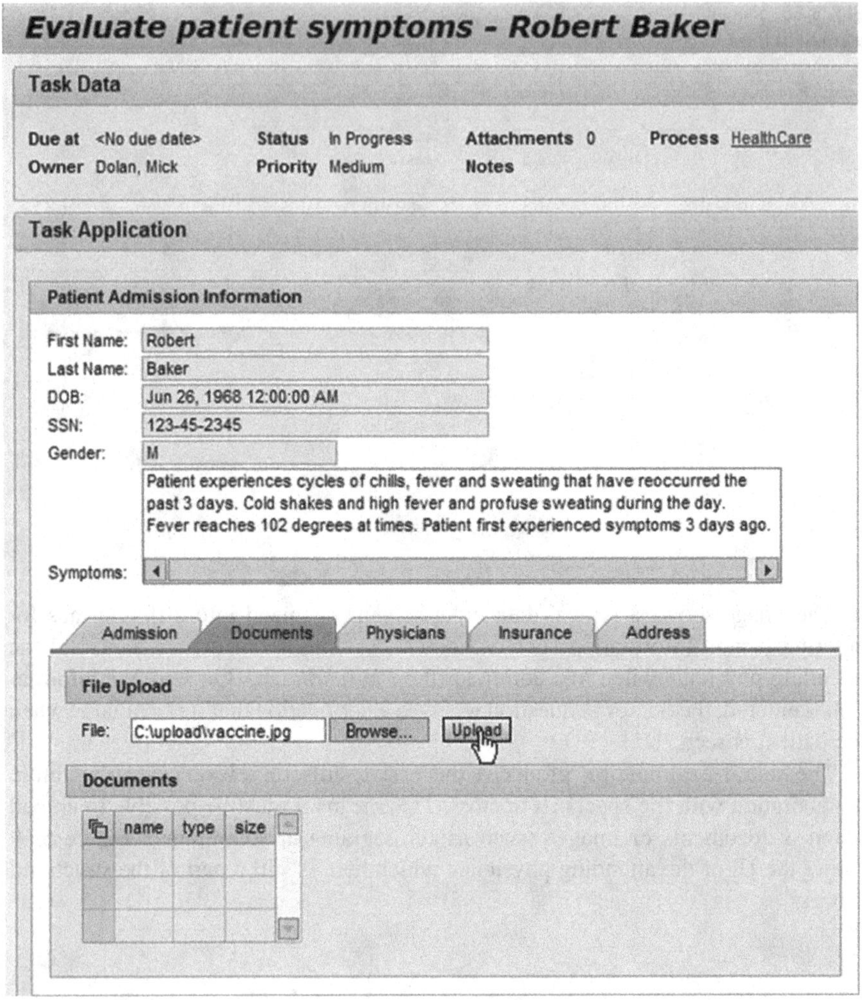

Evaluate patient symptoms - Robert Baker

Task Data

Due at <No due date>	**Status** In Progress	**Attachments** 0	**Process** HealthCare
Owner Dolan, Mick	**Priority** Medium	**Notes**	

Task Application

Patient Admission Information

First Name:	Robert
Last Name:	Baker
DOB:	Jun 26, 1968 12:00:00 AM
SSN:	123-45-2345
Gender:	M

Symptoms:

Patient experiences cycles of chills, fever and sweating that have reoccurred the past 3 days. Cold shakes and high fever and profuse sweating during the day. Fever reaches 102 degrees at times. Patient first experienced symptoms 3 days ago.

| Admission | Documents | Physicians | Insurance | Address |

File Upload

File: C:\upload\vaccine.jpg   Browse...   Upload

Documents

	name	type	size	

Fig. 5.69 Form for entering the initial examination

In this example, the vaccination certificate of the patient is being uploaded, but otherwise the UI is nearly identical to the admission screen just shown. Only the initiation of collaboration has been added to the *Physicians* tab. Here, those specialist doctors are selected that are required to add further data, such as test results, ECGs, x-rays, or sonograms. Figure 5.70 shows the specialists selected by the attending physician Mick Dolan.

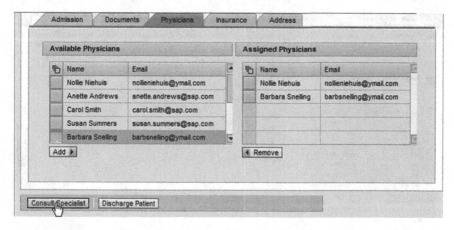

Fig. 5.70 Selection of specialists for collaboration

Choosing the *Consult Specialist* pushbutton creates the collaboration in SAP StreamWork. SAP StreamWork has a REST API (REST: REpresentational State Transfer) that does not just start a collaboration but also makes it possible to upload documents, the existing data, and the people involved. All this information is passed to SAP StreamWork from the UI program. Once the collaboration has been created, its initiator (Mick Dolan) can connect to the platform immediately. A dialog box informs the doctor that the collaboration is there and that the workspace can now be accessed (Fig. 5.71).

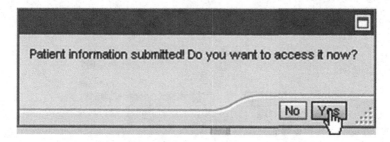

Fig. 5.71 Confirmation of successfully created collaboration

After the doctor has accessed the collaboration platform, the SAP StreamWork environment shown in Fig. 5.72 appears. We can see clearly here that the screen is split into a left half, containing patient data and a vaccination certificate, and a right half, where any people involved can create comments about the information on the left. It is the results from these kinds of discussion that are often poorly documented or not documented at all. SAP StreamWork makes these discussion threads an important part of the solution while also linking them clearly to the relevant information on the left.

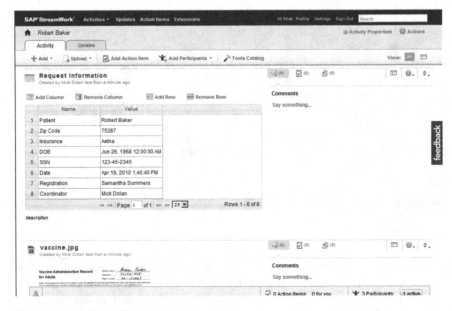

Fig. 5.72 SAP StreamWork collaboration environment

The people involved in the collaboration are shown in the bottom right corner of the screen. Three people are currently working together here, and one of them is active. Clicking the text *3 Participants* displays the three specialists selected by the attending physician, who were also passed successfully to SAP StreamWork (Fig. 5.73).

Fig. 5.73 List of the doctors in the collaboration

The specialists can now access the data in the case record when they see the patient and have a full picture of the situation. If current or future examinations require further specialists to be consulted, this can be done at any time by choosing the *Add Participants* menu item.

Once the collaboration has ended, the waiting main process must be released from its wait situation. This is done by sending a Web service call from SAP StreamWork to SAP BPM. The process waits at an intermediate message event, associated in SAP BPM with an interface that can be called using a Web service. SAP StreamWork obscures this function within an activity called *Decision* (see Fig. 5.74).

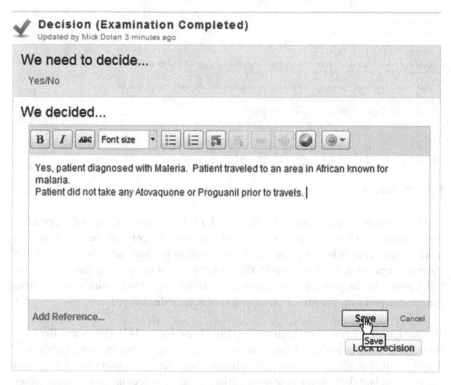

Fig. 5.74 Completing collaboration and reactivating the waiting main process

As soon as the *Save* button is chosen, communication takes place with the waiting process. This process now reaches the next step for the coordinating physician and requests a diagnosis, a plan of treatment, and further steps. Figure 5.75 shows the associated form in detail.

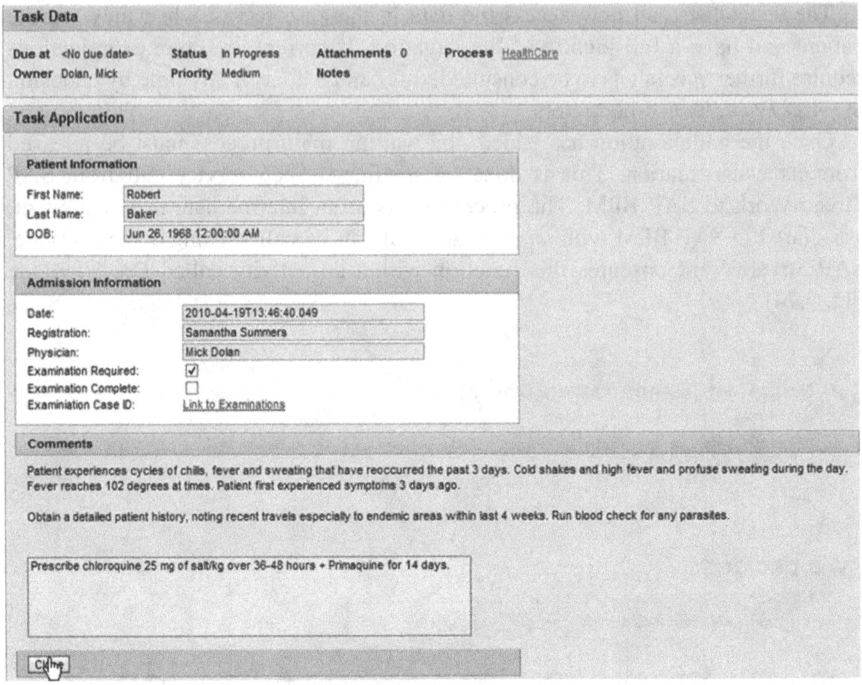

Fig. 5.75 Form for completing treatment

Here, the doctor can also use the hyperlink *Link to Examinations* in the center of the screen to navigate the case record and study the progress of the examinations again. These results help him or her when deciding the next actions to take in the patient's treatment. In this example, this just consists of prescribing medication. As you can see in the process model, this information is passed to admissions, where the patient picks up the prescription and is officially discharged.

Discussion of Alternative Approaches for "Case Records" The "Case Record" topic (also known as Case Management) has attracted attention recently, since it could seem that all classic business process management approaches have been made redundant. Whenever new topics arise, it's easy to feel unsure about whether you are taking the right approach yourself, particularly when ambitious statements are heard such as "Give up your process-centric approach and take a great leap into the future by putting the case record at the center of your concept". If this were the case, you could stop reading this book right now and hope that it might at least make a good door stopper. My approach is, after all, strongly oriented toward business processes. It is impossible to be 100 % convinced about any approach, which is why it makes sense to step back and take a more careful look at the new holy grail of process management ☺. The following discussion is based on a white paper written by Frank Buytendijk called *Embrace Complexity, Simplify Your Organization*

(Buytendijk 2012). It is an effective summary of the main ideas in the adaptive process approach and a good substitute for all publications on this topic that present similar solutions.

By now, the *Case Record* topic has become known under a variety of names, such as *Adaptive Case Management* (ACM), *Adaptive Processes, Dynamic Case Management*, or simply *Case*. It is, after all, a significant paradigm change when the case in question is at the center of attention and not the process. Associated with this is a different kind of process execution involving a supporting use of a new generation of process software rather than execution-driven process engines. This new software enables end users to decide which steps are performed to achieve their specific targets. This means that the driver of the process is the user and not the central process engine and the software is a utility supporting end users to perform their tasks. This is unlike the approach in classic predefined processes, which dictate to the end users exactly *what* they have to do. The new idea, therefore, presents us with target- or goal-oriented processes in which each instance runs in a slightly different way to the other instances, making it unique. This is made possible by changing our perspective and our way of thinking to concentrate on solving only the case in question (defined as the number of steps needed to achieve a specified result). The solution of the case is at the center of our attention and the software aids us when we identify the appropriate steps for a specific context and collect them in a group. The end user then selects an action to perform from this group of steps. The context we are talking about here is certainly similar to the process context already discussed, since new or existing data is added to it when an activity is completed. This produces a new context and a new situation from which a new group of appropriate steps has to be determined to move us closer to completing our case. This is a method known from navigation systems in cars, where if the conditions change (if traffic is encountered or a turnoff is missed) the system immediately calculates an alternative route. This is also how we should imagine adaptive processes.

We can now describe the process flow when we handle a case relatively easily as follows:

1. Based on the current context C, the software calculates the set A of activities that move us closer to completing the case.
2. The end user chooses *one* activity from the set A and executes it.
3. Once the activity in question has been completed, the software updates the context C.
4. If the case has not yet been completed, the cycle starts again with step 1.

This means that the software does not dictate to end users what they need to do and they can choose to proceed with any of the potential activities. This is made possible by preconditions and post-conditions defined for the activities in question. The precondition defines the conditions under which an activity can be executed and the post-condition determines the state of the process context after the activity has been completed. Based on the preconditions and post-conditions, the process software can divide the activities into three sets, called the *dynamic activity plan* by Buytendijk in his paper:

– The set of active *current activities* that can be executed immediately. The order of execution within this set is not significant.
– The set of completed *processed activities*. If new data emerges that was not known when the steps were executed for the first time, the activities can be executed again.
– The set of *future activities* that cannot be activated due to the current context and the preconditions of these steps, but which can be activated at a later point in time.

These concepts make the overall solution strongly target-oriented. A prerequisite for this is, of course, suitable preconditions and post-conditions that ensure that the case can be completed. Another thing you may have noticed in this approach is that all potential activities, together with their preconditions and post-conditions, need to be defined or modeled in advance. There is, therefore, no complete freedom here either. Adaptive processes claim to handle the explosion in potential combinations in a single process, with all its nuances and exceptions, which is why Buytendijk's paper has the name *Embrace Complexity*. We should not try to simplify our (highly complex) reality using reduced process models and instead regard this complexity as something completely normal and look for solutions to it. Buytendijk believes that we already have a solution in the concepts described above.

One interesting question remains, namely how do we formulate specific conditions? You may notice the resemblance to business rules here and this similarity is real. In his paper, Buytendijk states that "everything is a business rule" and these rules are used to "separate the "know" from the "flow"". These concepts should be very familiar to us. In the chapter about business rules, we already considered making processes more flexible by combining business rules with BPMN and we should now ask whether there is a BPMN alternative to the flow logic above for handling cases. Hence, let us take a look at the model shown in Fig. 5.76.

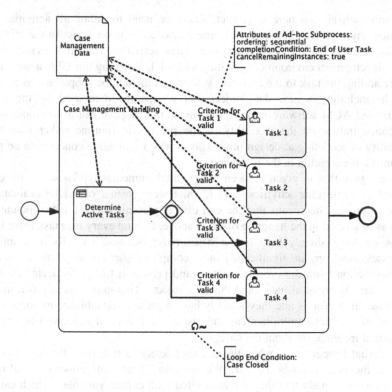

Fig. 5.76 Case record handling as BPMN model

This solution is based on a combination of an ad-hoc subprocess, a loop across the ad-hoc subprocess, and rules. Let us now take a look at this process flow in more detail. If the token reaches the ad-hoc subprocess, its definition (see the discussion of the ad-hoc subprocess at the start of Sect. 5.8) dictates that only those tasks are activated that do not have an inbound sequence flow, in our case only the business rule task *Determine Active Tasks*. All activity criteria are defined in this task centrally. It is, after all, an evaluation of the current process context (shown symbolically in the model using the *Case Management Data* data object) with respect to the preconditions of each activity. You may wonder whether it is a good idea to group all activity conditions in a central location, since they are preconditions for *Activities* and need to be assigned to them. I would argue that defining them centrally is actually much simpler than needing to examine each activity in turn to establish which conditions apply to it, but this is a matter of preference. I personally find being able to define and edit conditions centrally highly practical. No matter what we decide, the business rule task provides us with a list of potential activities. This list is evaluated by the exclusive gateway and the sequence flows pass the token to those associated tasks that are relevant for our case as detected by the rules. I have only chosen four tasks in the example, but the list naturally contains the set of all tasks that can potentially complete the case.

The approach chosen here is correct, since we need to define all activities in advance anyway. This is where we come across a slight weakness in the BPMN solution, namely that it is not that easy to add new activities. This involves returning to the development environment, creating a new UI, assigning this UI to a task, and finally adding the task to the inclusive gateway in the ad-hoc subprocess as a new branch (including a new data object that groups the data used by the UI). Specialized ACM software is more flexible in this respect, but at the moment I am concentrating on the flexibility of the process at runtime rather than the flexibility of modeling at design time. This is why I will again concentrate on the semantics at execution in the following.

Every task that is given a token is activated immediately. To stay with our example, we select the activities *1* and *3*, which were given a token after evaluation at the gateway. This means that the end user is presented with a list of potential tasks as described in the handling of cases above. Behind every user task there is a UI as we have already seen in the structured processes. The UIs in adaptive processes, however, are significantly more complex. After all, they have to group all information from the completed steps and present it (this is indicated by the associations between all tasks and the data object). This makes them much more than just simple forms and they actually have a greater resemblance to portal UIs that are divided into multiple areas and display both context-dependent and role-dependent information about the case.

But what happens now when the end user selects a task from the list? Let us assume the user chooses *Task 1*. We now see a special property of ad-hoc subprocesses, namely that they are associated with certain variables, which cause the ad-hoc subprocess to behave in a certain way. One of these variables is called `ordering` and is used to define which non-selected tasks remain active and can be completed in parallel. There is no visual representation of these variables in the BPMN model, so I have added a comment to the ad-hoc subprocess. This states that the variable is set to *sequential*, meaning that no further tasks are active while the current task is being edited. The end user can work on *Task 1* without being disturbed and at the same time the associated UI, as usual, is provided with the data from the data object *Case Management Data*. In the same way, the data object is updated by an output mapping once the input has been completed. This corresponds to the post-conditions in the description above.

If we were able to complete *Task 1* successfully, the BPMN specification dictates that we now test whether the ad-hoc subprocess can be completed. To do this, the ad-hoc subprocess uses a further variable, `completionCondition`. As also detailed in the comment mentioned above, the ad-hoc subprocess must be completed whenever a user task is processed in full. *Task 1* is a user task of this kind, which means that the condition is met and the ad-hoc subprocess is completed. However, we should not forget a third variable, `cancelRemainingInstances`, also typical for ad-hoc subprocesses, which dictates what happens with other tasks also expected by tokens and which could theoretically be executed. The comment states that the variable is set to `true`, which means that all tokens are cleared (in our example, from *Task 3*), without a further activity needing to be performed. Finally, the ad-hoc subprocess is completed as planned. We still need to evaluate the loop condition that we added to the subprocess and I have explained this in a comment too. This states that the call of the ad-hoc subprocess is repeated until the case record has been processed in full. If this is not yet the case, we start the subprocess again, run through our rules, and we are given a new set of active tasks produced by the now modified process contexts. Again, this is exactly the behavior we expect, since the grouping of the tasks must be oriented to the modified conditions every time. As you can see from this description, it is perfectly possible to implement the core ideas of dynamic behavior in Adaptive Case Management using BPMN.

It is not my goal at this point to prove that dynamic behavior can be mapped using BPMN, what is more important to me is to qualify absolute statements such as "the process-centric approach is obsolete and we need to switch to dynamic case handling." There are, of course, instances where an adaptive approach is highly useful, particularly in knowledge-intensive areas (characterized by *Knowledge Workers*). This requires fresh new ideas and solutions that rejuvenate the market-place and promote progress in the domain of business processes. But there will still be many classically defined processes that can only run economically using a process engine, not to mention the integration-centric processes that are performed practically without human interaction. There will be no point looking for adaptive solutions here in the future, and hence we will rely on a harmonious combination of both solutions, as we saw in the hospital scenario. This is why I think this development is a positive thing and why I'm excited about further developments to come.

I would also argue as follows against an overly strong focus on processes with heavy human involvement. The desire of enterprises to increase automation has already been discussed in Sect. 5.7.3. The many customer interviews I have held stress the fact that people interaction is associated with aspects such as time delays, susceptibility to errors, and costs. This is why I view a wide distribution of strongly user-oriented solutions with skepticism.

Despite this, standardization is also making itself felt in the area of process management. Once again, the OMG is tackling this topic and, together with leading enterprises (such as Agile, BizAgi, Cordys, IBM, Oracle, SAP, and Tibco), are developing the new modeling standard *Case Management Model and Notation* (CMMN), which can be viewed as a complement to BPMN. An explicit goal here is to integrate it with BPMN and to expand BPMN. Other central aims are to specify a meta model, a graphical notation, and operational semantics for the special domain of case record handling. As in BPMN, efforts are being made to produce a uniform exchange format for the process models.

You might well wonder at this point about the effects of adaptive processes on process-driven applications, as we have handled them in this book. You might be surprised to read that there are NO effects and you can keep reading this book right until the end, keep it on your shelf, and not, as feared, as a door stopper. Let me explain why this is the case, firstly by stating that the structured processes are, after all, only switched with adaptive processes or the adaptive processes are added to them. And, of course, these processes also have communication and integration requirements. It goes without saying that these adaptive processes also work in heterogeneous landscapes, and hence the same rules apply to these processes as to any other application, as do the same risks. In other words, if we do not apply the tried and tested architecture concepts for IT landscape abstraction, we stumble into the same forest of relationships and dependencies that weighed us down in all the other application approaches. ACM-based solutions do not relieve us of this responsibility either. The situation remains that, since only the business process layer is expanded using ACM, you do not get very far without a sustainable architecture concept in the case of adaptive processes. All other layers (and the associated concepts) remain untouched here and can continue to be described as process-driven applications.

BPMN Extension for Improving Modeling Flexibility I mentioned navigation systems already in the last section and I do not want to finish this chapter without pointing out one interesting development. An article by Stefan Jablonski (Jablonski 2011) also discusses a navigator, more precisely a process navigator that supports the user when navigating through its processes. Jablonski addresses the problem of a more compact representation of complex business situations in process models. These situations often arise because the reality of process execution does not match the theory. Hence, the models need to be redesigned to reflect the reality. Instead of the defined execution order in the model, steps are moved up since, for example, it takes too long to wait for a preceding step. Jablonski provides a journey to a conference as an illustration and the ideal execution order is as follows:

1. Travel requested by the employee
2. Travel request approved by the manager
3. Travel booked by the employee or the secretaries' office

In reality, if it is known that the manager is going to approve the request, the employee does not always wait for confirmation just because the manager is busy right now. The employee or secretary goes ahead and books the transport and hotel anyway.

If we wanted to visualize this variant and all potential execution paths using BPMN, we would have to model all possible permutations. Figure 5.77 shows what a model for just these three steps would look like.

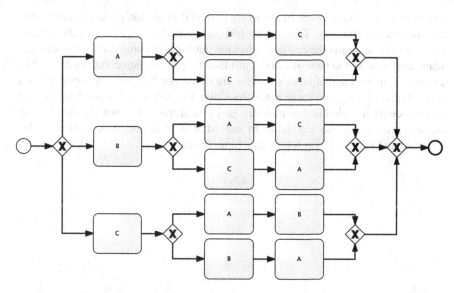

Fig. 5.77   Explicit representation of all possible execution paths in BPMN (from Jablonski 2011)

We now have all execution paths, but the preferred order of execution has been lost. How can we solve this problem? Jablonski suggests a notation extension that enables far more compact representation of the same scenario while also increasing the flexibility of execution. Figure 5.78 shows what this could look like:

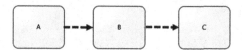

Fig. 5.78   Implicit representation of all possible execution paths using a notation extension (from Jablonski 2011)

Here, the dashed line between the activities is new and its semantics state that tasks linked with this dashed line can be executed in any order. At the same time, the preferred order of execution, namely the sequence *A—B—C* is preserved. This last point is important, since a parallel execution of the steps can, in principle, also be modeled using the parallel gateway.

There is, however, a far more generic approach behind this simple example. The core idea is to use notation elements with rich semantics to produce more compact models. BPMN models often become highly complex in real-life scenarios and are difficult to follow. Using elements that are rich in semantics makes complex scenarios easier to illustrate. There is though a steep learning curve here, since the modeler and the readers of the model must understand the semantics hidden behind the elements. This does not make it simpler to read and comprehend models and there is also the problem of the many potential execution paths at runtime that can confuse the end user. This is why Jablonski introduces the idea of the process navigator that supports the end user when navigating these processes and which can adapt automatically to new situations, just like the car navigation system does when a turnoff is missed and alternative routes are needed by the driver. I consider this a very interesting idea, but these notations either succeed or fail depending on their acceptance by a wide number of users, and this proposal has not yet got this far. Despite this, it will be intriguing to see what new developments arise in this direction and I suggest you follow this topic further.

Conclusion and Outlook

Today's companies are facing enormous challenges. They have to sustain their position in the face of fierce competition and continually adapt the processes that give them their competitive advantage in ever shorter cycles. I have presented a particular type of application in this book: the process-driven application, which can support companies in this difficult task. Its central idea is a sustainable application architecture; this enables companies to keep their applications flexible for as long as they continue to be used, which is where most monolithic applications fail. You can only accomplish this if all the relevant components are aligned and follow certain principles; it has therefore been the objective of this book to explain these principles and propose real implementations to help you with your projects. One of the main points I have tried to put across is that a process-driven application brings together a number of very different components and enables them to work with each other *in true harmony*; it is in the interaction of these components that we see the true extent of its capabilities. We will only be able to leverage the potential of this increased flexibility, however, if there is a change in the mindset of architects and developers: If they continue to apply the development strategies used for monolithic applications to this new, loosely coupled, distributed world, their efforts are doomed to failure. Another of the main objectives of this book was to explain the differences between these two worlds and propose suitable solutions. In this respect, I refer you back to the aspects covered in Chap. 5: increased flexibility, the use of rules (alone or together with analytical applications), and the collaboration between standard, structured, and unforeseeable processes. We now have tools such as collaboration software, rules engines and process engines, and analytical applications at our disposal; these, paired with the sustainable architecture presented here, *give companies the freedom they need to be able to develop their business-critical processes*. We can avoid the risk of running into the dead end that is so often the final destination for monolithic applications when software can no longer be maintained and any innovative ideas are smothered before they can flourish. Of course, this architecture comes at a price, and as with any project, you have to weigh up the costs against the benefits you expect to achieve. However, as the only other alternative is to stick with what you know, with all its attendant risks and shortcomings, you can hardly afford to do this either. In today's business environment you have to be able to adapt your processes to changes and it is crucial to be able to differentiate your processes from those of your competitors. The architecture developed in the course of this book and the associated methodology help you to balance the pros and cons and come to a solution that makes sound business sense.

6.1   Outlook

This book would not be complete without some analysis of current IT trends and what they mean for process-driven applications. I will put forward a few thoughts about modification-free extensions to process-driven applications, followed by a discussion of current topics such as cloud and on-demand computing, software as a service, main memory databases, mobility, and REST as an architectural style, and their impact on process-driven applications.

6.1.1   Increasing Flexibility Using Modification-Free Extensions

Flexibility is a central theme in this book. The entire architectural approach is based around the requirement from management that the IT department implements company strategy as quickly as possible in the form of executable processes (business-IT alignment). It is absolutely essential to incorporate flexibility into your architecture, and one particular type of flexibility warrants further examination: the possibility of external extensions to process-driven applications without having to make any changes to the original models or source code (also known as modification-free extensions). For example, how can a customer add new fields to a composite without having to access the original software?

Once a composite application had been shipped and installed, it is usually not long before customers start to ask how they can adapt the application to meet their specific requirements. We have not yet addressed this extension aspect; our discussions on flexibility so far have centered on finding the best approach for componentization and how to configure components dynamically, perhaps using rules. We know that it is possible to replace complete components, but non-invasive modification-free extensions relate to new fields resulting from a business need and have a new quality that affects all layers of the process-driven application. The consequences for the process-driven application are as follows:

- The new field is persisted in the composite: Therefore, either a field has to be added to the existing database table, or a new database table has to be created for the extension fields and managed by the composite.
- The new field is filled and written back by external services: This requires the interface   contract   between   the   composite   and   the   service   contract

implementation layer to be changed. This can be done by extending the existing
interface or using a completely new service that deals solely with the new fields.
- Since the new field must be included in the user interfaces, the architecture of
  composite user interfaces must allow such extensions.
- The new field must be added to the process context at the process level and must
  be able to be forwarded to process steps that encapsulate services or interfaces.
- The new field has consequences for the business logic as well, and this may also
  have to be changed.

As well as dealing with these immediate issues, you also need to decide what
will happen if the vendor of the composite releases a new version and encounters
the customer's extensions during the upgrade? How can the vendor's changes be
merged with the customer's extensions?

Object Orientation as the Key to Modification-Free Extensions The most
promising approach in relation to this question seems to be a consistent application
of the object-orientation concept. If a composite uses objects throughout, customers
can make the necessary extensions by simple derivation from the original objects.
The prerequisite for this approach is that these objects are used consistently across
all levels of the process-driven application. As well as attributes, the objects should
also contain the typical CRUD lifecycle methods (Create, Read, Update, Delete)
and search methods (we will discover the reason for this later on). This approach
requires a framework that allows the customer to access the modifiable objects and
the user interfaces used in the composite, and make the required changes.

To illustrate how this concept works, let us use a supplier object as an example.
The supplier object for this example contains the usual required fields such as
company name, address, telephone number, fax number, email, contact person, and
so on. If the supplier object is saved locally in the composite, there is a
corresponding database table; if the object is managed externally, a dedicated
service interface is responsible for reading, updating, and deleting the object. The
service interface is part of our service contract. The object is transferred to the UI
(s) using interfaces and exists in the process context as an object as well. You could
use a reference to the original object in the process context instead, to save memory;
this makes no difference to the behavior described below.

The vendor of the composite allows its customers to add new fields to the
supplier object through object derivation. In our example, we want to add a field
for a Skype name; this field was not provided in the original composite, but is very
important to our fictional customer. A framework enables the customer to view the
extendable objects without having to use the development environment (for example, Eclipse). The customer can then decide which object to extend, and which
fields to add. Once the changes have been made, a generation run ensures that the
extension is deployed across the application:

- In the local persistence: An extra database table is generated for the extension fields. The CRUD and search methods are automatically overwritten by the extended object so that any calls from the composite now use the new methods instead of the original object versions.
- In external management: New interfaces containing the new fields are automatically generated for the service contract implementation layer.
- Since objects are also transferred to the user interfaces, the new fields are automatically made available to these UIs, using the derivation mechanism. The framework allows you to add new tabs to user interfaces for the new fields.
- The process context also profits from object orientation. It is irrelevant whether the process context contains just a reference to the supplier object or a complete copy, the mechanism works here as well.
- You can include new business logic if the framework allows dedicated extensions of the original software. In SAP software (SAP 2010c) this concept is known as BAdI (Business Add-In) and is applicable here. The interface to the extension point remains stable and, in our example, contains the supplier object as a new parameter as well. The customer can use this type of extension to include new logic in the composite.
- If the vendor of the process-driven application releases a new version, the method described here ensures that customer extensions and vendor software updates can be merged without any conflicts. From the customer perspective, all they have done is derive a new object from an existing one, and they can just as easily apply this method to the object modified by the vendor. A regeneration is necessary in this case to bring the modifications into the new software. Since new fields on the user interface are put into separate tabs anyway, there is no conflict here. Last but not least, the new business logic created by the customer is still applied, since the interface to the extension point remains stable and contains the object as a transfer parameter in any case.

Modification-free enhancement of process-driven applications certainly looks possible if we have the following combination:

- Programming conventions for the vendor of the process-driven application (consistent use of objects)
- Principles of object orientation (object derivation)
- A framework for the external extension of objects, user interfaces, and business logic; and a regeneration of the entire application after the changes have been made

However, this approach has not yet been implemented in this form, so we cannot verify if it works. What is certain though is that being able to extend process-driven applications is an exciting prospect, especially for customers, and warrants further research.

6.1.2 What About Cloud and On-Demand Computing , Software as a Service, Mobile Applications, and Main Memory Databases?

The IT sector is currently buzzing with new trends, and although this is quite a normal state of affairs in our industry, it does pose the following questions: What effect will these developments have on process-driven applications? I don't want to invest in a particular solution to solve a problem today, only to find out tomorrow that new technological developments have rendered my problem obsolete. Can I use the new solutions to approach the problem in a different way? Is my architecture still up-to-date? My discussions with customers have revealed a certain degree of unease about new technologies and solutions and their implications. But I can reassure you on this point; none of the much-hyped topics mentioned above will have any serious implications for the methodology and architecture addressed in this book. Quite the opposite in fact: If anything, they actually increase the need for an intelligent approach. I will expand on why exactly this is in the following sections. Of course, predictions do have a way of coming back to haunt you. Thomas J. Watson, former chairman of IBM, is alleged to have stated: "I think there is a world market for maybe five computers" (Wikipedia-Watson 2014). Well Mr. Watson, it is certainly a few more than that now.

6.1.2.1 Software as a Service, On-Demand and Cloud Computing

What exactly can we expect from these new developments? Let's look at them in more detail. In my view, software as a service, on-demand and cloud computing are all moving in a similar direction: Software services are being offered by a host of new providers at attractive prices to enable companies to externalize part of their IT and business processes (although this should be limited to those processes that are not part of the core business of the company and do not provide a competitive advantage). For our process-driven application, this means increased fragmentation in the back-end area. The systems that process-driven applications work on are being changed with ever-increasing frequency. Applications that previously ran on systems on the company's server (on-premise) will, in the future, be run by service providers outside the company and only called when they are needed (on-demand). In other words, this trend actually works in favor of our application architecture. Let us look at this development from another perspective. If we look at what is currently on offer in the on-demand area, we find standard processes that appeal to a large customer base, with the aim of attracting as many customers as possible. Classic examples are CRM On Demand for the customer support area, HR/CRM On Demand for human resources, and ERP On Demand for enterprise resource planning. But companies are surely not going to outsource their entire CRM/HR/ERP functionality in one go. It is much more likely to be an evolutionary process, with the company outsourcing individual functions to service providers one at a time, with the end result that a process-driven application that previously had to communicate with three systems within the company network eventually has to exchange data with six systems, some of these outside the company boundaries. Do not forget that the various on-premise and on-demand solutions themselves have to be integrated as well, to enable them to communicate with each other. We were indeed correct in our assumption that the topic of *integration* is being revived!

Since process-driven applications address innovative and business-critical solutions, they are unlikely to be outsourced. And thanks to the service contract implementation layer, we are protected on the back-end side from any changes in the system landscape anyway. However, companies that are not equipped with a flexible architecture will find it very difficult to benefit from these new trends in the future. Forward-looking companies with aligned layer architectures, on the other hand, can face future developments head-on and make their decisions based on the maturity of the on-demand solutions on offer, their requirements, their financial possibilities, and their strategic direction.

6.1.2.2 Mobile Applications

The biggest changes in the front-end area are in the mobile area: The long-awaited mobile solutions breakthrough seems to be almost upon us (although I'll believe it when I see it ☺). In far as our architecture is concerned, mobile solutions can be seen as an alternative technology for the front-end area of our process-driven application, and in this respect are simply another UI technology that we have to deal with. The front-end area has always been subject to frequent change; barely a year goes by without new frameworks and technologies springing up. It would seem an almost impossible task to stay on top of all these new developments, but is there a way to equip ourselves to deal with this? Let us take a closer look at the way in which user interfaces are used in process-driven applications. Think back to our implementation example from Sect. 4.2.2, where we had two primary use scenarios:

1. Standalone UIs to Start a Process
2. UIs as part of processes for executing particular business subtasks

Both usage types clearly require collaboration with the respective process framework. The standalone UI must be able to start processes and transfer the entered data to the process instance. The user interfaces that are called during the execution of the process have to collaborate with the process framework insofar as they have to exchange status changes (step completed, step canceled, set error status) and process data. Therefore, it is a good idea for vendors of process environments to provide a callable API that can be used universally and independently of the UI technology and programming language used. (RESTful) Web service interfaces, for example, can perform this function. Companies are then free to choose their preferred UI technology and programming language (one is often linked to the other), and of course the mobile technologies, although the mobile frameworks of the respective vendors are a factor to be considered as well. Apart from this, the behavior of mobile interfaces is identical to that of their non-mobile counterparts. The statements in the chapter about the basic architecture of process-driven applications are equally valid here. At the end of the day, mobile interfaces are simply another type of UI technology (yet another client technology) to deal with.

6.1.2.3 Main Memory Databases

To finish, I want to look at main memory databases, which are a much-discussed topic at the moment. Could they possibly eclipse the concept of process-driven applications? The basic idea of main memory-based databases is to keep all the data of an application in the main memory, and then run incredibly high-speed evaluations on this data. This technology enables analyses and *what-if* simulations that would not previously have been thought possible. Its objective is a "real realtime". So far, this technology has primarily been used to analyze aggregated data, which only requires read access to the data. Using its HANA (High-performance ANalytical Appliance) technology (SAP 2012; Plattner and Zeier 2011) at its customer Yodobashi, SAP managed to improve performance by a staggering factor of more than 100,000 (Sikka 2012). With HANA, the time taken to calculate incentive points in the customer loyalty program was reduced from three days to just 2 s. And now transactionally-secure handling of write calls is almost ready to be shipped productively as well. Looking at these astonishing figures, we have to ask ourselves what this could mean for process-driven applications. Not much initially, as at the moment in-memory systems can only read. This improves read calls triggered from UIs, but nothing more. Asynchronous write processing in the considerably slower back-end systems will therefore remain unchanged for the time being, as does our case for using a process-driven architectural approach.

But what will happen if write processing in the in-memory database becomes possible as well? Even then, not much will change. We are talking about one single application that would be replaced by in-memory processing. Companies would continue to have numerous legacy systems in their landscapes, and it would be no easy task to convert these to in-memory. Even if you did, you would have to coordinate between multiple in-memory systems, which brings us back to the familiar landscape problem. We can put forward the same arguments as for on-demand as we are yet again facing a situation where the IT landscape is becoming ever more fragmented, this time complicated even further by the addition of main memory-based applications. In fact, we can add in-memory to the list of examples that argue *for* a loosely coupled approach.

The problem can only really be solved by a single homogenous in-memory system, but I for one cannot begin to imagine how this would work...

Main Memory Databases and Event Processing I do, however, see in-memory technology as a significant development in event processing which is important if we think about new trends such as the Internet of Things (Wikipedia-IoT 2014). In current systems for processing events, complex event processing (CEP) analyzes the individual fine-grained events *while they are happening* and aggregates them into coarse-grained business events when predefined features and relationships between different events are recognized. You use a special query language such as Oracle's CQL (Continuous Query Language—Oracle 2012) or EPL (Event Processing Language), which is used in Esper (2012), a Java-based CEP engine. What they all have in common is that they are streaming languages, which execute their functionality *while* the event is happening. This is also referred to as event stream processing (ESP). One of the main disadvantages of this approach, again, is its inflexibility: If I have not accounted for situations or formulated them using the appropriate query language constructs before the event happens, they cannot be discovered after event processing. If, however, I do not have to handle the events while they are happening, but simply put them in a main memory database instead, I have other analysis options *after* they have happened. Most notably, I can run through many more constellations and dependencies than would be possible with the streaming technology. As well as the normal streaming queries, which I could also execute against the in-memory database, on-the-fly queries enable me to perform new *what-if* analyses on fine-grained events, which helps companies to identify favorable or unfavorable constellations much earlier on. This is certainly a significant development in event processing. I do not, however, see a change for process-driven applications, as explained above.

6.1.3 Does REST Have Implications for Process-Driven Applications?

There has been a great deal of heated debate on the Internet recently on the subject of REST (REpresentational State Transfer), and the implications of this architectural style for established Web service technologies. Since Web service technologies have been our constant companion throughout this book, the discussion is certainly relevant to us. Let us examine the available information about REST and try to draw conclusions about what it means for process-driven applications. In the following statements I refer to Roy Fielding's dissertation "Architectural Styles and the Design of Network-based Software Architectures" (Fielding 2000) and an article by Cesare Pautasso, Olaf Zimmermann, and Frank Leymann (2008), which compares classic Web services with RESTful Web services.

REST is first and foremost an architectural style for creating a globally connected information system. It follows particular principles, which have contributed significantly to the success of the World Wide Web:

– Resources and their representations

  Everything is a resource. This is just a simplistic way of explaining one of the principles. A resource can be reached and called using a stable, unique address, irrespective of whether it is an order, a customer, a supplier, a product, or a cancellation, or whether it is used to contact a service for converting currencies, for example. To call a resource, you use a URI (Universal Resource Identifier); this is a global namespace where each resource is uniquely identified. The resources themselves can be represented in different ways, and the same resource can have different representations, for example, as an HTML or XML file, in JSON (JavaScript Object Notation) or in PDF format. Resources are thus separated from their representations.

– Hypermedia

In the communication between the client and the server, URIs are returned as a component of the response message. They define what the client can do next. For example, a search service returns a hitlist, where each entry contains a link to the detailed data, in the form of a URI. We are quite familiar with this linking of content from our daily work with Web applications. At the same time, an application state (hence the "State" in REST) is transported to the client, and when we follow these links, the application moves from one valid state to the next. This hypermedia mechanism is used to process the states for the whole application, although the actual services themselves are stateless. Therefore, the messages from the client to the server must contain enough information to enable the server to react appropriately.

– Consistent, uniform interfaces

The communication between the client and the server exploits all the possibilities of the HTTP protocol. This is particularly evident in the actions that can be executed on resources. You use the HTTP standard request methods: GET, PUT, POST, and DELETE. Their behavior is defined in the HTTP specification (IETF 1999). GET returns a possible representation of a resource; PUT updates an existing resource or creates a new one if it does not already exist; POST also creates a new resource; DELETE deletes it. GET, PUT, and DELETE must support idempotent behavior. Also, the HTTP protocol uses metadata to support other technical services during communication that control caching behavior, access control, authentications, behavior in the event of transfer errors, and negotiations about the representation format that the server should provide to the client. The HTTP protocol is used as it was originally intended, namely as an application protocol and not a transport protocol. Since these mechanisms have been used successfully in the Internet for years, REST is based on a well-established, tried-and-tested, scalable infrastructure for clients and for servers.

Admittedly, these concepts all sound very promising and are worth looking into. However, I do see a problem in projecting them onto process-driven applications. We need to consider carefully if and where it would make sense to use RESTful Web services in our architecture. I will not be swayed when it comes to the separation of the application and the service contract implementation layer. If we back down on this point, we would have direct communication again between the application and back-end systems, with all the problems that this entails.

The only thing left to consider is the communication between the process-driven application and the service contract implementation layer and the communication between the service contract implementation layer and the back-end systems. Of course, I can design the service contract between the application and the implementation layer in line with the REST style. In Sect. 3.3.5.1, I referred to alternative formats in the discussion of the service contract. It does not have to be WSDL, nor classic Web services; what is important is *that* a contract is made at all. But what advantages does a REST-compliant interface bring me in this case? I find it difficult to summon up much enthusiasm for REST. It is the same story for the communication between the service contract implementation layer and the back-end systems. At this point, we are restricted by the capabilities of the back-end systems anyway, and imposing a REST-compliant layer on top of this would be about as helpful as bestowing Web services on all systems even though established communication channels are available. Much orchestration is necessary between the service contract implementation layer and the numerous different systems, and in this respect, a REST-based system is simply another backend that has to be integrated. The REST-specific advantages do not apply here. At this juncture, I can only concur with the last sentence of Pautasso, Zimmermann and Leymann's paper, which needs no further comment:

> The main conclusion from this comparison is to use RESTful services for tactical, ad hoc integration over the Web (à la Mashup) and to prefer WS-* Web services in professional enterprise application integration scenarios with a longer lifespan and advanced QoS requirements.

Epilogue

I began this book with a quote from Charles Darwin about how chances of survival are improved by the ability to adapt swiftly to changes in the environment. Process-driven applications are a response to this challenge; they enable companies to implement management strategy immediately and thus ensure their survival. The method I describe for designing and implementing process-driven applications supports a sustainable architecture that you can continue to maintain and develop for many years to come. The foundation stone has been laid.

V. Stiehl, *Process-Driven Applications with BPMN*, DOI 10.1007/978-3-319-07218-0,
© Springer International Publishing Switzerland 2014

Appendix A
BPMN Notation

Appendix A.1 Core Elements of BPMN

Table A.1 Core Elements of BPMN 2.0 (OMG 2011)

Element	Description	Notation
Event	An event is something that happens during the course of a process. Events affect the subsequent flow of the process. They either have a cause (trigger) or they reflect a result that is passed on, and can be referred to as catching or throwing events, respectively. Events are depicted as circles. There are three types of events: start, intermediate, and end. A start event is displayed as a circle with a single line and indicates where a process starts. An intermediate event has a double line and always appears in the sequence diagram between the start and end event. An end event is drawn with a thick single line (see notation) and indicates where a process ends. The basic elements can be filled with markers depending on their trigger or impact.	○ ◎ ⭕
Activity	An activity is a generic term for actions that are performed during the process flow. An activity can be atomic or non-atomic (compound). Accordingly, there are two activity types: task and subprocess, which are both displayed as rounded rectangles.	Task or Subprocess

V. Stiehl, *Process-Driven Applications with BPMN*, DOI 10.1007/978-3-319-07218-0,
© Springer International Publishing Switzerland 2014

Gateway	A gateway is used to control the divergence and convergence of sequence flows in a process diagram. It determines the conditions under which particular paths are taken and how paths are joined. Gateways are displayed as diamonds. Special markers within the diamond shape indicate different gateway types and their behavior.	◇
Sequence flow	A sequence flow is used to show the order that activities will be performed in a process. It is displayed as a line with an arrowhead.	──────────▶
Message flow	Message flows are used to show the flow of messages between two or more processes. This represents the collaboration between the processes. The direction of the message exchange is indicated by a dashed line with an arrowhead.	o‑ ‑ ‑ ‑ ‑ ‑ ▷
Association	An association is used to link information and artifacts with BPMN graphical elements. It is represented as a dotted line, with or without an arrowhead, depending on what the BPMN element is linked to. Directional associations can be used to visualize data flows for data objects. Text annotations on the other hand are associated without a direction.	······················· ······················▷
Pool	A pool is a container for a complete process that thus comprises the entire sequence flow. Pools also play an important role in collaboration diagrams, to represent the collaboration between several processes. A pool is a graphical representation of a participant in a collaboration. Since collaboration diagrams focus mainly on the message exchange between the participants, the content of the pool, that is, its sequence flow, can be hidden (collapsed pool). It then becomes a *black box* rather than a *white box* (which displays all details of a process). Pools can be multi-instance. In this case, they have a special marker (**⫴**), which indicates that the pool has a number of participants of the same type.	**Pool** **Collapsed Pool** **Multi-Instance Pool**

(Swim)Lane	A (swim)lane is a subpartition within a pool and is used to organize and categorize activities within the pool. For example, lanes are used to assign roles or company organizational units: All activities that are assigned to a particular lane are performed by this role or organizational unit. Similarly, a lane can be an IT system or an application that executes particular activities. Pools and lanes can extend either horizontally or vertically.	
Data object	Data objects provide information about the data that activities require to perform their task. This can be input or output data. Data objects can be simple fields, complex structures, or lists (collection) of objects. A data object that is a list (collection) has a multi-instance marker (**III**).	
Message	A message is used in collaboration scenarios to depict the contents of a communication between the participants.	
Group (a rectangle around a group of objects)	A group puts BPMN elements together for documentation or analysis purposes. This type of grouping does not affect the sequence flow within the group.	
Text annotation (attached by an association)	Text annotations are a mechanism for a modeler to provide additional text information for the reader of the model. These texts can be connected to BPMN elements with an association to indicate which BPMN element the text refers to.	

Appendix A.2 Events

Table A.2 Events of BPMN 2.0 (OMG 2011)

Element	Description	Notation
Catching message events	Catching events are displayed with an unfilled marker. For message events, this means that the envelope marker is not filled in black (see the notation on the right). A catching event can be used as a start or intermediate event. If used as a start event, this means the process waits for a message to arrive before starting. Similarly, if a catching event is used as an intermediate event, the process flow is interrupted until a message arrives.	
Throwing message events	Throwing events are displayed with a filled marker. For message events, this means that the envelope marker is filled in black. A throwing event can be used as an end or intermediate event. If used as an end event, a message is sent when the process ends. Similarly, if a throwing event is used as an intermediate event, a message is sent and the process continues immediately to the next step in the process flow.	
Message boundary events	As well as using events directly in the process flow, you can also attach them to activities(also known as boundary events). This indicates that if the event occurs *during* processing of the activity to which it is attached, the process flow assigned to the boundary event is followed. In the figures on the right, activity 3 is performed as soon as a message arrives during the processing of activity 1. In the upper figure, where the line of the boundary event is dashed, activity 1 is not interrupted. In the lower figure, where the line of the message boundary event is solid, the assigned activity is interrupted when a message arrives.	

Appendix A.3 Gateways

Table A.3 Gateways of BPMN 2.0 (OMG 2011)

Element	Description	Notation
Exclusive gateway	At an exclusive gateway, indicated by the **X** marker within the diamond, the process flow follows exactly one of the alternative paths. Each path must have a condition, and these conditions must be mutually exclusive. Therefore, only *one* token leaves the gateway. If none of the conditions are met, the flow follows the default branch, indicated by a diagonal slash through the sequence flow. If a converging exclusive gateway is used, as soon as an incoming token arrives from one of the paths, a corresponding outgoing token is produced by the gateway. Thus, in some circumstances the activity following the gateway is executed several times.	
Parallel gateway	At a parallel gateway, indicated by the + marker within the diamond, a token is passed to each outgoing path, irrespective of the conditions. Parallel process flows are started and the number of tokens increases. If a converging parallel gateway is used, the process waits at the gateway until tokens have arrived from all incoming sequence flows. Then, exactly one token leaves the gateway; the number of tokens is reduced.	

| Inclusive gateway | At an inclusive or "or" gateway, indicated by the **O** marker within the diamond, the process flow follows the outgoing paths whose conditions are met. Therefore, each path must have a condition. The gateway can thus pass on one or more outgoing tokens. It is possible to model a default path here as well; this path is followed if none of the specified conditions are met.

If a converging inclusive gateway is used, the process waits at the gateway until all tokens that can reach the gateway have arrived. The gateway is informed how many tokens have been generated by the foregoing process logic and may yet still reach the gateway. Then, exactly one token leaves the gateway; the number of tokens is reduced. | |
| Complex gateway | At a complex gateway, indicated by the asterisk marker (✳) within the diamond, any conditions can be used in branching and in merging to determine how the tokens are handled. This covers the remaining cases that cannot be implemented by the other gateways. For example, you can implement n-of-m mergers (with n <= m): "If 3 of 5 paths are completed, the process should continue and all subsequent tokens should simply be eliminated without being passed on." | |

Event-based exclusive gateway	The event-based exclusive gateway branches the process flow depending on which events happen. The gateway is connected to several events. The process follows the sequence flow whose event happens first. In the example on the right, the process is waiting for a message or a timeout. Whichever happens first determines the outgoing path that is followed.	
Instantiating exclusive event-based gateway	A variant of the event-based gateway can be used to instatiate processes. The start of the process is triggered by one of the events following the gateway. Once one of these events happens, the process starts and follows the sequence flow that belongs to that particular event. The process does not wait for the second event to happen.	
Instantiating parallel event-based gateway	The instantiating parallel event-based gateway is another variant of the instantiating event-based gateway. Here as well, the process starts as soon as the first of the events following the gateway fires. However, once one event has happened, the other events remain active, and the process continues to wait for them. If, as shown in the figure on the right, the branches are also merged by the parallel gateway, all events must have fired before the process can continue. In the example on the right, message A and message B must both have arrived before the process can continue.	

Appendix A.4 Task Types

Table A.4 Tasks of BPMN 2.0 (OMG 2011)

Task Types	Description	Notation
Manual	Manual tasks are used in a process model if the task is performed without any computer support. This could be a task performed by a maintenance worker, for example, or a task where particular tools or devices are used.	Manual Task
User	A user task is a typical "workflow" task, where the end user performs the task with the assistance of application programs. Users are informed by task lists or dedicated messages that they need to participate in a process.	User Task
Service	A service task is a task that uses some sort of automated service. This could be a Web service or some other automated application function.	Service Task
Receive	It is possible for a process to wait for messages from external process participants before continuing. If you need this function, use the receive task. This task waits until the message has been received. In collaboration diagrams, external participants are usually connected to the receive task using a message flow.	Receive Task
Send	The send task is used to model tasks for sending messages to external process particants. Once the message is sent, the task is completed. In collaboration diagrams, external participants are usually connected to the send task using a message flow.	Send Task

Script	Some process engines are shipped with an in-built macro language. This enables process modelers to solve minor problems by using scripts in programs. These scripts run in the process engine itself. The script task is used for such cases. Once the execution of the script is completed, the task is also completed, and the process flow continues.	Script Task
Business rule	Business processes and business rules complement each other perfectly: Business rules can be used to capture decision logic in preparation for gateway decisions, and to make the result available to the gateway. This keeps the process stable and makes it easier to isolate the decision logic from the process logic in the form of business rules, which can be changed easily and independently of the process model. This is why the business rule task provides for the invocation of business engines.	Business Rule Task

Appendix B
Excursus on Service Management:
A Comparative Study of Approaches

In Sect. 3.4 (Service Repositories and Process-Driven Applications) we examined the differences between a service repository and a services registry. We learned where information about services is stored and how you can use this information while designing service-oriented software and at runtime. Our findings were based on the solutions that are currently available but, of course, new concepts continue to emerge and are the subject of ongoing research projects to optimize and innovate service management, searches, and calls. This excursus provides a brief overview of current projects to give you an idea of the improvements that can be expected in this area in the near future.

Appendix B.1 Three-Schema Architecture

The first approach we will look at is based on the three-schema architecture for service management (Fischer et al. 2010). This paper proposes an organizational structure for services that takes the schema architecture used for database systems as its basis. The structure has three schemas, arranged in layers one on top of the other, that interact as shown in Fig. B.1.

V. Stiehl, *Process-Driven Applications with BPMN*, DOI 10.1007/978-3-319-07218-0,
© Springer International Publishing Switzerland 2014

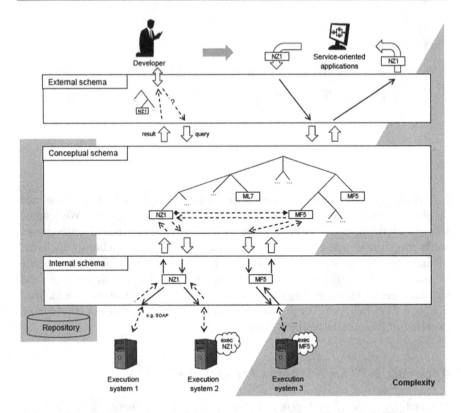

Fig. B.1 Three-schema architecture for service management (from Fischer et al. 2010)

Each layer is self-contained and provides services by means of well-defined interfaces. This layer approach has three main objectives:

1. Consistent access to services, so that they are easier to use. This is represented by the external schema.
2. Consistent description of services, so that it is easier to find services with the particular properties that meet the requirements of your application. This is supported by the conceptual schema.
3. Independence from concrete service implementations and, with this, the freedom to optimize or exchange services without having to modify the consuming applications. This is achieved by the internal schema, which manages the physical service instances.

These three schemas form the pillars of service-based management systems (based on database management systems). There are two main types of consumer for these systems. First, application developers, who need to find the services that will enable them to implement their application requirements, and thus access the system for search purposes. The result of this search is a consistent interface (the external schema), which the developer can use to call the service. Second, the calling application itself, which needs the system at runtime to access services.

The conceptual schema clearly plays an important role in both types of interaction. It is not merely a categorized overview of all services and their metainformation; it also uncouples the use of services from their implementations, by mediating between the external schema used to make the call and the actual implementation represented by the internal schema.

To be able to perform these tasks, the conceptual schema has to fulfill certain requirements and provide certain content. The following points must be taken into account:

- Consistent semantic description of services (What task does the service perform?)
- Link between external and internal schema
- Connections to other services (Which services are used by the current service during execution? Which other services use the current service?). This point also illustrates the fact that service-based management systems do not only manage atomic services, but also support services that themselves use other services (composite services)
- Prerequisite for using services
- Post-conditions once call is completed
- Side effects when using the service (for example, database changes)
- Costs of using services
- Expected response times

Redundancies are not an issue when collecting this information as it is often not possible to categorize services uniquely. On the contrary, redundancies can help the developers with their search and can actually be a good thing.

For this approach to work, the metadata listed above must be provided in such a way that it can be evaluated automatically, and then searched (using an SQL-type language, for example) and changed. Current projects are working on the technical realization of the three schemas and the implementation of a prototype.

Appendix B.2 Semantic Web Technologies

The problem of providing services with metadata and semantic information in a form that allows automatic evaluation is the subject of other research projects as well. In recent years, real progress has been made in the area of semantic Web technologies in particular. I refer here to two dissertations (Stein 2009; Lautenbacher 2009); these go into great detail about the standards and approaches in this area. Essentially, we need to be able to automatically match the business requirements as formulated by business departments with the available services that will implement them. For this to be possible, both the requirements from the business experts and the metainformation about the services must be available in a machine-readable format. The representation of requirements and metadata is specified formally in ontologies. Ontologies for business requirements can differ from ontologies for service metadata; they are, after all, produced by different groups (business requirements by business experts, service metadata by IT experts). To make it possible for a requirement to be assigned automatically to a service or a chain of services, the respective ontologies must be mapped to one another. Only with this information can computers deduce which services are required to implement particular requirements. This procedure, whereby business requirements are automatically assigned to one or a chain of services, is also known as machine reasoning.

This basic idea has paved the way for the development of entire approaches, even semantic business process management, where process models are modeled in BPMN as normal, but the modeler can add semantic annotations to the model to represent the business requirements for a process step or an event. A wide range of different ontologies is now available for this purpose. For example, there are ontologies for processes, for company organization, for various specialist domains, and for Web services. Even at the modeling stage, the business expert gets help from the system: a semantic search for existing processes, process fragments, or services in a semantic repository can be used to complete a model automatically. It is also possible to verify a process using semantic criteria.

One particularly interesting feature is the automated composition of Web services to fulfil a business function. If a search in the repository reveals that the functionality needed to implement a requirement cannot be provided by one service alone, the system attempts to provide the required functionality by combining different services. This is possible because the input and output of the service is annotated ontologically and can be used in the algorithms of machine reasoning.

These approaches certainly have promise, but are not without their own set of problems. Florian Lautenbacher lists the challenges that have yet to be addressed. Interestingly, most of these issues center on the ontologies themselves:

1. Ontologies are extremely fragile and change constantly to reflect domain-specific dynamics (new elements are added, others are removed).
2. Companies are unlikely to invest valuable time and resources in the development of new ontologies if they do not envisage a substantial benefit from it.
3. Even though ontologies are usually created by a small group of experts, consumers may still ask (and quite rightly): How do I know I can trust an ontology? Can I make my own additions to it?
4. Getting up to speed with new ontologies is no easy task. Consumers are not involved in their design and only have the formal specifications to guide them.
5. How is the intellectual property of the individual or group that created the ontology protected, if at all?
6. It is difficult to decide how big an ontology should be: Too small and it is of limited use to consumers; too large and it becomes unmanageable.
7. Who is actually prepared to take on the task of creating ontologies?

Understandably, there is still some skepticism when it comes to semantic Web technologies, even though research projects in this area are producing very promising results.

Appendix B.3 Self-Organization and Collective Intelligence

A fundamental problem of ontologies is that they are developed centrally. Whenever committees work centrally on the requirements for specifications, formats, or similar, they have to reconcile differing objectives, opinions, needs, and points of view, and the danger is that the resulting solutions are a poor compromise, or that nothing is achieved at all. Therefore, it is worth considering whether a decentralized approach might be preferable. Vanderhaeghen et al. (2010) describe some very interesting and innovative approaches for using the decentralized design principles of Web 2.0, with *self-organization* and *collective intelligence* both playing an important role. These aspects have long been a feature of Web 2.0 applications such as Wikipedia, interactive review platforms (for products, hotels, travel, etc.), and blogs. In their paper, Vanderhaeghen et al discuss these characteristics in the context of process management, but the ideas are equally applicable to the semantic description of services and an intelligent search for services for a particular business requirement. The core idea is the central tagging of services, whereby metadata is added as tags (for example, the tagging of bookmarks on the Delicious social bookmarking service). The tags are initially provided by whoever is responsible for the service, as they know the functionality and can provide basic information about the service. After that, the consumer is free to add supplementary tags and share these with others. These tags can contain information such as prerequisites for use, post-conditions, required experience, errors, runtime behavior, different languages, reviews, frequency of use, and versions. What is especially interesting is the linking of services (and the tags) to visualize how the services can be combined to produce new value. You can then add tags to these new, higher-value composite services as well, just as you would with an atomic service. The collective knowledge about the service is thus made available to everyone. Furthermore, consumers have the option of adapting domain-specific terms to meet their own requirements. For example, the *customer* of a lawyer is called a *client*. If this supplementary information is added to a service, the service can be found using the search term *client*, whereas previously it could only be found using the search term *customer*. Since there are no formal guidelines, anyone can make such enhancements using a Web platform. A Google-type search lets you quickly find suitable services. In time, a highly intelligent network of semantic service descriptions develops; due to its decentralized nature, it is more comprehensive and efficient than anything a centrally-controlled committee could ever hope to achieve.

We have covered several service management approaches in this section: the three-schema architecture, semantic Web technologies, and self-organization with collective intelligence. It remains to be seen how these approaches will develop over time; what we can be sure of is an exciting future for service management.

Appendix 3.2 Self-Organization and Collective Intelligence

Appendix C
List of Abbreviations

2PC	Two-Phase-Commit
A2A	Application-to-Application
ABAP	Advanced Business Application Programming
ACM	Adaptive Case Management
ADEPT	Application Development based on Encapsulated Pre-modeled Process Templates
B2B	Business-to-Business
BAPI	Business Application Programming Interface
BAL	Backend Abstraction Layer
BPD	Business Process Diagram
BPEL	Business Process Execution Language
BPM	Business Process Management
BPMI	Business Process Management Initiative
BPMN	Business Process Model and Notation
BPMS	Business Process Management System
BRG	Business Rules Group
BRM	Business Rules Management
BW	Business Warehouse
CAF	Composite Application Framework
CCTS	Core Component Technical Specification
CEP	Complex Event Processing
CMMN	Case Management Model and Notation
CQL	Continuous Query Language
CRM	Customer Relationship Management
CRUD	Create, Read, Update, Delete
CSV	Comma Separated Values
DSL	Domain Specific Language
EAI	Enterprise Application Integration
EAM	Enterprise Architecture Management
EIP	Enterprise Integration Pattern
EJB	Enterprise Java Beans
EPC	Event-driven Process Chain
EPL	Event Processing Language
ERP	Enterprise Resource Planning

V. Stiehl, *Process-Driven Applications with BPMN*, DOI 10.1007/978-3-319-07218-0,
© Springer International Publishing Switzerland 2014

ESB	Enterprise Service Bus
ESP	Event Stream Processing
ESR	Enterprise Services Repository
FEH	Forward Error Handling
FPN	Federated Portal Network
GDT	Global Data Types
GoF	Gang of Four
HANA	High-performance ANalytical Appliance
HCM	Human Capital Management
HR	Human Resources
HTTP	Hyper Text Transfer Protocol
IBPM	Integrated BPM Project Methodology
iCOD	Industry Composite Development
IDoc	Intermediate Document
ISO	International Organization for Standardization
ISV	Independent Software Vendor
Java EE	Java Platform Enterprise Edition
Java SE	Java Platform Standard Edition
JAX-WS	Java API for XML Web Services
JMS	Java Message Service
JMX	Java Management Extensions
JPA	Java Persistence API
JSF	Java Server Faces
JSON	JavaScript Object Notation
JSP	JavaServer Pages
KMC	Knowledge Management and Collaboration
LDAP	Lightweight Directory Access Protocol
MDA	Model Driven Architecture
MDD	Model Driven Development
MDM	Master Data Management
MEP	Message Exchange Pattern
MOM	Message Oriented Middleware
NWDI	SAP NetWeaver Development Infrastructure
NWDS	SAP NetWeaver Developer Studio
OAGi	Open Applications Group
OAGIS	Open Applications Group Integration Specification
OSI	Open Systems Interconnection
P2P	Point-to-Point
PDA	Process Driven Architecture
	Process Driven Application
PDF	Portable Document Format
POC	Proof of Concept
POJO	Plain Old Java Object
QoS	Quality of Service
RCA	Rich Client Application

REST	REpresentational State Transfer
RFC	Remote Function Call
RFM	Remote Function Module
RPC	Remote Procedure Call
SaaS	Software-as-a-service
SAP BPM	SAP Business Process Management
SAP BRM	SAP Business Rules Management
SAP CE	SAP Composition Environment
SAP PO	SAP Process Orchestration
SAP PI	SAP Process Integration
SAP NetWeaver VC	SAP NetWeaver Visual Composer
SCIL	Service Contract Implementation Layer
SDO	Service Data Objects
SHIL	Service-Human-Interaction-Layer
SLA	Service Level Agreement
SME	Small and Medium Enterprises
SOA	Service Oriented Architecture
SOAP	Simple Object Access Protocol
SQL	Structured Query Language
S.W.I.F.T.	Society for Worldwide Interbank Financial Telecommunication
SWOT	Strength, Weaknesses, Opportunities, Threats
SysML	Systems Modeling Language
TCO	Total cost of ownership
UDDI	Universal Description, Discovery, and Integration
UI	User Interface
UML	Unified Modeling Language
UN/CEFACT	United Nations Centre for Trade Facilitation and Electronic Business
URI	Universal Resource Identifier
URL	Uniform Resource Locator
UTA	User Trained Agents
VC	Visual Composer
VCD	Variant Component Diagram
WAN	Wide Area Network
WSDL	Web Services Description Language
W3C	World Wide Web Consortium
WTP	Web Tools Platform
WYSIWYG	What You See Is What You Get
XML	Extensible Markup Language
XSD	XML Schema Definition
XSLT	Extensible Stylesheet Language Transformations

Appendix D
Glossary[1]

2PC, Two-Phase-Commit*	An approach for maintaining consistency over multiple systems. In the first phase, all backends are asked to confirm one or more planned changes. Once all have confirmed, the changes are committed in a second phase. In accordance to the principles of *loose coupling*, in *SOA compensation* is usually used instead of 2PC.
Activity*	Possible term for one step in a *business process*. In the context of a *process-driven application*, an activity is typically implemented by a *service* or as a user interaction.
Aggregator	An *enterprise integration pattern* that collects and compresses *messages* that belong together. Once the set of messages is complete, the package is sent as a single message to a target system so that it can be processed there in its entirety.
Architecture*	The architecture of a computing system is the structure or structures of the system, which comprise software (and hardware) components, the externally visible properties of those components, and the relationships among them.
Asynchronous communication*	A form of communication where there is a measurable time interval between the sending and receiving of the content of any *message*. *Message-oriented middleware* is typically implemented based on this concept by introducing message queues that queue (persist) messages sent by a system until they are accepted by the receiving system(s).
	Asynchronous communication is a form of *loose coupling* because it avoids the requirement that the sender and receiver of a message must be available at the same time.
Asynchronous request/response*	Another name for the *request/callback message exchange pattern*.

---

[1]All glossary terms marked with (*) are reproduced with the kind permission of Nicolai Josuttis (Josuttis 2007).

Backend*	A system that maintains the data and/or business rules of a specific *domain*. Usually, it provides a specific role or has a specific responsibility in a system landscape. In a *process-driven application*, a backend is usually encapsulated in the *service contract implementation layer*.
Bottom-up approach	Method for the development of new applications that starts with the existing *services* and implements complex *business processes* by combining reusable services. The opposite of the *top-down approach*.
BPEL*	Business Process Execution Language. An *XML*-based language used to *orchestrate services* to composed services or process services. The resulting services are *Web services*. *IDE*s allow you to create BPEL files using graphical user interfaces. BPEL engines allow you to interpret these files as service implementations at runtime and run the corresponding *business processes*. In the future, this functionality will be increasingly provided by *BPMN* models and BPMN engines.
BPM*	See *Business process management* and *Business process modeling*.
BPMN*	Business Process Model and Notation. A graphical notation for *business processes* maintained by the *OMG*. Thanks to the executability of BPMN models that is specified in version 2.0, it is increasingly replacing *event-driven process chains* (EPCs) on the business side and also *BPEL* models on the technical side.
Bus*	An abstract software pattern used to transfer data between multiple systems. In contrast to the *hub and spoke* pattern, it uses a federation of components that all follow a common *policy* or protocol to send, route, and receive *messages*.
Business process*	A structured description of the *activities* or *tasks* that have to be done to fulfill a certain business need. The activities or tasks might be manual steps (human interaction) or automated steps (IT steps). Business processes might be managed (see *Business process management*) and implemented using modeling notations such as *BPMN* or *EPC* or execution languages such as *BPEL* (as of version 2.0, BPMN is executable as well). Some people differentiate between *workflows* and business processes by stating that business processes describe more generally *what* has to be done while workflows describe *how* activities or tasks should be carried out.

Business Process Execution Language*	See *BPEL*
Business process management, BPM*	A general term that refers to all activities carried out to manage (i.e. plan, implement, document, observe, and improve) *business processes* as well as *business process modeling*.
Business Process Model and Notation*	See *BPMN*
Business process modeling, BPM*	According to Bloomberg and Schmelzer (2006), "a set of practices or tasks that companies can perform to visually depict or describe all the aspects of a business process, including its flow, control and decision points, triggers and conditions for activity execution, the context in which an activity runs, and associated resources".
Business rule	From (Wikipedia-Rules 2014): "Business rules describe the operations, definitions and constraints that apply to an organization. Business rules can apply to people, processes, corporate behavior and computing systems in an organization, and are put in place to help the organization achieve its goals."
	Business rules are created by business users and can be adapted to changing business and market conditions at runtime. They thus contribute to a company's agility. They also help to separate the business process and the business logic.
Business rule management system	A system for developing, executing, and managing *business rules*. It consists of a *business rules engine*, a *business rule repository*, and tools for developing and maintaining business rules.
Business rules engine	A business rules engine executes the *business rules* saved in a *business rule repository* and thus ensures compliance with the business logic and strategy. It is part of a *business rule management system*.
Business rule repository	A central storage location for *business rules* for managing different versions and to support the lifecycle of business rules (definition, development, production, and so on). The business rule repository is part of a *business rule management system*.
Canonical data model	A universal cross-system data model that is completely independent of the applications that are to be integrated.

Choreography*	A way of aggregating *services* to *business processes*. In contrast to *orchestration*, choreography does not compose services to a new service that has central control over the whole process. Instead, it defines rules and *policies* that enable different services to collaborate to form a business process. Each service involved in the process sees and contributes only a part of it.
Compensation*	An approach for maintaining consistency over multiple systems. In contrast to *2PC*, compensation doesn't update all the *backends* synchronously. Instead, it defines compensating activities to be performed in the event that not all corresponding updates of different systems succeed (regardless of whether the updates are performed sequentially or in parallel). As a consequence, this approach leads to *looser coupling* of systems; however, it might require more effort to implement.

BPEL and *BPMN* have direct support for compensation. |
| Composed Message Processor | An *enterprise integration pattern* where a *message* within the *ESB* passes through multiple processing steps. First, a *Splitter* splits the message into independent parts. Each submessage is sent (independently of the other submessages) through a *Content-Based Router* to a target system, where it gets a response as a reaction. An *Aggregator* collects all the responses, compresses them into a message, and sends the aggregated message to the sender of the original message as a response to its request.

A typical example is a check whether an order comprising several items can be processed fully. An availability check must be performed for each item. The message has to be split into the individual items and sent to the respective warehouse management systems that are responsible for the products corresponding to these items. The responses about the product availability are collected and made available to the requester in a message. |
| Composed service* | Common term for *services* that are composed of basic services and/or other composed services. Unlike *process services*, these are "microflows", which are stateless (at least from a business perspective). |
| Composite Application, Composite | Synonym for *process-driven application* |

Consumer*

General term for a system that has the role of calling ("consuming") a *service* (which is offered by a service *provider*). Another term used for this role is (service) *requestor*.

Content Based Router

An *enterprise integration pattern* where *messages* are sent to target systems based on their content. Unlike the *Recipient List* pattern, a message is sent to one target system only.

Content Enricher

An *enterprise integration pattern* where a received *message* is enriched during its processing in the *ESB* with information that is called synchronously from another system and that the target system needs for further processing.

Content Filter

An *enterprise integration pattern* where a received *message* is simplified by the removal of fields because the target system does not need this information for further processing.

Contract*

The complete description of a *service* interface between one *consumer* and one *provider*. It includes the technical interface (signature), the semantics, and non-functional aspects such as *service-level agreements*.

Sometimes a contract is also called a "well-defined interface".

CORBA*

Common Object Request Broker Architecture. An *OMG* standard that allows remote access to objects of different platforms. Although its initial purpose was to provide an infrastructure to access distributed objects, CORBA can be used as an *SOA* infrastructure by focusing on its concept of Object by Value (OBV).

Domain*

A definable (business) area or scope that plays a specific role and/or has a specific responsibility. In *process-driven applications* this might be a company, a division, a business unit, a department, a team, a system, or a component.

Domain-specific language, DSL*

A specific graphical or textural notation for a *meta model*. It allows you to specify the concrete behavior of a *model* in a precise, condensed, readable, and complete form.

EAI*

Enterprise Application Integration (sometimes also just called Enterprise Integration, or EI). An approach to integrate distributed systems such that they use a common infrastructure (middleware and/or protocol). With this approach, for each system it is enough to provide and maintain only one adapter to the infrastructure, instead of a specific adapter for each of the systems it communicates with. The infrastructure might use a *bus* or *hub and spoke* approach.

Process-driven applications can usually be described as an extension of EAI where EAI provides the technical aspect of *interoperability*. For this reason, the concepts of EAI can be considered as being a major part of or even the same as an *enterprise service bus* (ESB).

EDA*	See *Event-driven architecture*
Enterprise application integration*	See *EAI*

Enterprise integration pattern, EIP

Well-established patterns for message-based integration of heterogeneous IT landscapes in companies. They are cataloged in Gregor Hohpe and Bobby Woolf's book of the same name (Hohpe and Woolf 2004). Classic examples also used in the context of *process-driven applications* are *Aggregator*, *Resequencer*, and *Composed Message Processor*.

Enterprise service bus, ESB*

The infrastructure of an IT landscape that enables the *interoperability* of *services*. Its core task is to provide connectivity, data transformations, and (intelligent) routing of *messages*, as well as options for monitoring, logging, and debugging. The ESB might provide additional abilities that deal with security, reliability, service management, and even *business process* composition. However, there are different opinions as to whether a tool to compose services is a part of an ESB or just an additional platform to implement composed and process services outside the ESB.

In addition, tool vendors tend to define an ESB as something to buy, while you might also consider a standard such as *Web services* to be an ESB because conceptionally they define all that is necessary to provide interoperability between systems (without the need to buy some specific hardware or software).

An ESB might also be heterogeneous, using various middleware and communication technologies.

You can consider *EAI* solutions as (part of) an ESB.

EPC*	See *Event-driven process chain*
ESB*	See *Enterprise service bus*
Event*	A notification sent from a sender (*provider*) to a more or less well-known set of receivers (*consumers*). Usually, the receivers of an event have to subscribe for a certain type of event. This can be at development time, start time, or runtime.

You can consider events as part of the *publish/subscribe message exchange pattern* and *event-driven architectures* as part of or an enhancement of *process-driven applications.*

Event-driven architecture, EDA*	A software architecture pattern promoting the production, detection, consumption of, and reaction to *events.*

Some consider EDA to be an extension of or complement to *process-driven applications*; others consider EDA to be part of a *process-driven application* (a special *message exchange pattern* where the service *provider* sends a message to multiple *consumers*).

Event-driven process chain, EPC*	A graphical notation for *business processes*, mainly promoted by ARIS and SAP. Becoming less important.
Fire-and-Forget*	Another name for *one-way* messages (a *message exchange pattern* where a service sends a message without expecting a response).
Frontend*	A system that initiates and controls *business processes* by calling the necessary *services*. That is, it acts as a service *consumer*. It might be a system with human interaction or a batch program.
Governance*	In general, a term that describes the task of "making sure that people do what's right". In *SOA*, governance is about architectural decisions, *processes*, tools, and *policies*.
HTTP*	Hypertext Transfer Protocol. The fundamental protocol of the World Wide Web. In a secure form (using *SSL* transport-layer security), it is called HTTPS.
Hub and spoke*	An abstract software pattern used to transfer data between multiple systems. In contrast to the *bus* pattern, it uses one or more central components (hubs) that coordinate all communication between senders and receivers.
IDE*	Integrated development environment. A (usually graphical) project-oriented environment for the development of specific software.
Idempotence*	In a *process-driven application* idempotence describes the ability of *services* to deal with *messages* that are delivered more than once so that redeliveries do not have unintended effects.

In an unreliable network or protocol (such as *HTTP*), if you want to be sure the message gets delivered and send the message again, the receiver should be able to deal with this second message in such a way that it does not produce an effect different from that of receiving the message only once.

Services can be or be made idempotent on a business or technical level.

Interoperability*	The ability of different systems to communicate with each other. Interoperability between different platforms and programming languages is a fundamental goal of *process-driven applications*.

Note that standards do not necessarily ensure interoperability. For this reason, in the *Web services* world a special organization called *WS-I* provides *profiles* to make the standards interoperable. |
| JMS* | Java Message Service. The standard Java API for *message-oriented middleware* (MOM). Because it is only an API standard, it provides portability (allowing you to change the middleware while keeping the interfaces) but not *interoperability* (allowing you to use different JMS implementations). |
| Loose coupling* | The concept of reducing the dependencies between systems. There are different ways to decrease the tightness of coupling between systems, such as having different object models, using *asynchronous communication*, or using *compensation* instead of *2PC* to maintain consistency.

In general, loose coupling leads to more complexity. For this reason, in a specific *process-driven application* you have to find the right amount of loose coupling. |
| MDSD* | Model-driven software development. An approach where a significant amount of schematic code, which has the same structure but varies depending on the concrete situation (such as the data types used), is generated out of an abstract *model*. |
| Message* | A chunk of data sent around as part of a *service* call. *Message exchange patterns* define typical sequences of messages to perform service calls. |
| Message exchange pattern, MEP* | A definition of the sequence of *messages* in a *service* call or service operation. This sequence includes the order, direction, and cardinality of the messages sent around until a specific service operation is done.

The most important *MEPs* are *one-way*, *request/response*, and *request/callback* (asynchronous request/response).

For example, the request/response MEP defines that a *consumer* sends a request message and waits for the answer, which is sent by the *provider* as a response message. |
| Message Filter | An *enterprise integration pattern* where entire *messages* are not forwarded to the target system if they are not relevant for this system. |

Message-oriented middleware, MOM*	Middleware that is based on the concept of *asynchronous communication*. Examples are SAP Process Integration, WebSphere MQ (formerly MQ Series) by IBM, MSMQ by Microsoft, Tibco Rendezvous, SonicMQ, and *JMS*.
Message Translator	An *enterprise integration pattern* that converts between different message formats. It is used whenever the interfaces of the sender and receiver systems are different.
Meta model*	A (formal) description of a *model*. A meta model refers to the rules that define the structure a model can have. In other words, a meta model defines the formal structure and elements of a model.
Model*	An abstraction. The structure of a model is typically described with a *meta model*. For the model, there are typically one or more specific graphical or textural notations (sometimes called *domain-specific language* (DSL)).
Model-driven software/ service development*	See *MDSD*
OASIS*	Organization for the Advancement of Structured Information Standards. An international not-for-profit computer industry consortium for the development, convergence, and adoption of e-business and *Web services* standards. See http://www.oasis-open.org.
OMG*	Object Management Group. An international, not-for-profit computer industry consortium for the development of enterprise integration standards. OMG's standards include UML, MDA, and *BPMN*. See http://www.omg.org.
One-way*	A *message exchange pattern* where a *service* sends a message without expecting a response. Another name for this pattern is *fire and forget*.
Orchestration*	A way of aggregating *services* to *business processes*. In contrast to *choreography*, orchestration composes services to a new service that has central control over the whole process. For *Web services*, *BPEL* is a standard for orchestration, for which development tools and engines are available. In the future, *BPMN* will increasingly assume this role as the coordinator of service calls.
Participant*	General term for a *consumer* or *provider*.
Process*	A structured set of the steps (*activities* or *tasks*) to fulfill a certain need or reach a certain goal.

Different processes are involved in *process-driven applications*: The goal is to implement *business processes*. To do this, you must have processes to establish and manage solutions and *services* (solution lifecycles, service lifecycles, and so on). Also, on a meta level, you have the process of establishing process-driven applications and their *governance*.

Process-driven application (PDA)
Process-driven applications are business-oriented applications that support differentiating end-to-end business processes spanning functional, system, and organizational boundaries by reusing data and functionality from platforms and applications. Process-driven applications are part of a *process-driven architecture*.

Process-driven architecture (PDA)
An application architecture resulting from a top-down process-driven method (see also *Top-down approach*). The core elements of the architecture are the *process-driven application* itself, the *service contract*, and the *service contract implementation layer*.

Process service*
A *service* that represents a long-term *workflow* or *business process*. From a business point of view, this kind of service represents a "macro flow", which is a long-running flow of *activities* (services) that is interruptible (by human intervention).

Unlike *composed services*, these services usually have a state that remains stable over multiple service calls.

Profile*
In the context of *Web services*, a profile is a set of standards each of a specific version combined with guidelines and conventions for using these standards together in ways that ensure *interoperability*.

Most profiles are specified by *WS-I*.

Provider*
General term for a system or a component that has the role of offering ("providing") a *service*, which might then be used/called by different *consumers*.

Publish/subscribe*
A *message exchange pattern* where a service *consumer* subscribes to get a notification message from a service *provider* when a certain condition or state occurs or changes.

The subscription might happen at development time, start time, or at runtime. If the provider doesn't know the consumer, this pattern is the base of *event-driven architecture* (EDA), where the notification is an *event*.

Recipient List
An *enterprise integration pattern* where *messages* are sent to target systems based on their content. Unlike the *Content-Based Router* pattern, a message can be sent to multiple target systems.

Registry*

Registries manage *services* from a technical point of view, unlike *repositories*, which manage services from a business point of view.

Registries manage all the technical details necessary for using services at runtime (signatures, deployment information, and so on). Usually, a registry is considered to be a part of the infrastructure (*ESB*).

Repository*

Repositories manage *services* from a business point of view, unlike *registries*, which manage services from a technical point of view. That is, they manage interfaces, *contracts*, *service-level agreements*, dependencies, etc., to help to identify, design, and develop services. Unlike for a *registry* the service description should be independent of technical details and infrastructure aspects. That is, it should not be necessary to change a repository when a company switches to a new infrastructure (*ESB*).

Request*

A *message* that is sent by a *consumer* as an initial message in most *message exchange patterns* (see *Request/response* and *Request/callback*).

Sometimes this term is also used as a synonym for a *service* call.

Request/callback*

A *message exchange pattern* where a service *consumer* sends a *request* message but does not block and wait for a reply. Instead, it defines a callback function that is called later, when the *response* message sent by the service *provider* arrives.

Sometimes request/callback is called *asynchronous request/response*.

Requestor*

Alternative term for *consumer* (mainly used in the context of *Web services*).

Request/response*

A *message exchange pattern* where a service *consumer* sends a *request* message and expects an answer.

Usually the consumer blocks until the *response* message sent by the service *provider* arrives. Sometimes, however, the blocking is not required. In that case, there is a separation between synchronous and asynchronous *request/response*. The latter is also known as the *request/callback* message exchange pattern.

Resequencer

An *enterprise integration pattern* where *messages* arrive unsorted and are sent to a receiver system in the correct sequence according to particular sort criteria.

Response*

A *message* that is sent by a *provider* as an answer to a service *request* (see *Request/response*).

Policy*	A general rule or guideline. In *SOA*, policies have an impact on the infrastructure (*ESB*), the *provider(s)*, and the *consumer(s)*. A policy might be a mandatory law (such as a required naming convention) or a goal (such as the maximum number of versions of a *service* in operation).
Rule	See *business rule*
Rules engine	See *business rules engine*
Scatter-Gather	An *enterprise integration pattern* where a *message* within the *ESB* passes through multiple processing steps. It is similar to the *Composed Message Processor* pattern, but the incoming message is not split into several parts. Instead, it is sent unchanged to multiple target systems, from which it expects a response. However, the pattern only waits a certain time for responses. It may be the case that response messages arrive but are no longer taken into account because the response time was exceeded. Specific criteria are used to select exactly one message from the responses received in the allotted time; this message is sent to the sender of the original message as a result.

This behavior can be illustrated using a request for a quote as an example: A request for a quote is sent to several business partners. After a certain time, or once a certain number of responses have arrived, the pattern stops waiting and the received responses are evaluated. Finally, the best quote is sent to the initiator of the request.

Service*	The IT realization of some self-contained business functionality.

Technically, a service is a description of one or more operations that use (multiple) *messages* to exchange data between a *provider* and a *consumer*. The typical effect of a service call is that the consumer obtains some information from the provider and/or modifies the state of the providing system or component.

Services can have different attributes and can be of different categories.

A service is usually described by an interface. The complete description of a service from a consumer's point of view (signature and semantics) is called a "well-defined interface". Together with the non-functional requirements of a service, this data is formulated into a *contract* between a provider and a consumer.

Service contract	See also *Contract*. The service contract (as used in this book) is part of a *process-driven architecture* and is defined using the *top-down approach*. The service contract contains interfaces comprised of only those fields that are necessary from the perspective of the *process-driven application*. The data types used are based on the *canonical data model*. The interfaces in the service contract do not have to be reusable.
Service contract implementation layer (SCIL)	Implements the business requirements of a *process-driven application*, which expresses these in a *service contract*. In this way, the process-driven application is protected from the technical implementation of its requirements by system calls. This layer reduces the dependency (see also *loose coupling*) of the process-driven application on the system landscape, and ensures that changes in requirements resulting from changing market conditions can be implemented as quickly as possible. The service contract implementation layer is part of a *process-driven architecture*.
Service-level agreement, SLA*	A formal negotiated agreement between two parties with the main purpose of agreeing on the quality of the service. For a specific subject an SLA usually records the common understanding about priorities, responsibilities, availability, performance, operation, or other attributes of the service (such as billing and even penalties in the case of violations of the SLA).
	In the context of *process-driven applications*, these parties are usually a *service provider* and a service *consumer*. The main agreements usually concern availability (for example, "7 × 24"), response times (for example, "80 % <0.5 s"), and throughput (for example, "max. 10,000 calls per hour").
	An SLA is usually part of a *contract*.
Service-oriented architecture, SOA*	There are various definitions for SOA. Some specify only that it is an approach for *architectures* where the interfaces are *services*. However, in a more specific sense, SOA is an architectural paradigm for dealing with *business processes* distributed over a large and heterogeneous landscape of existing and new systems that are under the control of different owners.
	The key concepts of SOA are *services*, *interoperability*, and *loose coupling*. The key ingredients of SOA are the infrastructure (*ESB*), *architecture*, and *processes*. The key success factors for SOA are understanding, *governance*, management support, and homework.

	Note that *Web services* is not a synonym for SOA; Web services are *one* possible way of realizing the infrastructure aspects of SOA.
SOAP*	SOAP is the basic protocol of *Web services*. As an *XML*-based format, it defines the format of the header and body of a Web services *message*.
	Formerly the acronym stood for "Simple Object Access Protocol," but because SOAP was neither simple nor for objects or access, the term now stands for itself.
	The protocol still allows different types of message exchange. The most commonly used is the "document/literal wrapped" pattern.
Software architecture*	See *Architecture*
Splitter	An *enterprise integration pattern* where a complex *message* is split using particular criteria into smaller units, which can then be handled independently.
SSL*	A cryptographic protocol that provides secure communication on the Internet protocol *HTTP* (which is often called HTTPS then).
Task*	Possible term for one step of a *business process*. In the context of a *process-driven application*, a task is typically implemented by a *service* or as a user interaction.
Top-down approach	A method for determining the main artifacts of a *process-driven application* where you start with the business *processes* that you want to implement and, from this perspective, derive processes, user interfaces, business objects, and *services* (new services to develop internally and external services to reuse). The business functions expected externally and the interfaces provided by the process-driven application form the *service contract*. The top-down approach is the opposite of the *bottom-up approach*.
Two-phase commit*	See *2PC*
UDDI*	"Universal Description, Discovery, and Integration". A *Web services* standard for *registries*. Initially designed for the UDDI Business Registry, it now serves as a standard for the technical management and brokerage of Web services.
W3C*	World Wide Web Consortium. An international consortium for the development of standards for the World Wide Web, which also develops *SOA* standards such as *XML* and *SOAP*. See http://www.w3.org/.
Web services*	A set of standards that serves as *one* possible way of realizing a *SOA* infrastructure.

	Initially started with the core standards *XML*, *HTTP*, *WSDL*, *SOAP*, and *UDDI*, it now contains over 60 standards and *profiles*, developed and maintained by different standardization organizations, such as *W3C*, *OASIS*, and *WS-I*.
Well-defined interface	See *Contract*
Workflow*	Similar to a *business process*, a description of the *activities* or *tasks* that have to be done to fulfill a certain business need.
	Some people differentiate between workflows and business processes by stating that business processes describe more generally *what* has to be done while workflows describe *how* activities or tasks should be carried out.
WS*	General abbreviation for *Web services*. Also used as common prefix for Web services standards.
WSDL*	Web Services Description Language. An *XML*-based language that describes *service* interfaces from a technical point of view. Although it is a *Web services* standard, WSDL can also be used for other infrastructures.
WS-I*	Web Services Interoperability Organization. An open industry organization that standardizes *Web services* standards as *profiles* to make them *interoperable*. See http://www.ws-i.org/.
XML*	eXtensible Markup Language. A human-readable general-purpose notation widely used for the description and exchange of data. Specific XML formats can be defined by and validated against an *XML schema definition*.
XML schema definition, XSD*	A language used to describe a set of rules to which a corresponding *XML* document must conform in order to be considered valid. It includes a set of basic data types.

References

ADEPT2 (2014) Web site University Ulm regarding ADEPT2 research project. https://www.uni-ulm.de/in/iui-dbis/forschung/projekte/abgeschlossene-projekte/adept2.html (08.04.2014)

Allweyer T (2010a) Unternehmen als Prozess Engine? Möglichkeiten und Grenzen mit BPMN. http://www.tele-task.de/archive/lecture/overview/5376/ (08.04.2014)

Allweyer T (2010b) BPMN 2.0. Introduction to the standard for Business Process Modeling. Norderstedt: Books on Demand

Anstey J (2009) Apache Camel: Integration Nirvana. http://architects.dzone.com/articles/apache-camel-integration (08.04.2014)

Balko S (2010a) Understanding intermediate events, asynchronous message receipt and correlation in NetWeaver BPM 7.20. http://www.sdn.sap.com/irj/scn/index?rid=/library/uuid/f0369539-e876-2d10-ef93-8f30e112ee6d&overridelayout=true (08.04.2014)

Bloomberg J, Schmelzer R (2006) Service orient or be doomed!: how service orientation will change your business. Wiley, Hoboken, NJ

BRG—Business Rules Group (2003) The business rules manifesto. The principals of rules independence. http://www.businessrulesgroup.org/brmanifesto.htm (08.04.2014)

Buytendijk F (2012) Embrace complexity, simplify your organization. http://www.beinformed.com/BeInformed/webdav-resource/binaries/pdf/whitepapers/embrace-complexity.pdf?webdav-id=/Be%20Informed%20Bibliotheek/0000%20WEBDAV/WebDAV%20StatContent.bixml (08.04.2014)

Camel (2011): Apache Camel Homepage. http://camel.apache.org/ (08.04.2014)

Dadam P, Reichert M (2009a) The ADEPT Project: a decade of research and development for robust and flexible process support - challenges and achievements. Comput Sci Res Dev 23 (2):81–97

Dadam P, Reichert M, Rinderle-Ma S, Lanz A, Pryss R, Predeschly M, Kolb J, Ly LT, Jurisch M, Kreher U, Göser K (2009b) From ADEPT to AristaFlow BPM suite: a research vision has become reality. http://dbis.eprints.uni-ulm.de/620/1/ER_BPM_Workshop.pdf (08.04.2014)

EIP (2011) Enterprise integration patterns Tools and downloads. http://enterpriseintegrationpatterns.com/downloads.html (08.04.2014)

Erl T (2008) SOA design patterns. Prentice Hall, Upper Saddle River, NJ

Erl T (2013) About the SOA manifesto. http://www.soa-manifesto.org/aboutmanifesto.html (08.04.2014)

Erl T, Arsanjani A, Booch G, Boubez P, Chappell D, deVadoss J, Josuttis N, Krafzig D, Little M, Loesgen B, Thomas Manes A, McKendrick J, Ross-Talbot S, Tilkov S, Utschig-Utschig C, Wilhelmsen H (2009) SOA Manifesto. http://soa-manifesto.org/ (08.04.2014)

Esper (2012): Event processing with Esper and NEsper. http://esper.codehaus.org/ (08.04.2014)

Fielding RT (2000) Architectural styles and the design of network-based software architectures. Doctoral dissertation, University of California, Irvine. http://www.ics.uci.edu/~fielding/pubs/dissertation/top.htm (08.04.2014)

Fischer M, Link M, Ortner E, Zeise N (2010) Servicebase management systems: a three-schema-architecture for service-management. In: Fähnrich K-P Hrsg.): Informatik 2010 - Service

Science. Neue Perspektiven für die Informatik, 27.09 - 01.10. 2010, Leipzig. Ges. für Informatik, Bonn, S. 730–735

Freund J, Rücker B (2012) Real-life BPMN: Using BPMN 2.0 to analyze, improve, and automate processes in your company. CreateSpace Independent Publishing Platform

FuseSource (2011a) Enterprise integration pattern reference. http://fusesource.com/docs/ide/2.0/eip_ref/eip_ref.html (08.04.2014)

FuseSource (2011b): Enrich pattern. http://fusesource.com/docs/ide/2.0/eip_ref/eip_ref.html#enrich (08.04.2014)

Gamma E, Helm R, Johnson R, Vlissides J (1995) Design patterns: elements of reusable object-oriented software. Addison-Wesley, Reading, MA

Graml T, Bracht R, Spies M (2008) Patterns of business rules to enable agile business processes. Enterprise Inform Syst 2(4):385–402

Hammer M, Champy J (1993) Reengineering the corporation. Harper, NY

Hill M, Dimitrova D (2008) Exceptional scheduling of shift workers. http://www.sdn.sap.com/irj/scn/index?rid=/library/uuid/40ab3554-58b1-2b10-ceb9-80861dacd5cf&overridelayout=true (08.04.2014)

Hohpe G, Woolf B (2004) Enterprise integration patterns. Designing, building, and deploying messaging solutions. Addison Wesley, Boston

Ibsen C, Anstey J (2011) Camel in action. Manning, Stamford

IETF (1999) RFC 2616 – Hypertext transfer protocol—HTTP/1.1. http://www.ietf.org/rfc/rfc2616.txt (08.04.2014)

Jablonski S (2011) Der ProcessNavigator – Ein Navigationssystem für das Prozessmanagement. In: Zeise N, Fischer M, Link M (eds) Anwendungsorientierte Organisationsgestaltung. Baar, Hamburg, pp 259–275

Josuttis N (2007) SOA in practice: the art of distributed system design. O'Reilly Media, Sebastopol

Josuttis N (2010) Das SOA-manifest—Kontext, Inhalt, Erläuterung. Dpunkt, Heidelberg

Krafzig D, Banke K, Slama D (2004) Enterprise SOA – Service-oriented architecture best practices. Prentice Hall, Upper Saddle River, NJ

Lautenbacher F (2009) Semantic business process modeling: principles, design support and realization. Doctoral dissertation, University Augsburg, Augsburg

Malek T, Dimitrova D (2008) Master data management: Create customer data. http://www.sdn.sap.com/irj/scn/go/portal/prtroot/docs/library/uuid/005808cd-59b1-2b10-b589-c7016d221092?QuickLink=index&overridelayout=true (08.04.2014)

Manes AT (2009) SOA is dead; long live services. http://apsblog.burtongroup.com/2009/01/soa-is-dead-long-live-services.html (08.04.2014)

Margulius DL (2005) Process-driven architectures. http://www.infoworld.com/t/business/process-driven-architectures-121 (08.04.2014)

OAGIS (2009) OAGIS release 9.4.1. http://www.schemacentral.com/sc/oagis941/ss.html (08.04.2014)

OMG (2010a) Business process model and notation, V2.0 Beta 2. http://www.omg.org/cgi-bin/doc?dtc/10-06-04. (08.04.2014)

OMG (2010b) BPMN 2.0 by example. http://www.omg.org/cgi-bin/doc?dtc/10-06-02.pdf (08.04.2014)

OMG (2011) Business process model And notation (BPMN), V2.0. http://www.omg.org/spec/BPMN/2.0/PDF/ (08.04.2014)

Oracle (2012): Introduction to Oracle CQL. http://docs.oracle.com/cd/E16764_01/doc.1111/e12048/intro.htm (08.04.2014)

Pautasso C, Zimmermann O, Leymann F (2008) RESTful web services vs. "Big" web services: making the right architectural decision. In: WWW '08: Proceedings of the 17th International World Wide Web Conference. ACM.

Plattner H, Zeier A (2011) In-memory data management: an inflection point for enterprise applications. Springer, Berlin, Heidelberg

Pohl K, Rupp C (2011) Requirements engineering fundamentals: a study guide for the certified professional for requirements engineering exam - foundation level - IREB compliant. Rocky Nook, Kingston, MA

Pucher MJ (2010): Adaptive process: theory and reality. http://isismjpucher.wordpress.com/2010/05/28/adaptive-process-theory-and-reality/ (08.04.2014)

Rauscher J, Stiehl V (2008) The developer's guide to SAP NetWeaver Composition Environment. Galileo, Bonn

Ross RG (2009) Business rule concepts. Getting to the point of knowledge, 3rd edn. Business Rule Solutions, LLC, Houston, TX

SAP (2002a) SAP launches cross applications - New breed of cross-functional business applications drives continuous business improvement. http://www.sap.com/about/newsroom/press.epx?pressID=1334 (08.04.2014)

SAP (2002b) SAP delivers mySAP™ technology and details SAP xApps™ vision. http://www.sap.com/about/newsroom/press.epx?pressID=1634 (08.04.2014)

SAP (2002c) SAP xApps™ Gain market momentum - first customer deploys xApp to deliver increased visibility to plant assets; SAP announces new SAP xApp to support product design and development. http://www.sap.com/press.epx?pressID=1636 (08.04.2014)

SAP (2010a) BPM use case – Handling issue reports submitted by citizens. http://wiki.scn.sap.com/wiki/display/BPMUC/Streamlining+multi-channel+services+example+-+Handling +issue+reports+submitted+by+citizens (08.04.2014)

SAP (2010b) Enterprise services repository and enterprise service workplace. http://esworkplace.sap.com (08.04.2014)

SAP (2010c) Business add-ins (BAdIs). http://help.sap.com/saphelp_nwpi71/helpdata/de/8f/f2e540f8648431e10000000a1550b0/frameset.htm (08.04.2014)

SAP (2010d) Forward error handling – documentation. http://help.sap.com/saphelp_nw73/helpdata/en/cd/798aa3c7754c61b2f2d50ea7b66aac/content.htm (08.04.2014)

SAP (2011) SAP streamwork. http://www.sapstreamwork.com/ (08.04.2014)

SAP (2012) Experience SAP Hana. https://www.experiencesaphana.com/community/learn (08.04.2014)

SAP (2014) UI development toolkit for HTML5 developer center. http://scn.sap.com/community/developer-center/front-end (08.04.2014)

SAPJAM (2014): Collaborate in the cloud – with our social network solution, SAP Jam. http://sapjam.com (08.04.2014)

Schuller A (2007a) Architecture guideline series for composite applications. Introduction and basic overview. http://www.sdn.sap.com/irj/scn/go/portal/prtroot/docs/library/uuid/20f7c4ef-b73d-2a10-a2b9-d9833908130c?QuickLink=index&overridelayout=true (08.04.2014)

Schuller A (2007b) Architecture guideline series for composite applications. Portal and process layer. http://www.sdn.sap.com/irj/scn/go/portal/prtroot/docs/library/uuid/1078e3b0-ec5d-2a10-f08a-c9b878917b19?QuickLink=index&overridelayout=true (08.04.2014)

Schuller A (2007c) Architecture guideline series for composite applications. Business logic, abstraction layer and connectivity. http://www.sdn.sap.com/irj/scn/go/portal/prtroot/docs/library/uuid/00caf8bd-487a-2a10-36a9-93d840309310?QuickLink=index&overridelayout=true (08.04.2014)

Sikka V (2012) A renewal of enterprise landscapes. http://vishalsikka.blogspot.com/2012/01/renewal-of-enterprise-landscapes.html (08.04.2014)

Silver B (2011) BPMN method and style, 2nd Edn, with BPMN implementer's guide: a structured approach for business process modeling and implementation using BPMN 2.0. Aptos CA: Cody-Cassidy Press

Slama D, Nelius R (2011) Enterprise BPM – Erfolgsrezepte für unternehmensweites Prozessmanagement. dpunkt, Heidelberg

Stein S (2009) Modelling method extension for service-oriented business process management. Doctoral dissertation, Christian-Albrechts-University Kiel, Kiel

Stiehl V (2004) Gain a real-world understanding of how your applications will operate on a new platform—porting a J2EE application to .SAP web application server. SAP Professional J 6(3); Dedham, MA: Wellesly Information Services (WIS)

Stiehl V (2006) Guidelines for specifying composite applications. https://www.sdn.sap.com/irj/scn/index?rid=/library/uuid/20844e88-0d01-0010-de9a-eb2d302df7b7&overridelayout=true (08.04.2014)

Stiehl V, Deng J (2008) Project issue management. http://www.sdn.sap.com/irj/scn/go/portal/prtroot/docs/library/uuid/0087457d-65b1-2b10-c1b0-93f02bd60434?QuickLink=index& overridelayout=true (08.04.2014)

Strnadl CF (2006) Aligning business and IT (2006): the process-driven architecture model. Inform Syst Manage 23(4):235–241

SysML (2010) OMG systems modeling language, Version 1.2, OMG Document Number: formal/2010-06-01. Object Management Group, 2010

Togliatti A (2008) The value of process driven architecture. http://soa.sys-con.com/node/536116?page=0,0 (08.04.2014)

UN/CEFACT (2003) Core components technical specification—Part 8 of the ebXML Framework. Version 2.01. http://www.unece.org/cefact/ebxml/CCTS_V2-01_Final.pdf (08.04.2014)

van der Aalst W (2010) Process mining—research, tools, applications. http://www.processmining.org (08.04.2014)

van der Aalst W (2011) Process mining—discovery, conformance and enhancement of business processes. Springer, Berlin, Heidelberg

van der Aalst W, ter Hofstede A, Kiepuszewski B, Barros A (2003) Workflow patterns. Distrib Parallel Databases 14(3):5–51

Vanderhaeghen D, Fettke P, Loos P (2010) Organizational and technological options for business process management from the perspective of Web 2.0—results of a design oriented research approach with particular consideration of self-organization and collective intelligence. Bus Inform Syst Eng 2(1):15–28

W3C (2004) XML schema part 2: datatypes, 2nd edn. http://www.w3.org/TR/xmlschema-2/ (08.04.2014)

Waldo J, Wyant G, Wollrath A, Kendall S (1994) A note on distributed computing. Technical Report, SMLI TR-94-29. Sun microsystems laboratories, November 1994. http://citeseerx.ist.psu.edu/viewdoc/summary?doi=10.1.1.41.7628 (08.04.2014)

White S (2004) Process modeling notations and workflow patterns. http://www.bpmn.org/Documents/Notations_and_Workflow_Patterns.pdf (08.04.2014)

Wikipedia-IoT (2014): Internet of things. http://en.wikipedia.org/wiki/Internet_of_things (08.04.2014)

Wikipedia-Rules (2014): Business rule. http://en.wikipedia.org/wiki/Business_rule (08.04.2014)

Wikipedia-Watson (2014): Thomas J. Watson. http://en.wikipedia.org/wiki/Thomas_J._Watson#Famous_misquote (08.04.2014)

Woods D (2003) Packaged composite applications. O'Reilly, Sebastopol

Zur Mühlen M (2004) Organizational management in workflow applications—issues and perspectives. Inform Technology Manage 5(271–291):2004

Index

Printed in the United States
By Bookmasters